LIST OF FIGURES

List of Tables

PREFACE

In October 2007, the 11th International Conference on Finance and Banking took place at the Silesian University, School of Business Administration in Karviná, Czech Republic. Each time, the conference focuses on a specific new development in the banking and financial sector. This year, the theme was *Future of the European Monetary Integration*. All submitted papers were reviewed by the international programme committee and, finally, 55 papers were accepted for presentation.

This volume contains ten of the best papers presented at the conference and two invited papers. In spite of the fact that the book is a collection of independent studies it represents a comprehensive and cohesive work. All studies (book chapters) are tied together by common themes. Through original research, the book covers various aspects of the European monetary integration, giving a comparison of its impacts in the euro area and non-euro EU Member States, in the traditional, new and newest EU Member States. Special attention is paid to prospective integration of the euro-candidate countries to the euro area and the implications for national economic policies.

The book contains twelve chapters arranged in four thematic parts focusing on the exchange rate policy, financial markets, monetary policy, and optimal currency area issues.

In the first chapter, *Fernando Seabra, Lisanda Flach & Tatiana Santos* argue that despite deregulation of the international capital flows there is still a "home bias" to investment decisions. Geographical and institutional proximity, trade linkages, common currency or exchange rate regimes induce local portfolio allocations. Therefore, the authors analyse the determinants of foreign portfolio investment from the main European countries into 21 host countries. In the second chapter, *Ralph Setzer* aims to answer what factors determine a country's exchange rate policy. He argues that the exchange rate policy is the outcome of a political process with strong distributional and welfare implications. Such an assumption is applicable in the circumstances of the European economic and monetary integration. An innovative approach of survival analysis is used on a large sample of 47 countries over the period 1975 – 2000. In the third chapter, *Daniel Stavárek* applies a non-conventional approach to assess the convergence of the exchange rate development between the euro-candidate currencies and the euro. Sufficient degree of the exchange rate convergence is one of the conditions that must be fulfilled by any euro-candidate country. Various alternative types of correlation coefficients are calculated using time series of both exchange rate returns and volatility. In the fourth chapter, *Tomáš Tichý* applies the simplest approaches to the dependency modelling of subordinated Lévy models in order to estimate the probability distribution of returns of a small exchange rate sensitive portfolio. He uses daily exchange rates of euro-candidate currencies as well as the major world currencies during a seven-year period.

In the fifth chapter, *Dimitris Georgoutsos & Petros M. Migiakis* stem from the empirically documented fact that European financial markets share increasing degrees of financial integration. However, they focus on issue that still remain to be answered – a strength of the linkages among the European bond markets. The authors aim to find dominant characteristics for some of the government bonds. Regime switching structures are adopted on data of 11 euro area countries. In the sixth chapter, *Marie Brière & Florian Ielpo* analyse how new information on economic fundamentals influence interest rates in Europe. They propose an original methodology allowing separation of the impacts due to European economic announcements from the influence of the US yield curve. Moreover, the innovative approach allows measuring the impact on the entire European yield curve. The impacts of announcements of 18 fundamentals are examined over the period January 2000 – July 2007. The next important part of financial system is stock market. In the seventh chapter, *Lumír Kulhánek* focuses on the stock market volatility in selected new and traditional EU Member States. He provides an overview of the stock markets' development with emphasis on risk and return; and also investigates linkages among the markets analysed. In the eighth chapter, *Salih Turan Katircioglu & Elif Katircioglu* concentrate the research on the relationship and direction of causality between financial development and economic growth in the euro area countries. They apply Granger causality tests on a comprehensive cross-sectional data set of 12 countries and 45 years.

The part of the book focused on monetary policy starts with the ninth chapter, in which *Felix Hammermann* analyses the potential cost of regional monetary integration while being at the same time integrated with third countries. For this purpose, he develops a New Keynesian three-country model. He evaluates the central bank loss function with and without ERM 2. Subsequently, he assesses the costs of ERM 2 and derives the implications of production sharing for monetary policy. In the tenth chapter, *Bogdan Muraraşu & Nicoleta Ciurila* analyse the interest rate channel of the monetary policy in selected new EU Member States. A special attention is paid on degree and speed of the interest rate pass-through as well as on contemporary adjustment to the long-term equilibrium. The analysis leads to conclusions on effectiveness of the monetary policy in the new EU Member States.

In the eleventh chapter, *Gerhard Fink, Peter Haiss, Wolfgang Rainer & Magdalena Oeberseder* point out that the accession of Bulgaria and Romania to the EU raised some concerns about the catch-up process in these countries. Therefore, the authors apply a scoring model to assess comprehensively the counties' risk. Besides the ex-post assessment in 2001 – 2006 the chapter also offers a country risk projection for the period 2007 – 2010. In the twelfth chapter, *Gabriel Bobeica, Elena Bojesteanu & Ionela Costica* also analyse Bulgaria and Romania. From the perspective of the Optimum Currency Area theory, the authors investigate the shock synchronicity between the EU newcomers and the euro area. Using inflation rate, nominal interest rate and real GDP growth rate a similarity in supply, demand and monetary shocks are empirically analysed.

Karviná, July 2008

Daniel Stavárek
Stanislav Polouček

ACKNOWLEDGEMENTS

There are many people to thank for their input in making the conference and this book possible. We would like to thank everyone who helped to make this conference so successful. We appreciate the speakers giving their valuable time to share their expertise as well as the discussants and audience participants who actively contributed to very interesting debates. In this context, we should express our gratitude to the invited keynote speakers: John Lewis, economist from De Nederlandsche Bank; Viktor Kotlán, Chief Economist of Česká spořitelna; and Marek Dohnal, Chief Financial Officer of Energy 21 and a graduate of Silesian University, School of Business Administration in Karviná. We also would like to thank the members of the International Programme and Organizing Committee and to all reviewers of the papers. A deep sense of gratitude is owed to members and staff of the Department of Finance, School of Business Administration in Karviná.

We offer our deepest appreciation to all the contributors for their enthusiasm about this project and their hard work in completing the chapters to a universally high standard.

We are glad to acknowledge the support provided by the Czech Science Foundation within the project ***GAČR 402/08/0067 "Financial integration of New EU Member States with the Eurozone"*** in editing the book and elaborating Chapter Three and Chapter Seven. And a final word of appreciation to Amanda Millar, Carol Koulikourdi, Andy Nercessian, and their colleagues at the publishers, who approved the project and helped to finalize it.

CHAPTER ONE

FOREIGN PORTFOLIO INVESTMENT, EUROPEAN ECONOMIC AND MONETARY UNION AND EXCHANGE RATE UNCERTAINTY

FERNANDO SEABRA, LISANDA FLACH AND TATIANA SANTOS

Cross-border flows of portfolio investment are by nature more unstable than foreign direct investment (FDI). Clearly, portfolio holdings are not subject to the high sunk costs and the market irreversibility that affect FDI. The literature has given less attention to foreign portfolio investment (FPI) due to its less predictable behaviour. More recently, however, the deepening of international financial integration has brought about an unprecedented movement of capital in bonds and equity markets. As barriers to flow are lower, portfolio holdings tend to move across countries according to higher returns and to a better sharing and diversification of risk.

Although portfolio diversification can be reasoned by investors' optimal behaviour – based on the international capital asset pricing model – information asymmetries between domestic and foreign investors can represent restrictions to invest overseas and establish a "home bias" to portfolio investment decisions. The literature points out that investors tend to include too little of their wealth in foreign assets as a consequence of investors' preferences for holding equities that they are more familiar with (Huberman, 2001).

In the context of a currency union, as the European Economic and Monetary Union (EMU), we can argue that a higher degree of financial integration enhances savings availability – increasing potential GDP growth – and risk sharing among the member countries. Besides, within the currency union area and also for those countries with a greater degree of financial integration, the volatility of asset prices tends to be lower, motivating a more efficient allocation of financial capital.

Portfolio holdings in foreign countries are also subject to transaction and information costs. Geographical and institutional proximity, trade linkages, common language, and exchange rate arrangements reduce these costs and induce local portfolio allocations (Grinblatt and Keloharju, 2001). Hence, the "home bias" effect at the euro area level is likely to occur not only as a consequence of the European integration process (e.g., increase in intraregional trade and common legal systems) but also as a result of the lower volatility of asset prices, implied by the common currency or some level of exchange rate coordination.

Therefore, the objective of this study is to analyse the determinants of FPI from the main European countries into 21 main host countries. The focus is on both financial and real variables, especially exchange rate uncertainty, monetary integration and geographic and institutional distance. An FPI model is developed and estimated based on a panel dataset over the period 2001-2006. The remainder of this work is organized as follows. In the next section we provide a summary of the relevant literature. In the further sections, we develop the basic model, report the empirical results and, finally, draw some conclusions.

Portfolio Investment Behaviour

The experience of the EMU provides an opportunity to discriminate between different theoretical explanations for investment behaviour. There are basically two competing theoretical approaches to explain investment behaviour given the implementation of a currency union. From the diversification motive standpoint, the monetary union should reduce the attractiveness of European portfolio holdings in other euro area countries. On the other hand, the asymmetric information hypothesis argues that reduced transactions costs due to the EMU should increase the share of European portfolio investment within the euro area.

The basic intuition of the diversification motive was first developed by Grubel (1968) and Solnik (1974). In the line of these early works, Harvey (1991) and De Santis and Gérard (1997) argued that portfolio investors hold foreign securities because of the risk reduction benefits. The principle is that if securities in a portfolio are less than perfectly correlated, then some degree of diversification is desirable to counterbalance adverse shocks that disproportionately affect security returns. Levy and Sarnat (1970) demonstrate that the diversification motive across countries yields benefits because of the imperfect correlation that may exist among returns from assets in different countries.

The literature supporting the asymmetric information hypothesis argues that there are significant indirect barriers that lead investors to concentrate their portfolio investments in the domestic market; that is, the "home-bias" effect. According to Al-Khail and Berglund (2003), the explanations for the "home bias" phenomenon fall into to two different categories. The first one explains the concentration of portfolio investment in the domestic countries by the existence of some inertia in financial markets and severe institutional restrictions. The other explanation to the asymmetric information motive – put forward, for instance, by Tesar and Werner (1995) – relies on geographic proximity, strong trade linkages and common language. Coval and Moskowitz (1999) and Grinblatt and Keloharju (2001) provide significant empirical evidence that geography, language and culture induce a "home bias" effect on portfolio allocations. Huberman (2001) shows that the "home bias" is a consequence of investors' preferences, since they tend to hold equities that they are more familiar with. Cooper and Kaplanis (1994) test whether the "home bias" in equity portfolio decisions is caused by investors attempting to hedge purchasing power parity deviations. They find that the bias towards domestic stocks is not reconcilable with investors need for hedging the domestic inflation.

Overall, the literature points out that while international financial markets have been witnessing a higher degree of integration in recent years, there still remain many considerations that prevent investors from taking advantage of large diversification strategies. The evidence also suggests that at least some fraction of the home bias may be the result of the inability of simple mean-variance theory to capture other sources of risk. International investing introduces additional risk arising from different currencies, political, legal and institutional difference across countries that makes information gathering on foreign markets an expensive and imprecise task.

Model Used in the Empirical Analysis

In the context of international investment theory, portfolio decisions are assumed to be affected by the expectation of return differential at the domestic and the foreign capital markets. The underlying model for this hypothesis is provided by the well-known uncovered interest parity (UIP) condition. Besides, portfolio decisions are argued to be influenced by the investment climate at the source and at the host country. Therefore, the nature of the investment determinants is twofold: financial variables, as interest rate differentials, and real variables, as the quality of institutions.

On the financial side, interest parity conditions recognize that investors have the choice of holding assets denominated in the currency of the source country (in bilateral terms, named as country *i*), which offer a domestic rate of return $\left(r_t^i\right)$, and of holding assets denominated in host currency (named as country *j*), which offer a foreign rate of return $\left(r_t^j\right)$. Since investors are concerned with returns denominated in their own currency, foreign rates of returns have to be adjusted by the expected devaluation of the foreign currency with respect to the domestic one. Therefore, the uncovered interest parity can be written as:

$$r_t^i = r_t^j + E_t[s_{t+1}^{ij} - s_t^{ij}] \tag{1.1}$$

where s^{ij} is the (log of the) nominal bilateral exchange rate.

The empirical evidence of the UIP condition has been widely tested. Most of the studies have pointed out the empirical failure of the UIP (e.g., Engel, 1996); although more recently, attempts to estimate long-run horizon regressions have found support for the uncovered interest parity.[1] For the purpose of this study, we are not concerned with the assumption of whether the UIP holds; but we rather assume that the investment decision is driven by the interest differential, including the expected devaluation.

Since future exchange rates are unknown, we estimate the value of s_{t+1}^{ij} using a simple autoregressive AR(1) process. The underlying uncertainty related to the future exchange rate is also assumed to condition the investment decision. The future exchange rate and the conditional uncertainty are estimated based on an Autoregressive conditional heteroscedasticity (ARCH) model:

$$s_t^{ij} = a_0 + a_1 s_{t-1}^{ij} + \varepsilon_t^{ij} \tag{1.2}$$

$$(\hat{\varepsilon}_t^{ij})^2 = \alpha_0 + \sum_{k=1}^{q} \alpha_k (\hat{\varepsilon}_{t-k}^{ij})^2 + \omega_t^{ij} \tag{1.3}$$

where $(\hat{\varepsilon}_t^{ij})^2$ is the conditional variance of the nominal bilateral exchange rate and ω_t^{ij} is an error term.

The real side of the FPI determinants can be based on the well-established gravity equation. We assume, therefore, that portfolio investment is not only conditioned by financial variables but also by real factors. The literature on theoretical and empirical studies using the gravity model is quite vast. The gravity equation has been extensively used to explain bilateral trade and foreign direct investment.[2] However, applications to portfolio flows are more limited, partly due to lack of available information. One of the earliest studies on bilateral financial flows using the gravity approach is Portes and Rey (1999) who find support for gravity variables – mainly distance as a measure of information costs – in explaining bilateral equity flows between 14 countries. More recently, Guerin (2006) also estimated a modified gravity model to examine the determinants of bilateral foreign direct investment, trade and portfolio investment. Bilateral portfolio investment is found to be significantly affected by information costs and also to be more sensitive (as compared with FDI) to control variables, as macroeconomic fundamentals.

The original gravity theory is given by the Newtonian law, which states that attraction between two bodies is directly proportional to their mass and indirectly proportional to their distance. This notion applied to international trade and capital movements means that bilateral flows of goods and capital can be explained by the economic size, geographical distance and a set of variables that capture common institutional characteristics such as language, trade agreements, common borders and cultural aspects.

In a simple specification, the gravity equation can be expressed as:

$$F_{ij} = {Y_i Y_j}/{D_{ijj}} \tag{1.4}$$

where F_{ij} are flows (e.g. trade or capital flows), Y_i and Y_j are economic sizes, and D_{ij} is a separation measure. If the flows are portfolio holdings, the attraction forces are financial and real sector variables and the measures of separation are geographical and institutional distances, the gravity equation can be written as:

$$\begin{aligned} fpi_t^{ij} &= \beta_0^{ij} + \beta_1\left((r_t^j - r_t^i) - E_t(s_{t+1}^{ij} - s_t^{ij})\right) + \beta_2 eru_t^{ij} + \beta_3 EMU_t^i + \\ &+ \beta_4\left(gdp_t^j - gdp_t^i\right) + \beta_6 geodist^{ij} + \beta_6 instdist_t^{ij} + u_t^{ij} \end{aligned} \tag{1.5}$$

The dependent variable is bilateral foreign portfolio investment (*fpi*). Source countries *i* are the largest eight European countries: Belgium, France, Germany, Ireland, Italy, Netherlands, Spain and the United

Kingdom. Host countries *j* are the main destination of FPI within the European Union (all the source countries except Belgium), two Eastern European countries (Hungary and Poland), seven emerging markets (Brazil, China, India, Malaysia, Mexico, Russia, South Africa, South Korea and Turkey) and three non-European developed countries (Canada, Japan and the United States). Annual data are from 2001 to 2006.

As for the financial variables, the UIP deviation – given by $(r_t^j - r_t^i) - E_t(s_{t+1}^{ij} - s_t^{ii})$ – is calculated based on the difference between nominal bilateral interest rates and the expected bilateral exchange rate devaluation.

Differently from the other variables, the expected exchange rate uncertainty (*eru*) is estimated for each exchange rate series (host country currency with respect to the euro or the British pound) based on monthly data. When the ARCH effect is found to be significant, the uncertainty variable is given by the square root of $(\hat{\varepsilon}_t^{ij})^2$ in equation (1.2). If there is no ARCH, the uncertainty variable is simply computed by the absolute value of error term in the mean equation (1.1). To compute the relevant *eru* variable, we take the annual average of either the first or the second measure.

To capture the EMU effect, we consider a dummy variable, which is 1 when the host and the source country adopt the euro and 0, otherwise. The reduction of transaction costs achieved by a monetary union stimulates portfolio investment and tends to magnify the "home bias" evidence to the level of regional integration areas. In fact, financial integration has progressed more remarkably within countries that are part of preferential trade agreements than at a multilateral level. As found by De Santis and Gérard (2006), the establishment of the EMU enhanced regional financial integration in the euro area and motivated equity and bonds flows within the region. Al Khail and Berglund (2001) reached similar results for the case of Finland. They concluded that the allocation of Finnish portfolio investment is predominantly influenced by the information based assumption, which supports that reduced information asymmetry produced by the EMU increases portfolio holdings in other euro area countries.

Two of the real sector variables are conventional gravity factors: the difference in economy sizes, given by GDP differentials $(GDP_t^j - GDP_t^i)$; and the geographic distance (*geodist*^{ij}) – taken by the distance between countries' capitals (see www.chemical-ecology.net). Interest rates, exchange rates and GDP (in USD) as well as bilateral FPI come from the IMF datasets (International Financial Statistics and www.imf.org/external/np/sta/pi/geo.htm).

The institutional distance variable (*instdist*^{ij}) was proxied by the six indicators computed by Kaufmann et al. (1999): government effectiveness (*gov*), regulatory quality (*reg*), voice and accountability (*vac*), political stability (*pol*), rule of law (*law*) and control of corruption (*cor*). Institutional distance is given by the difference in the indicator value at the host country and at the source country. The extension and quality of institutions have been often related as a structural change with significant impacts on economic development. In international financial sectors, institutions play a significant role since foreign investors are subject to uninsurable instability arising from different currencies and political and legal systems across countries. According to Al-Khail and Berglund (2003), asymmetric information is a significant restriction to financial capital movements. He includes institutional variables as proxies for the information costs, as long as these institutions provide a regulatory and legal environment that reduces the non-familiarity conditions with respect to the host country.

Empirical Results

Before dealing with the estimation of the determinants of bilateral portfolio investment, we focus on some preliminary results regarding our main variable FPI and the exchange rate uncertainty measure.

Table 1-1 shows the FPI stocks that the eight source European countries hold in the main destinations: European Union (EU), USA, Canada, Japan and the emerging countries in our sample. The EU bias is quite evident for most of the European countries, since the EU region is the main recipient of portfolio investment: Belgium (85.3 percent of FPI is allocated in EU countries); Spain (84.8 percent); Germany (80.1 percent); Italy (78.2 percent) and France (74.6 percent). On the other hand, for the UK, foreign portfolio holdings are more homogeneously distributed, with the highest shares among European countries in terms of destinations as the USA (42.4 percent of total British FPI) and emerging markets (9.2 percent).

Table 1-1 Foreign portfolio investment in 2006 (USD mln)

Source country	Host country					
	EU	**USA**	**Canada**	**Japan**	**Emerg. markets**	**Total**
UK	907.20	816.89	25.56	231.25	178.09	1,927.74
France	1,114.74	253.64	15.57	86.08	23.74	1,493.77
Ireland	781.63	397.39	19.35	56.99	34.62	1,289.97
Germany	986.93	179.10	12.28	28.27	24.77	1,231.34
Netherlands	603.19	305.53	9.40	37.29	35.21	990.63
Italy	486.33	103.64	2.98	13.92	15.08	621.95
Spain	384.84	52.16	1.65	2.59	12.29	453.52
Belgium	384.29	54.88	3.64	4.27	3.49	450.57

Source: International Monetary Fund

The results for the exchange rate uncertainty variable for selected countries are depicted in Figure 1-1 and Figure 1-2. The highest uncertainty values are consistently found in Brazil and Mexico. The relatively low exchange rate uncertainty estimated for China is due its pegged exchange rate system. Among the lowest uncertainties are the exchange rates for the UK (with respect to the euro), Hungary and Japan (both with respect to the euro and the British pound).

Figure 1-1 Exchange rate uncertainty measure: host country against the euro

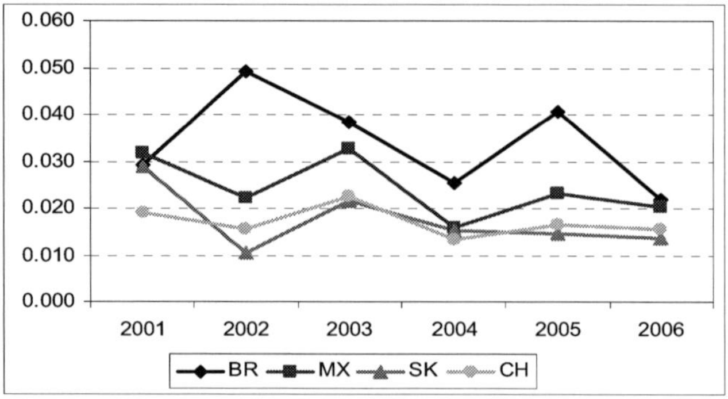

Figure 1-1 (cont.)

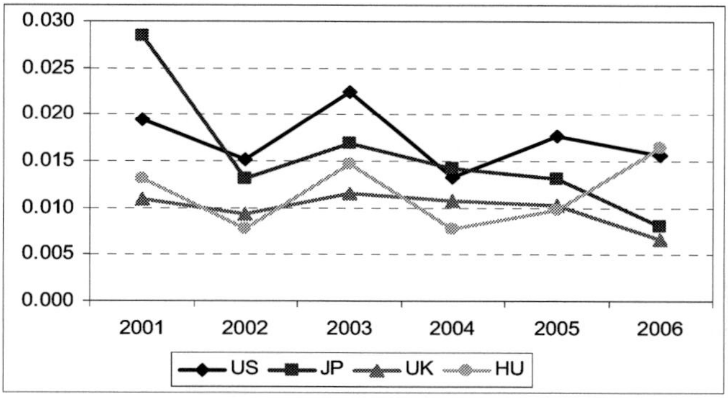

Source: Authors' calculations
Note: BR, Brazil; MX, Mexico; SK, South Korea; CH, China; US, United States; JP, Japan; UK, United Kingdom; HU, Hungary.

The ARCH model of the bilateral exchange rate, outlined in equations (1.2) and (1.3), was estimated for each exchange rate series (relating the host country currency against the euro and the British pound). The estimation was based on monthly data from 2001 to 2006. Appendix 1-A summarises the results. Out of 15 exchange rate series, the ARCH effect was statistically significant (at 5 percent significance) for 4 rates of the host country currency against the euro and for 3 rates of the host country currency against the pound. ARCH was found significant for some emerging markets (e.g., Brazil, Mexico, South Korea and Turkey) and for Japan.

Figure 1-2 Exchange rate uncertainty measure: host country against the British pound

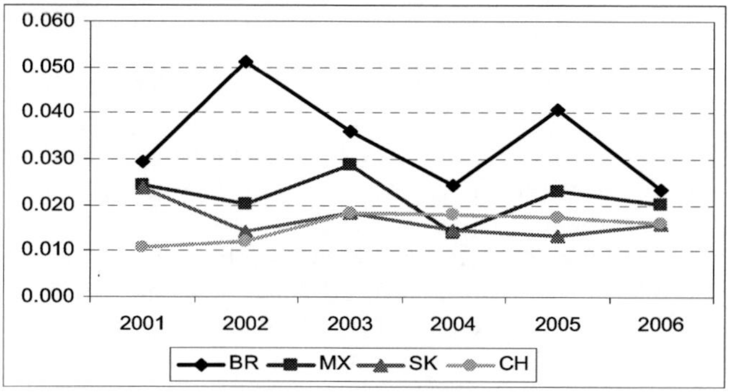

Figure 1-2 (cont.)

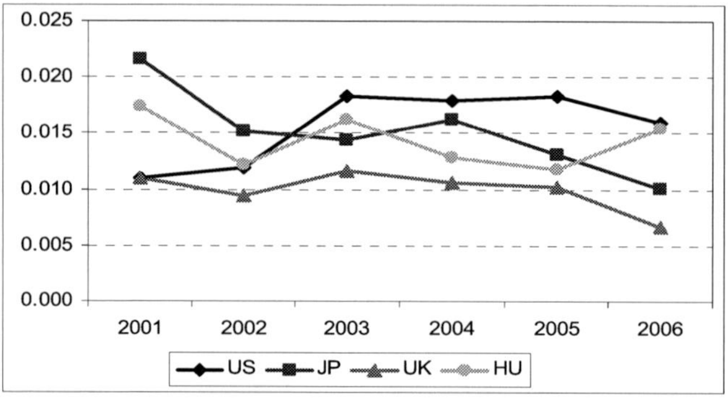

Source: Authors' calculations
Note: Countries denoted as in Figure 1-1

Table 1-2 Panel unit root tests

Null hypothesis: unit root	Statistic	Probability
fpi_t^{ij}	-18.279	0.000
ERU_t^{ij}	-44.170	0.000
$(r_t^j - r_t^i) - E_t(s_{t+1}^{ij} - s_t^{ii})$	-14.308	0.000
$(GDP_t^j - GDP_t^i)$	-24.185	0.000
$(gov_t^j - gov_t^i)$	-2.140	0.016
$(reg_t^j - reg_t^i)$	-11.391	0.000
$(vac_t^j - vac_t^i)$	-8.391	0.000
$(pol_t^j - pol_t^i)$	-15.462	0.000
$(law_t^j - law_t^i)$	0.021	0.508
$(cor_t^j - cor_t^i)$	-0.946	0.172

Source: Authors' estimation. Note: Test proposed by Levin et al. (2002).

The panel data model (equation 1.5) was estimated by the random effects method since geographical distance is invariant over time for a given country pair. In Table 1-3, we report the results for the FPI equation.

Specification (1) includes all variables in the model, while specification (2) only the statistical significant ones. In specification (3), we dropped the two institutional measures estimated with a negative sign – since such result is not compatible with theory. The withdrawal of these two variables does not change the qualitative results.

Table 1-3 Foreign portfolio investment determinants

	(1)	(2)	(3)
Constant	14.733*** (1.062)	14.787*** (1.111)	13.606*** (1.143)
$(r_t^j - r_t^i) - E_t(s_{t+1}^{ij} - s_t^{ii})$	0.016*** (0.004)	0.016*** (0.004)	0.023*** (0.004)
ERU_t^{ij}	-0.125*** (0.036)	-0.125*** (0.036)	-0.177*** (0.037)
EMU_t^i	1.108*** (0.338)	1.122*** (0.353)	0.699*** (0.363)
$(GDP_t^j - GDP_t^i)$	0.684*** (0.070)	0.673*** (0.071)	0.585*** (0.073)
$geodist_t^{ij}$	-0.730*** (0.129)	-0.735*** (0.135)	-0.505*** (0.137)
$(gov_t^j - gov_t^i)$	1.028*** (0.162)	1.017*** (0.162)	0.491*** (0.152)
$(reg_t^j - reg_t^i)$	0.768*** (0.170)	0.755*** (0.168)	0.431*** (0.172)
$(vac_t^j - vac_t^i)$	-0.591*** (0.129)	-0.614*** (0.130)	
$(pol_t^j - pol_t^i)$	0.650*** (0.120)	0.642*** (0.121)	0.565*** (0.126)
$(law_t^j - law_t^i)$	-0.989*** (0.244)	-1.018*** (0.200)	
$(cor_t^j - cor_t^i)$	-0.048 (0.192)		
Common language	0.691** (0.370)	0.691** (0.370)	0.624* (0.385)
Number of observations	966	966	966
Adjusted R^2	0.361	0.357	0.311
F-statistic	50.43	54.46	55.24

Source: Authors' estimation

Note: ***, **, * Significant at the 1, 5, and 10% level. Standard errors are in parentheses.

Among the financial variables, the UIP differential was found to be statistically significant and with a positive sign coefficient, indicating that FPI is attracted by higher rates of return (discounted of the expected exchange rate devaluation). Conditional exchange rate uncertainty – measured by the ARCH model – was estimated to significantly decrease portfolio holdings in the host economy. The coefficient for the *eru* variable is higher than the coefficient for the UIP deviation, which means that FPI tends to be more responsive to changes in uncertainty than to changes in excess returns.

At last, the coefficient of the EMU variable was estimated to be positive and significant. This result confirms the asymmetric information hypothesis and indicates that the reduced transaction costs due to the EMU increase the share of European portfolio investment within the currency area.

As for the real sector results, the traditional gravity variables were found to be significant to explain European cross-border portfolio decisions. The coefficient for the difference in GDP levels was statistically significant and with a sizable magnitude. A ten percent GDP increase in the host market (relative to the source market) implies an increase of 5.8 percent in portfolio investment from European countries to host countries. Geographical distance was found to exert a negative and statistically significant influence to European FPI outflows. Common language was also a significant determinant of FPI.

Only three institutional variables were significant in the final specification. The non-stationarity result and some multicolinearity[3] are probably the main reasons for the non-significance of voice and accountability, rule of law and control of corruption. In the final specification, government effectiveness, regulatory quality and political stability are statistically significant and indicate that an improved institutional environment at the host country would attract FPI.

Conclusion

The literature on portfolio investment has pointed out two theoretical hypotheses: the diversification motive and the asymmetric information motive for cross-border portfolio holdings. Under the asymmetric information assumption, the launch of the EMU and the lower uncertainty among member countries should reduce transaction costs and facilitate capital movements within the currency area.

The estimation of a foreign portfolio investment equation for European countries confirms the general idea under the asymmetric information hypothesis. The EMU variable is statistically significant, indicating that there is a "regional bias" for European portfolio holdings. That result indicates that European investors prefer to invest more regionally (within the euro area) than internationally, given basically the lower transaction costs and familiarity aspects common to member countries. Besides, the results show that investors behave negatively to exchange rate uncertainty, indicating that a currency area and exchange rate arrangements might be preferable to other systems where the instability is inherently higher. The gravity variables also give support to the asymmetric information assumption since both geographic distance and institutional distance depress foreign portfolio investment. That is, the farther and the less reliable the host country, the higher the transaction and informational costs, and, therefore, the lower the portfolio investment inflows.

In addition, foreign portfolio investment from European countries was found to be positively influenced by the relative size of the host country economy – which ratifies the empirical appeal of the gravity model for portfolio holdings – and also positively affected by higher rates of return (net of exchange rate depreciation), validating the UIP differential as an arbitrage gain directing FPI flows.

References

Al-Khail, M.A. and T. Berglund. 2003. *What Drives the Country Allocation of International Portfolio Investments? Universally Available Versus Trade Related Information.* EFMA 2004 Basel Meetings Paper. Swedish School of Economics and Business Administration. Stockholm.

—. 2001. *The Impact of the EMU on International Portfolio Investments.* Departmental Working Papers 141. Tor Vergata University, CEIS. Rome.

Cooper, I. and E. Kaplanis. 1994. Home Bias in Equity Portfolios, Inflation Hedging, and International Capital Market Equilibrium. *The Review of Financial Studies* 7(1): 45-60.

Coval, J.D. and T.J. Moskowitz. 1999. Home Bias at Home: Local Equity Preference in Domestic Portfolios. *Journal of Finance* 54(6): 2045-73.

Deardorff, A.V. 1998. Determinants of Bilateral Trade: Does Gravity Work in a Neoclassical World? In *The Regionalization of the World Economy*, ed. J.A. Frankel. Chicago, IL: University of Chicago Press.

De Santis, G. and B. Gerard. 1997. International Asset Pricing and Portfolio Diversification with Time-Varying Risk. *Journal of Finance* 52(5): 1881-912.

Engel, C. 1996. The Forward Discount Anomaly and the Risk Premium: a Survey of Recent Evidence. *Journal of Empirical Finance* 3(2): 123-92.

Feenstra, R.C., J.R. Markusen and A.K. Rose. 2001. Using the Gravity Equation to Differentiate Among Alternative Theories of Trade. *Canadian Journal of Economics* 34(2): 430-47.

Grinblatt, M. and M. Keloharju. 2001. How Distance, Language, and Culture Influence Stockholdings and Traders. *Journal of Finance* 56(3): 1053-73.

Grubel, H. 1968. Internationally Diversified Portfolios: Welfare Gains and Capital Flows. *American Economic Review* 58(5): 1299-314.

Guerin, S.S. 2006. The Role of Geography in Financial and Economic Integration: A Comparative Analysis of Foreign Direct Investment, Trade and Portfolio Investment Flows. *The World Economy* 29(2): 189-209.

Harvey, C.R. 1991. The World Price of Covariance Risk. *Journal of Finance* 46(1): 111-57.

Huberman, G. 2001. Familiarity Breeds Investment. *Review of Financial Studies* 14(3): 659-80.

Kaufmann, D., A. Kraay and P. Zoido-Lobatón. 1999. *Aggregating Governance Indicators.* World Bank Policy Research Working Paper 2195. Washington, DC.

Levin, A., C.F. Lin and C.S.J. Chu. 2002. Unit Root Tests in Panel Data: Asymptotic and Finite Sample Properties. *Journal of Econometrics* 108(1): 1-24.

Levy, H. and M. Sarnat. 1970. International Diversification of Investment Portfolios. *American Economic Review* 60(4): 668-75.

Portes, R. and H. Rey. 1999. *The Determinants of Cross-Border Equity Flows*. NBER Working Paper 7336. National Bureau of Economic Research. Cambridge, MA.

Solnik, B. 1974. Why Not Diversify Internationally Rather than Domestically? *Financial Analysts Journal* 30(July): 91-135.

Tesar, L.L. and I.M. Werner. 1995. Home Bias and High Turnover. *Journal of International Money and Finance* 14(4): 467-92.

Notes

[1] See, for instance, Chinn and Meredith (2005).

[2] See, for instance, the seminal papers by Deardorff (1998) and Feenstra et al. (2001).

[3] High partial correlation are found, for instance, between *law* and *reg* (0.93) and between *cor* and *gov* (0.97). For more details see Appendix 1-B.

Appendix 1-A

Table 1-A1 ARCH Test for selected currencies against the euro and the British pound (2001-2006)

Host country	ARCH test against the euro		ARCH test against the British pound	
	χ^2	p-value	χ^2	p-value
Euro area	---	---	7.061	0.1326
UK	7.061	0.1326	---	---
USA	3.032	0.5523	1.393	0.8453
Japan	19.978	0.0005	13.142	0.0106
Canada	3.565	0.4680	3.612	0.4610
Hungary	0.047	0.9997	0.778	0.9413
Poland	2.200	0.6990	2.793	0.5929
Russia	8.428	0.0770	1.026	0.9057
Brazil	9.237	0.0554	11.383	0.0225
China	2.413	0.6601	1.144	0.8872
Korea	13.342	0.0097	4.964	0.2909
India	2.073	0.7222	1.290	0.8630
Malaysia	2.919	0.5713	0.966	0.5929
Mexico	12.143	0.0163	1.131	0.8891
South Africa	0.320	0.9884	0.513	0.9721
Turkey	22.117	0.0001	22.268	0.0001

Source: Authors' estimation

Note: The null hypothesis is that there is no ARCH. The test statistic TR2 follows χ^2 distribution with q degrees of freedom (here q=4).

Appendix 1-B

Table 1-B1 Partial correlations between institutional variables

	vac	reg	pol	law	gov	cor
vac	1					
reg	0.869	1				
pol	0.710	0.835	1			
law	0.833	0.926	0.817	1		
gov	0.789	0.943	0.808	0.956	1	
cor	0.831	0.943	0.799	0.969	0.970	1

Source: Authors' calculations based on Kaufmann et al. (1999).

CHAPTER TWO

THE POLITICAL ECONOMY OF FIXED EXCHANGE RATES: A SURVIVAL ANALYSIS*

RALPH SETZER

What factors determine a country's exchange rate policy? Since the collapse of the Bretton Woods system of fixed exchange rates in 1973, economists have been increasingly interested in answering this question. Analysts focused primarily on the possible influence of optimum currency area (OCA) criteria, such as a country's size, openness to trade, or factor mobility. More recent approaches emphasized the nature and the sources of shocks to which an economy is exposed or explicitly took imperfections on financial markets into account. However, despite a large body of work, little consensus has emerged about the determinants of exchange rate regime choice. The existing empirical literature could not identify a single variable as a clear predictor of exchange rate regime choice and even among economically comparable countries large discrepancies in exchange rate policy have been observed (Juhn and Mauro, 2002).

Possibly motivated by the financial crises in the 1990s that caused both economic and political turmoil, some economists have recently directed their attention to the impact of political-economic factors on exchange rate regime choice (see, e.g. Eichengreen et al., 1995; Simmons, 1997; Frieden et al., 2001; or the contributions in the fall 2002 special issue of International Organization). In this view, exchange rate policy is the outcome of a political process with strong distributional and welfare implications. Differences in exchange rate policy can be explained by factors such as different parties having different macroeconomic preferences or by incumbents' efforts to increase their reelection prospects. The aim of this chapter is to expand this branch of the literature. The central claim is that political and institutional factors have an important, predictable impact on the duration of fixed exchange rate regimes in developing countries. The focus is on currency devaluations (and not on regime choice) because historically the exit from currency pegs and the associated sharp losses in a currency's value have been those exchange rate episodes with the strongest political effects. For developing countries in particular, currency devaluations have often been accompanied by political turbulences and changes in government.

Although a number of empirical studies have been concerned with similar questions, this study differs from previous research on this subject in at least two significant ways: First, the sample consists of 47 countries within the time period from 1975 to 2000, and it is thus larger and more diverse than most other studies that have been conducted. This enables us to not only test the structure of one particular theory (as most previous research has done), but allows us to ask, when looking at a large set of data, whether different sets of political and institutional variables systematically influenced the duration of currency pegs in a number of developing countries.

The use of a survival analysis approach in the context of exchange rate regime duration is a second innovation to the literature and establishes greater empirical meaning than standard probit or logit models. Specifically, this method of estimation optimally exploits the data's nature of time dependency; that is, it accounts for the fact that the length of time already spent on a currency peg is an important determinant of the probability of exit into a more flexible exchange rate regime. To our knowledge, the only previous studies using survival analysis in the context of currency pegs are Bodea (2003) and Blomberg et al. (2005). Undoubtedly, the allowance for time dependence in these studies is an important improvement compared to previous research. However, what is missing in both studies is a clear picture of a serious discussion of the most adequate econometric model for this type of analysis. Another possible area of improvement is the application of the survival analysis approach for a global sample of developing countries.

The rest of this chapter proceeds as follows: First, we derive testable hypotheses for the following empirical analysis. After describing the dataset, we introduce the Cox model in the context of exchange rate regime shifts. We then present and comment the estimation results. Finally, some concluding remarks are derived.

Developing a Theory of Currency Peg Duration

A common feature to the explanation of currency peg breakdowns revolves around the policy trade off between the (short-term) political losses incurred if the political authorities resort to the devaluations option and the (long-term) macroeconomic gains achieved by doing so. The political losses arise because politicians fear that voters punish governments that violate exchange rate stability. The benefits are largely due to higher international price competitiveness. By making exports cheaper and imports more expensive, devaluations promise to provide relief from unsustainable current account deficits, low employment and low output growth. Additional economic gains are expected due to the possibility to pursue a more relaxed economic policy stance. Thus, if one assumes that in the short term governments have the ability to maintain a fixed exchange rate, the central question concerns the conditions that increase or lower the willingness of policymakers to sustain the exchange rate commitment. In the following we identify six political and institutional factors that are supposed to provide explanatory power with respect to the maintenance of currency pegs: the timing of elections, partisan motives, the number of veto players, the degree of central bank independence, the type of political system, and the strength of the government.

Elections

It is conventional wisdom that the state of the economy at the moment of an election has a major impact on voters' decisions (Remmer, 1991). The probability of reelection is higher when the economy prospers than when economic conditions are bad. Voters are taken to express a general dissatisfaction when the economy is in recession and hold the government responsible. Inasmuch exchange rates influence the economic key indicators price level, employment, and real income, the exchange rate regime may be of strategic value for the incumbent to maximize his reelection prospects. A number of studies have shown that abandoning an exchange rate commitment entails significant political costs and, at least in the short term, is usually accompanied by contractionary effects (Cooper, 1971). Hence, given that with an upcoming election the time horizon of governments is particularly short, incumbents will have a strong bias against devaluation in the pre-election period. Moreover, any potential gains from devaluing are presumably more than outweighed by the fact that devaluations cast doubt on the competence of the incumbent and its ability to govern.

Maintaining a fixed exchange rate regime that delivers monetary stability is seen as an important signal for successful economic policy. Thus, required exchange rate adjustments are likely to be delayed until after the election. The classical rule is, as Edwards (1994, 28) put it, to "devalue immediately and blame it on your predecessors." The incentive to delay devaluations until after the election is particularly strong in countries where the currency peg is part of an inflation-reducing exchange rate stabilization program. In such a case, the decision to abandon a fixed exchange rate regime and devalue is often interpreted in a way that other complementary parts of the stabilization program (such as a sound fiscal policy, liberalization of trade flows, or the privatization of state-owned companies) will not be maintained either. As a result, risk premium and public debt increase.

Additionally, market expectations that the government is eager to defend the exchange rate parity in the pre-election period should reduce the likelihood of a crisis in that period. Speculators with rational expectations will anticipate that policymakers have a higher willingness to defend an exchange rate peg prior to an election. Hence, they will delay a speculative attack until after polling day, when the political authorities will undertake fewer efforts to maintain the fixed regime (Leblang, 2003). This behaviour reduces the likelihood of the exit from a currency peg for the pre-election period and increases its likelihood for the post-election period.

Hypothesis 1a: In pre-election years, the probability of exit from a currency peg is lower than in non-election years.

Hypothesis 1b: In post-election years, the probability of exit from a currency peg is higher than in non-election years.

Partisan Actors

Hibbs (1977) argues that political parties represent different core constituencies, i.e. they pursue policies that favour only a subgroup of the population and thus maximize different objective functions. Parties from the ideological right traditionally have strong ties to the business and financial sectors. Since these social groups retain more wealth and are more secured from unemployment, the classical partisan theory presupposes that in terms of a stable Phillips curve trade off, right-wing parties attach a high priority to maintaining price stability while they are willing to tolerate certain level of unemployment rate because they dispose of safe jobs. Parties from the ideological left, on the other hand, have closer links to workers and trade unions, whose income strongly depends on employment opportunities. At the same time, inflation aversion is lower. Therefore, left-wing parties give priority to employment and distributional aspects, accepting a certain degree of inflation.[1] Consequently, they are more inclined to use expansionary macroeconomic policy to manage the domestic economy.

These distributional differences have important implications for the duration of exchange rate systems. Since left-wing governments are generally more inclined to use expansionary macroeconomic policy to manage the domestic economy, the danger of devaluation grows. As a consequence, left-wing parties are expected to experience the more short-lived duration of a currency peg. In contrast, right-wing governments, being more concerned about stabilizing the economy and securing the real value of investment and creditor savings, should have a greater incentive to maintain a currency peg.

However, empirical research has documented that when partisan influences are found, in about half of the studies partisanship worked the opposite of what theory would predict: i.e. that right-wing parties are less prone to currency pegs. While Leblang (2003) finds that right-wing governments are associated with a greater willingness to defend a currency peg than more leftist parties, results by Simmons (1997) and Bodea (2003) suggest that more conservative parties are less committed to currency pegs.

Such an opposing political cycle in the exchange rate regime may occur if one combines the partisan approach with the insights of the political business cycle theory. In fact, it might be precisely left-wing governments that seek to maintain a fixed exchange rate in the period prior to elections to signal concern for price stability. To illustrate this point, consider a left-wing government that has subsequently devalued its currency and is approaching an election. If this government cares about both remaining in office and setting policy, it would be unproductive to devalue even more in the election year. In fact, it could be useful to show some anti-inflationary concern and avoid devaluation. In this way, the government builds on an anti-inflationary reputation and increases its chances for re-election. Analogously, right-wing governments, which possess greater anti-inflationary reputations ex ante, can possibly afford to devalue in election years. The perceived political costs of an exchange rate adjustment will be lower because of their reputation of being tough with inflation (Milesi-Ferretti, 1995; Leblang, 2003).

Hypothesis 2a: In non-election periods, countries with a left-wing government have a higher probability of exiting from a currency peg than countries with governments from right-wing parties.

Hypothesis 2b: In pre-election periods, countries with a left-wing government have a lower probability of exiting from a currency peg than countries with governments from right-wing parties.

Veto Players

Exchange rate policy may also differ among countries because their policymaking is governed by different institutions. The number of veto players is a case in point. Following Tsebelis (2002, 19), veto players refer to the number of institutional or partisan actors whose agreement is necessary for a change of policy. The veto player theory contains important implications for economic policy. The main prediction is that the number of veto players correlates positively with the maintenance of the status quo. Hence, the problem with a low number of veto players is that a policy commitment such as a fixed exchange rate could suffer from credibility problems because it is too easy to change. However, societies characterized by many veto players can be plagued by indecision and gridlock and hinder many issues from being addressed for long periods of time because political consensus is more difficult to achieve. Countries in which there is a separation of powers, where the government coalition consists of multiple parties, where different relevant legislative chambers exist, and where states or provinces have authority over spending, taxes, or legislating, will find it hard to implement the necessary policy packages to sustain the exchange rate commitment in a timely fashion. Decision-makers in these countries are more likely to have different views regarding the required policy that will lead to the postponement of unpopular decisions. Delays in decision-making will in turn hamper effective policy adjustments in the face of adverse economic shocks or an unfolding crisis. In the absence of many veto players, however, political decision-making addresses sources of conflicts faster and conflicting positions can be better resolved (Alesina and Drazen, 1991).

Thus, one can interpret the insights of the veto player approach in two different ways. It is possible to think about many veto players as a credible commitment to not interfere in exchange rate matters. In this case, the existence of many veto players increases the sustainability of a fix. The assumption of the status quo bias in exchange rate policy is motivated by the idea that all veto players have to agree to the abandonment of the peg. But the belief of a longer duration of currency pegs with many veto players becomes more difficult to justify when exits from currency pegs are regularly enforced by the failure to respond to unfolding macroeconomic disequilibria. Alternatively, the status quo bias generated by many veto players can also lead to delays in the adjustment to economic shocks. In this case, political inertia increases exchange rate instability and leads to a lower persistence of currency pegs.

When will the direct effect of a stronger commitment device with many veto players prevail, and when will the indirect effect of the inability for political reforms take place? We argue that the relationship between veto players and the sustainability of currency pegs is U-shaped. A government's ability to maintain a currency peg is highest when there is an average number of veto players. A low number of veto players have difficulties to credibly commit. If political leaders face too few constraints to renege on the exchange rate commitment, markets cannot be confident that the exchange rate parity will not be subject to unpredictable changes. Therefore, with no (or few) institutional veto power options, currency pegs are expected to endure only briefly. By contrast, incompatible economic policy, which is more likely to persist with an institutional framework divided by a large number of veto players, has undoubtedly been at the core of most currency crises and large devaluations in the past. Inconsistent fiscal policies lead to real overvaluation, losses in reserves and to a more rapid exit from the currency peg.

Hypothesis 3: The probability of exit from a currency peg in relation to the number of veto players is U-shaped. A low number and a high number of veto players increase the probability of exit.

Central Bank Independence

Much has been written explaining why politicians willingly relinquish a sizeable part of their power and delegate policy tasks to an independent agency. Most of the authors see the inflation bias time inconsistency problem as rationale for such delegation. The time inconsistency problem exists because ex post politicians have a strong incentive to deviate from a preannounced monetary policy and surprise voters with inefficiently high inflation. Such a policy generates greater growth and employment and thereby improves the incumbent's re-election prospects. Rational forward-looking agents, however, will anticipate this loose monetary policy and adjust their inflation expectations. The result of this behaviour is higher inflation, but not higher growth.

Granting independence to central banks or pegging the exchange rate to a country with low inflation provides a solution to this dilemma. If successfully implemented, both forms of monetary commitment ensure a predictable and stable monetary policy that keeps inflation down and signals to economic agents that monetary policy will be insulated from short-term electoral manipulation (see Rogoff, 1985 for central banks and Giavazzi and Pagano, 1988 for currency pegs). In the case of independent central banks, monetary policy is delegated to a conservative central banker that has a longer time horizon and is more inflation averse than the government. In the case of pegged regimes, monetary policy is pursued by a foreign central bank with a high reputation of price stability. The implication is that independent central banks can be considered a substitute for a fixed regime to provide credibility. If the elimination of the inflation bias is achieved by an independent central bank, there is no need for countries with independent central banks to fix the exchange rate and give up domestic control over monetary policy. Proponents of this view suggest that countries with independent central banks have a lower propensity to peg than their more dependent counterparts (Broz, 2002).

While the previous considerations provide no satisfying answer to the question whether currency peg duration increases or decreases with central bank independence, a political-economic argument suggesting a negative impact of central bank independence on the duration of fixed exchange rate regimes is based on the constraints of the Mundell-Fleming model. If the currency is fixed and capital is mobile, monetary policy is rendered ineffective. Since the central bank is committed to a stable exchange rate, there is no leeway to use monetary policy for stabilizing output or adjusting the balance of payments. Whether the central bank is independent or not plays no role in this case. From a political-economic view, an independent central bank has its own interests that are likely to prefer a retreat from the peg. Such a change maximizes the central bank's influence on monetary policy on which it otherwise has (quite irrationally) hardly any influence. Only with flexible exchange rates can the central bank effectively use its policy instruments (discount rate, purchase and sale of government securities, and foreign currencies) and pursue its policy goals. This argument implies that the duration of a currency peg decreases with the implementation of central bank independence.[2]

Hypothesis 4: The probability of exit from a currency peg increases with the independence of the central bank.

Political Regime Type

The duration of currency pegs may also be influenced by a country's political regime type, i.e. whether a country has a democratic or an authoritarian political system. This study argues that greater transparency and accountability can be thought to increase the duration of a fixed exchange rate regime. Accountable politicians and a transparent institutional framework suggest that policymakers in democracies make better policy choices than those in autocracies. Since they provide markets greater quantities of accurate information, speculative attacks due to imperfect information (as suggested by Calvo and Mendoza, 2000) are less prevalent. This claim is consistent with Bonomo and Terra (1999, 9) who argue in their analysis of political cycles for the Brazilian Real, that "contrary to widespread belief, a dictatorship may be less able to take necessary bitter measures than a democratic regime". Cukierman et al. (1992) also provide evidence for this claim, concluding that totalitarian regimes are more prone to inflation than their democratic counterparts.

Moreover, democracies cannot only be expected to have a greater ability to maintain an exchange rate peg. They should also have a higher willingness to do so. Large devaluations are often followed by political turbulence and changes in government (Cooper, 1971). Government instability and the possibility of electoral defeat pose a much higher threat to decision-makers in democratic countries than to the political leaders in authoritarian regimes. Hence, democratic governments face higher political costs when a peg is abandoned. This implies that democratic governments have a large incentive to stabilize the exchange rate and maintain a currency peg.

Hypothesis 5: The probability of exit from a currency peg decreases with the level of democracy.

Political Instability

Méon and Rizzo (2002) model the influence of political instability on the credibility of a fixed exchange rate regime. They describe the choice of an exchange rate regime as a repeated game between the policymaker and the private sector in which the policymaker is subject to a time-inconsistency problem. In their model, only policymakers who can be assured that they will remain in office for an infinite amount of time, will resist the temptation to devalue and be able to defend the peg. Once political instability is taken into account and a policymaker's life expectancy shrinks, policymakers will choose to surprise the private sector and abandon the currency peg because the relief in the short-run through an unexpected devaluation exceeds the fear of an inflationary bias. Hence, political instability leads to a horizon-shortening effect that in most cases operates against the sustainability of currency pegs. This impact is intuitive. A more stable government should be more willing to pursue long-run economic goals than a less stable one. Fragile governments will heavily discount the future benefits of economic reforms that increase the long-run sustainability of currency pegs. A government's myopia will promote policies determined by short-term considerations. This behaviour is rational because, as second-generation currency crisis models have shown, short-term political inconsistencies will not necessarily lead to speculative behaviour.

Hypothesis 6: The probability of exit from a currency peg increases with political instability

The Dataset

In order to follow the theoretical propositions closely, we apply the methodology of duration models to a unique dataset for 47 developing countries for the period from 1975 to 2000.[3] The dependent variable in this study is the length of time until a currency peg collapses, or in other words, the number of years between the beginning and the end of a fixed exchange rate regime. We analyse together all currency pegs, regardless of the underlying reason for the peg's abandonment. The incentive for the inclusion of all exits in the analysis is given by the fact that in developing countries, where the prime rationale for fixing is to stabilize the economy, every abandonment of a currency peg signals the move from a stabilization-oriented policy toward a more discretionary policy orientation with presumably higher inflation rates. Thus, as argued by Edwards (1996) and Collins (1996), every exit of a pegged regime entails some political costs.

In order to determine the duration of a fix, it is important to choose an appropriate exchange rate classification. The IMF de jure exchange rate regime classification as published in the Annual Report on Exchange Rate Arrangements and Exchange Restrictions is inappropriate because it fails to capture macroeconomic policies that are inconsistent with a peg. For instance, if the institutional setting prevents a country from maintaining exchange rate stability, but the country still claims to have its exchange rate fixed, the failure to sustain to the currency peg would not be reflected in the regression results. The natural classification by Reinhart and Rogoff (2002) has severe drawbacks for the purpose of this analysis as well. In this classification, actual exchange rate flexibility is measured on a five-year moving average time period. While this procedure is useful to distinguish long-term regimes from short-term periods of exchange rate stability, it also results in very few regime transitions and makes it difficult to pinpoint changes in exchange rate policy due to political shocks. This problem is addressed by Levy Yeyati and Sturzenegger (2005), whose classification is chosen because it best captures the actual behaviour of policymakers. Exchange rate policy is measured on a yearly basis and deviations from exchange rate stability in a given year immediately reflect in a lower regime category.

The theoretical considerations outlined above have identified various potential political and institutional determinants of the duration of currency pegs. Data definitions for these variables are provided in Appendix 2-A. However, political and institutional factors alone cannot account for changes in exchange rate policy. As suggested by the OCA and currency crisis literature, a number of economic and financial variables are included as controls in the empirical model. However, one must also be aware that the inclusion of too many explanatory variables may lead to multicollinearity problems. The reason for the assumed occurrence of multicollinearity is the possibility that political variables may affect the exchange rate regime via the government's choice of macroeconomic policies. For instance, if a left-wing government engages in expansionary monetary policy, increasing inflation and thereby causing the exchange rate to devalue, estimation results could possibly attribute the abandonment of the peg to higher inflation rates although the underlying reason is the left-wing government's lower concern for economic stability. Hence, even purely economic variables may be related to political factors. Accordingly, an empirical specification that combines political variables with economic variables that can be influenced by the government might wash out the political effects, which are clearly more exogenous.[4]

Our solution to this dilemma is as follows: First, we collect a number of structural variables that are clearly exogenous to the political variables. These variables include external debt (*debt*), size of the economy (*gdp*), trade openness (*open*), standard deviation of export growth (*sdexport*), and a variable that accounts for a possible time trend (*share*). Then, we form a second group of economic variables that are under control of policymakers, or that could at least be related to domestic political factors. These are capital openness (*capop*) and fiscal balance (*fiscal*). Table 2-A1 in Appendix 2-A provides a definition of all variables. We will be more cautious when controlling for this second group of variables and only include them in some selected specifications.

Modelling Exchange Rate Regime Duration

Most previous studies on the political economy of exchange rates have employed probit or logit. While these approaches are useful because they consider multiple explanatory variables simultaneously in the prediction, one of their major shortcomings is the implicit assumption of a constant hazard rate. As such, these studies ignore the possible time dependence of exchange rate regimes. In other words, what these studies assume is that the time in which a certain exchange rate regime exists does not determine the likelihood of its abolition. However, failing to account for time dependence can only be justified under two crucial assumptions: First, time should not matter. That is to say that depending on the economic and political covariates in the model, the probability of a regime shift in any year must be the same as in any other year. Second, one must assume that the model is correctly specified. Since time can be used as a proxy variable for unmeasured occurrences, no uncontrolled variables should exhibit an impact on exchange rate regime duration. If one (or both) of these assumptions is not fulfilled, the regression result may be biased. However, both assumptions are hard to justify. For example, it seems inappropriate to assume that the probability that a country abandons an exchange rate peg is the same for a peg that has been in existence for one year than for a peg that has been maintained for ten years. The choice of an exchange rate regime is not a once-and-for-all decision, but is likely to change over time. Hence, it seems particularly useful to think of exchange rate regime choice in terms of the likelihood of the abandonment of the prevailing exchange rate regime. Studies of survival analysis account for these time effects and test for duration dependence, i.e. if exchange rate regime duration is a function of time.

In principle, three functions can be used to characterize the distribution of the survival time in a discrete time approach: the density function, the survivor function, and the hazard function.[5]

The density function is characterized by:

$$f(t) = \Pr(T = t_i) \tag{2.1}$$

where T is a non-negative random variable that takes values t that measure the time spent in a particular state. The survivor function is defined as the probability that the event of interest has not occurred by duration t, i.e. the random variable T exceeds (or at least equals) the specified time t. For the discrete case it is given by:

$$S(t) = \Pr(T \geq t_i) = \sum_{j \geq i} f(t_j), \tag{2.2}$$

where j denotes a failure time. $S(t)$ is a non-increasing function with a value 1 at the time origin and a value 0 as t goes to infinity.

The relationship between the failure (or exit) rate and the time already spent in that state is determined by the hazard function. The hazard function emphasizes conditional probabilities: It describes the probability of a spell ending at some time point, given that the spell has lasted to that time point. The discrete-time hazard rate is defined as:

$$\lambda(t) = f(t_i) / S(t_i)\,. \tag{2.3}$$

It depicts the conditional probability a regime ends at t_i, given that it lasts until t_i.[6]

Bodea (2003) and Blomberg et al. (2005) resort to the Weibull model, a parametric approach to fitting survival model. However, one should be cautious in terms of drawing conclusions about duration dependence from Weibull parameterisation because it only allows for a monotonic shape of the underlying or baseline hazard function. In fact, the hazard of exiting from a peg could increase (or decrease) non-monotonically with duration as well. In this case, the Weibull would fit the data poorly and the coefficient estimates would be biased. To allow for both non-monotonic and monotonic hazards, semiparametric approaches, such as the Cox proportional hazards model, are more appropriate because they allow for more flexibility in the shape of the baseline hazard function. The characteristic feature of the semiparametric models is that the baseline hazard $\lambda_0(t)$ is left completely unspecified. The hazards are made dependent on a vector of explanatory variables x with coefficients β that are to be estimated and the baseline hazard λ_0. The setting is then as follows:

$$\lambda(t, x, \beta, \lambda_0) = \lambda_0(t)\phi(x, \beta)\,, \tag{2.4}$$

where φ is a positive function of x and β, and $\lambda_0(t)$ characterizes how the hazard function changes as a function of time. The baseline hazard depends on t, but not on x, meaning that it captures individual heterogeneity that is unexplained by the covariates. Alternatively, the baseline hazard can be interpreted as the probability of an exchange rate regime to change conditional on all the covariates of zero. The most commonly used semiparametric procedure was developed by Cox (1972). He proposed to specify the relative hazard function $\phi(x, \beta)$ in the following way:

$$\phi(x, \beta) = \exp(x'\beta)\,. \tag{2.5}$$

The advantage of this model is that non-negativity of φ does not impose restrictions on β.[7] To estimate the hazard function, observed spells are ordered by length from smallest to largest, $t_1 < \ldots < t_n$. The conditional probability that the first observation abandons a spell at time t_1, given that any of the n observations could have been failed at t_1, is:

$$\frac{\exp(x_1,\beta)}{\sum_{i=1}^{n}\exp(x_i,\beta)} \qquad (2.6)$$

This quantity is the contribution of the shortest observation to the partial likelihood. Generally, the contribution of the j-th shortest observation j to the partial likelihood is given by:

$$\frac{\exp(x_j,\beta)}{\sum_{i=j}^{n}\exp(x_i,\beta)}. \qquad (2.7)$$

Translating this technique into that of exchange rate regimes, the numerator is the hazard for the country whose currency peg completes at time t_1, while the denominator is the sum of the hazards for countries whose spells were still maintained just prior to time t_j (i.e. those whose spells formed the risk set and could have ended at time t_j). The likelihood is formed as the product of these contributions and may be written as:

$$L(\beta) = \prod_{i=1}^{n}\frac{\exp(x_j,\beta)}{\sum_{i=j}^{n}\exp(x_i,\beta)}. \qquad (2.8)$$

The likelihood function depends only on the unknown coefficient vector β and can then be maximized using standard methods.[8] The functional form of the hazard rate does not need to be specified. The Cox log likelihood function is then as follows:

$$L(\beta)= \sum_{i=1}^{n}\left\{\ln\phi(x_i,\beta)-\ln\left[\sum_{j=i}^{n}\phi(x_j,\beta)\right]\right\} \tag{2.9}$$

where $\phi(x_i,\beta)=\exp(x_1,\beta)$.

One of the advantages of the survival analysis is that the partial likelihood framework accommodates for censored data.[9] This is done by including censored observations in the summation of the denominator of the partial likelihood function terms corresponding to observations that fail before their censoring point. Censored observations do not enter in the denominator of observations that fail after their censoring point and they are never included in the numerator of a contribution to likelihood.

Estimation Results

The main focus of the analysis is on the duration of currency pegs. Thus, some closer inspection of periods of fixed exchange rate regimes is in order. The variable *duration* characterizes the "life" of a fixed exchange rate regime or the consecutive number of years that a currency peg has persisted until it is abandoned. By definition, the minimum number of years that a pegged exchange rate regime lasts is one year and the maximum is 26 years (the number of years covered by the 1975-2000 sample). Overall, regime persistence is very low. The average currency peg duration is 3.97 years. It is important to note that this number has a downward bias because the operational design restricts the maximum length of a currency peg to be 26 years and since some of the pegs are either left- or right-censored.

Figure 2-1 further illustrates this point. It plots an estimate of the smoothed hazard function. The graph agrees with former analysis on currency peg duration (see, e.g., Duttagupta and Ötker-Robe, 2003), showing an increasing hazard first and a decreasing hazard afterward. In other words, the conditional probability of abandonment depends upon the amount of time that the peg has existed. The clearly non-monotonic pattern of duration dependence may be explained by a time lag between the introduction of a peg and gains in credibility. Achieving credibility is a long-lasting process and thus, only if the peg has persisted for a long time, the conditional probability of exit decreases. In any case, the non-monotonic pattern provides a strong case for the use of duration models such as the Cox that allow non-monotonity in the hazard rate.

Figure 2-1 Estimated hazard function for currency pegs, Kaplan-Meier

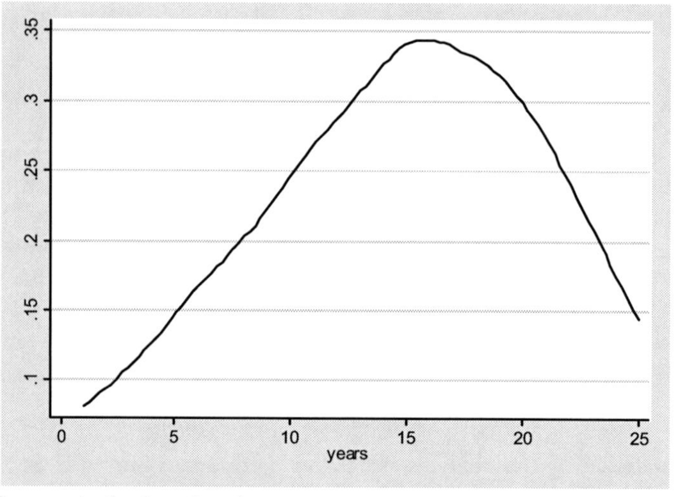

Source: Author's estimation

In the following, the semi-parametric approach by Cox (1972) is used to derive conclusions about the impact of the various variables defined above. In order to avoid the above-mentioned multicollinearity problems, four Cox models were measured. Some explanatory variables are alternately dropped from the regression equations.[10]

Table 2-1 presents the regression results. Let us begin with the interpretation of the results for the partial-likelihood estimate of the first political model presented in column (1). Coefficients for any β_i parameter significantly above zero indicate that an increase in the corresponding variable leads to a faster exit, and conversely for a negative coefficient parameter. Thus, we see that election years are significant and positively related to the risk of abandoning a peg. This is support for the notion that short time horizons raise the probability of abandonment. Statements about the magnitude of the impact can be drawn by calculating hazard ratios, which are exponentiated coefficients (i.e., e^{β_i}). For dummy variables, the exponentiated coefficients are easily interpreted as time-ratios. This implies that in election years the probability of exiting a currency peg is 111 percent higher than in non-election years. In line with hypothesis 2a, *left* has a higher probability of abandoning a currency peg than *center*. More exactly, the hazard at the same time for left parties is 15 percent higher than for more conservative parties.

Table 2-1 Duration of currency pegs, Cox model

	(1)	(2)	(3)	(4)
elect	0.746* (0.399)		0.555 (0.406)	0.488 (0.592)
left	0.142 (0.466)	0.181 (0.429)	0.600 (0.444)	-1.493* (0.770)
veto	0.567** (0.258)	0.548** (0.264)	0.518** (0.264)	0.821** (0.399)
cbi	-1.816* (0.946)	-2.241** (0.953)	-1.946** (0.916)	-6.044*** (1.521)
polity	0.100*** (0.038)	0.110*** (0.037)	0.089*** (0.034)	0.177*** (0.051)
partyinst	-0.512** (0.256)	-0.550** (0.269)	-0.529** (0.263)	-0.623* (0.346)
gdp	0.203* (0.121)	0.265** (0.108)	0.247** (0.105)	0.649*** (0.203)
debt	0.245 (0.168)	0.286* (0.169)	0.231 (0.157)	0.450 (0.397)
share	1.564 (1.807)	1.422 (1.680)		
sdexport	0.246 (0.511)			
open	0.000 (0.005)			
preelect		-0.764* (0.448)		
postelect		-0.538 (0.513)		
preleft			-1.976 (1.249)	-0.482 (1.372)
fiscal				-0.204*** (0.061)
capop				0.588 (0.597)
Observations	274	259	259	198
Wald chi^2	31.12	35.65	36.46	64.73
Link test	0.62	0.60	0.27	0.08
AIC	200.81	188.86	186.05	99.80
BIC	240.55	224.43	218.06	135.97

Source: Author's estimation

Note: *, **, *** indicate significance at the 10%, 5%, 1% level respectively. Standard deviations are reported below each value in brackets. Macroeconomic variables are used in lags.

The statistically significant positive parameter estimate of 0.57 for *veto* in model (1) means that every additional veto player above the mean (or, analogously, the loss of one veto player below the mean) increases the time-to-exit for a fixed exchange rate regime by 76 percent, a result that is consistent with the predicted U-shaped relationship between veto players and currency peg duration (hypothesis 3). The hazard ratio for *cbi*, as a proxy for the actual degree of central bank independence, is also significant at the 5 percent level. The negative coefficient indicates that independent central banks have a higher probability of abandoning a peg. This is in line with the idea of a substitutive relationship between independent central banks and fixed regimes (hypothesis 4). A one standard deviation increase in central bank independence would be predicted to increase the probability of exit by 16 percent. With respect to *polity*, the positive parameter estimate combined with the low p-value implies that the level of democracy does matter for explaining the duration of pegs. However, contrary to what has been suggested in hypothesis 5, more democratic countries display a faster exit from currency pegs. A one-point increase in the 21-point polity index increases the probability of exit by 11 percent. This result broadly survived when I experimented with the 11-point index of *democracy* as an alternative measure for the level of democracy.

Even more puzzling, the degree of political instability also influences currency peg durability in a counterintuitive way. A higher level of political instability leads, ceteris paribus, to a lower persistence of currency pegs. Again, the result is significant at the 5 percent level and the magnitude of the effect is quite large. A one standard deviation increase in political instability leads to a 50 percent lower probability of abandoning the currency peg. One possible explanation for this puzzle is that previous studies, such as those by Edwards (1996) and Berger et al. (2000) that found a positive relationship between political instability and the choice of a fixed regime have omitted to control for the type of political regime. Since the present study suggests that democratic countries are assumed to have a higher government turnover rate[11] and a lower currency peg duration, a correlation between political instability and the duration of a fix that does not control for these effects is spurious.

However, further (unreported) regressions reveal that even when omitting the democracy variable from the regressions, the puzzling coefficient for *partyinst* remains. This result does also hold if we exclude the countries with the highest political turnover ratio (Bolivia and Haiti) or when we use the government party turnover ratio (*govinst*) as a measure for political instability. Columns (2) through (4) display alternative specifications of the model. With respect to the basic variables just discussed, the results remain very much the same. All variables keep its sign from the first estimation model. Thus, we will only discuss the most important changes to these variables in the following. To the model in column (2), we add the two dummy variables *preelect* and *postelect*. The parameter estimates indicate a lower probability of exit in both pre-election and post-election periods. The former is consistent with hypothesis 1a. The negative sign for *postelect* contradicts the expectation of a higher risk of exit after the election. Thus, we obtain support for hypothesis 1a and no support for hypothesis 1b.

Model (3) asks whether there are any differences in the pre-electoral period between left- and right-wing parties. The interaction variable *preleft* has a negative sign. If pre-election periods are controlled for, the absolute magnitude of the impact of both left-wing parties increases considerably in this specification. Thus, data in column (3) reveal that in non-election periods, leftist parties have a higher probability to abandon a currency peg (the relative hazard for leftist parties compared to rightist parties is 1.82), while in pre-election periods right-wing parties are more likely to exit (in these periods the relative hazard for *left* is 0.14). This result is perfectly consistent with the view that despite its overall preference for flexible exchange rates, left-wing parties are unwilling to abandon a currency peg in pre-election periods to signal their concern for price stability (hypotheses 2a and 2b). Right-wing parties, by contrast, have a greater reputation for being tough on inflation and thereby have fewer electoral consequences to fear if they abandon a peg in election periods.

Model (4) adds further economic variables, which are not necessarily exogenous to the political variables. The positive coefficient for *capop* indicates that countries with capital controls have a higher likelihood of abandoning a peg. This result is consistent with previous empirical work on the relationship between exchange rate regime policymaking and capital controls (Leblang, 2003; Blomberg et al., 2005). Moreover, it also confirms the view that the introduction of capital controls may send a negative signal to currency and financial markets, and thus increases the likelihood of speculative attacks. The coefficient of *fiscal* enters statistically significant and displays the expected sign, indicating that countries with fiscal imbalances have difficulties in maintaining a fixed exchange rate system.

With the introduction of the macroeconomic variables most of the political and institutional variables lose their significant explanatory power. Interestingly, the coefficient of *left* changes sign. This suggests, e.g., that the higher probability of exit under left-wing governments can be partly attributed to their looser fiscal policy.

Quite importantly, the link test indicates that the specification seems to fit the data quite well. A common way to assess the model fit in Cox models is to calculate Cox-Snell residuals. If the fitted model is correct, the Cox-Snell residuals should have a standard censored exponential distribution with hazard ratio equal to one for all *t*. Therefore, a plot of the cumulative hazard function (based on the Nelson-Aalen estimator) for these data should lie on a straight line from the origin with slope equal to one. Figure 2-2 plots the Cox-Snell residuals for the different specifications of the political model. The graphic analysis indicates that the different models are reasonably specified. The plots satisfy the exponential requirement most of the time: model (4) in particular fit the data rather well. Note that some deviation of the 45° line is expected due to the reduced effective sample caused by censoring. The deviation is higher in the right-hand tail of the plot where the sparseness of data reduces the adequacy of the model, while the large number of smaller residuals in the left-hand tail of the figure cluster more closely around the straight line with slope equal to one.

In order to increase the robustness of the results, a second estimation routine resorts to complementary log-log (cloglog). The advantage of cloglog over alternative estimation strategies to handle discrete duration data, such as logit or probit, is that the response curve has a fat tail as it departs from *0*, whereas it approaches *1* more rapidly than both the logit and the probit function. This suggests that the cloglog function is particularly appropriate in datasets where there are relatively few failures (Box-Steffensmeier and Jones, 2004, 74).

Figure 2-2 Cox-Snell residuals (based on Cox estimates)

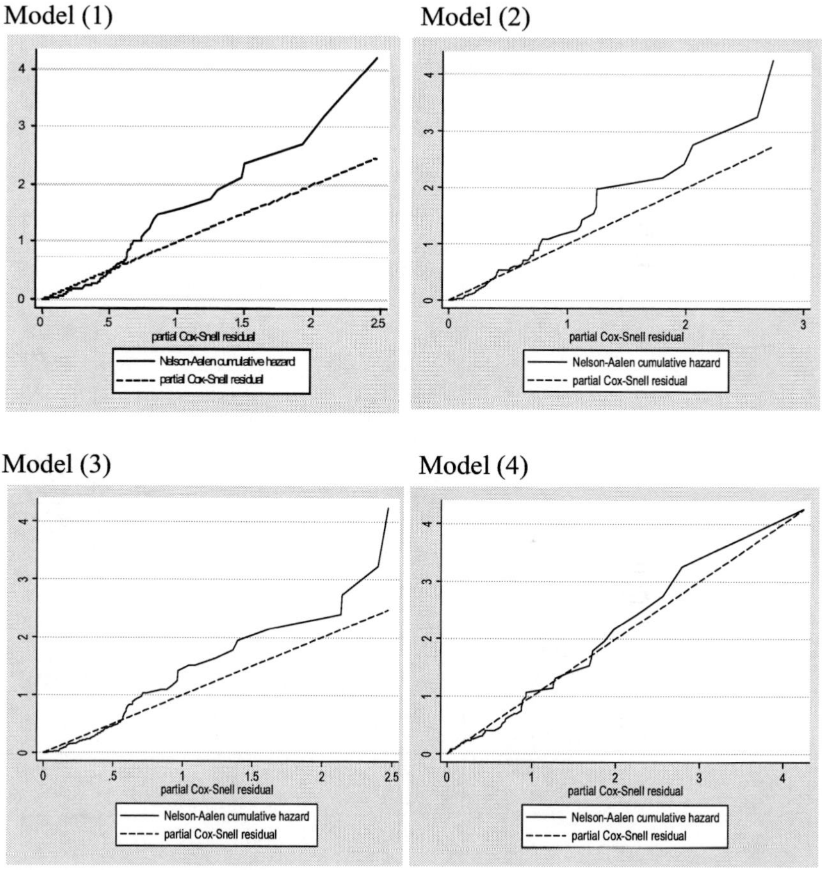

Source: Author's estimation

Table 2-2 presents the results for the re-estimation of the above specifications using the cloglog model. In order to get rid of the time dependence property, a cubic spline function on the basis of three knots was estimated (Beck et al., 1997, 11-12). Accordingly, the estimated model includes, in addition to the independent variables described above, three splines, which produce an estimate of the form of duration dependence.

Table 2-2 Duration of currency pegs, clog-log model

	(1)	(2)	(3)	(4)
elect	1.121*** (0.317)		0.984*** (0.281)	
left	0.168 (0.324)	0.024 (0.323)	0.215 (0.352)	-0.736* (0.402)
veto	0.163 (0.177)	0.167 (0.165)	0.143 (0.170)	0.239 (0.227)
cbi	-1.284 (0.905)	-1.619* (0.830)	-1.348* (0.814)	-4.163*** (1.333)
polity	0.048* (0.027)	0.069** (0.028)	0.059** (0.028)	0.130*** (0.042)
partyinst	-0.337 (0.242)	-0.323 (0.243)	-0.333 (0.232)	-0.410* (0.216)
open	-0.005 (0.003)	-0.006* (0.003)	-0.006* (0.003)	-0.019** (0.008)
debt	0.275 (0.259)	0.358 (0.262)	0.339 (0.260)	0.490 (0.378)
T1 cubed	0.416*** (0.156)	0.388*** (0.126)	0.408*** (0.139)	0.547*** (0.183)
T2 cubed	-0.271*** (0.104)	-0.254*** (0.084)	-0.265*** (0.093)	-0.367*** (0.126)
T3 cubed	0.022** (0.009)	0.022** (0.008)	0.022** (0.009)	0.036** (0.013)
sdexport	0.149 (0.410)			
gdp	0.047 (0.112)			
preelect		-0.381 (0.378)		
postelect		-0.558 (0.451)		
preleft			-1.208 (0.960)	-0.596 (1.081)
fiscal				-0.086*** (0.024)
capop				0.045 (0.584)

Table 2-2 (cont.)

Observations	273	259	259	198
Wald chi^2	82.90	40.59	62.50	79.98
Link test	0.52	0.60	0.99	0.83
AIC	274.63	272.55	261.90	168.60
BIC	325.16	318.79	308.14	217.93

Source: Author's estimation
Note: *, **, *** indicate significance at the 10%, 5%, 1% level respectively. Standard deviations are reported below each value in brackets. Macroeconomic variables are used in lags.

Overall, results are in line with the Cox models. Quite importantly in terms of robustness, all political and institutional variables keep its sign. The impact of the institutional variables is weaker than in the Cox specifications. However, the results confirm the important role of electoral and partisan motives.

Conclusions and Discussion

This study has examined political-economic determinants of fixed exchange rate regime duration in the framework of survival analysis. It has been argued that standard statistical methods such as logit or probit do not adequately capture the duration of currency pegs for three reasons: First, they ignore time dependence and do not account for the fact that the exit of a currency peg is more likely to happen at some time. Second, they are not suitable to handle multiple-failure data. Third, they treat censored and uncensored observations as the same. Therefore, the empirical analysis relied on discrete Cox regression models, in which the time dependent structure of the data is implicitly implemented.

Evidence was presented that political and institutional factors have an important impact on the duration of pegged exchange rate regimes. With regard to elections, hypothesis 1a (which proposes a lower likelihood of exchange rate adjustments in pre-election periods) was confirmed. By contrast, hypothesis 1b was clearly rejected. In terms of partisanship, we found also some evidence for the notion that the risk of exit from a peg is higher for left-wing governments than for conservative governments (hypothesis 2a). However, this result changed when macroeconomic variables, such as a country's fiscal balance, were included in the regression. Apparently, the lower duration of currency pegs under left-wing governments is caused by laxer fiscal policy. The negative sign of the interaction variable *preleft*, which measures the pre-election effects under left-wing governments, is consistent with such a view. Left-wing governments have a higher propensity to devalue; however, they may prefer maintaining a fixed regime in the pre-election period in order to build up some anti-inflationary credibility (hypothesis 2b).

Political institutions seem to be a weaker predictor of exchange rate instability than any electoral and partisan impacts. Still, the results suggest that as the variable *veto* increases (that is, as the deviation from the mean of veto players increases), the likelihood of abandoning a fixed exchange rate regime rises (hypothesis 3). The fourth hypothesis, which holds that the probability of exiting from a currency peg increases with the independence of the central bank could also be plainly confirmed. Contrary to expectations, highly democratic regimes and government stability tend to be negatively associated with a country's willingness to sustain exchange rate stability. The latter result in particular is robust to various specifications, which allows us to suggest that the greater political costs instable governments incur when they abandon the peg explain the difference.[12] Since weak governments are more desperately in need of the anti-inflationary credibility that accompanies a currency peg, they are expected to undertake large efforts to maintain exchange rate stability (Edwards, 1996, 159).

Thus, seen on the whole, five of eight hypotheses could be confirmed by the data. The date of elections, the ideological orientation of the governing party, the degree of central bank independence, and the number of veto players have a significant impact on a country's probability to maintain an exchange rate fix. These political and institutional differences may help to explain why some countries have maintained fixed exchange rates and others have not. In particular, the analysis might provide an explanation to why economically comparable countries pursue different exchange rate policies.

References

Alesina, A. and A. Drazen. 1991. Why are Stabilizations Delayed? *American Economic Review* 81(5): 1170-88.

Beck, T., G. Clarke, A. Groff, P. Keefer and P. Walsh. 2001. New Tools in Comparative Political Economy: The Database of Political Institutions. *World Bank Economic Review* 15(1): 165-76.

Beck, N., J.N. Katz and R. Tucker. 1997. Beyond Ordinary Logit: Taking Time Seriously in Binary Time-Series-Cross-Section Models. *American Journal of Political Science* 42(4): 1260-88.

Berger, H., J.E. Sturm and J. de Haan. 2000. *An Empirical Investigation into Exchange Rate Regime Choice and Exchange Rate Volatility.* CESifo Working Paper 263. Ifo Institute for Economic Research, Munich.

Blomberg, S.B., J.A. Frieden and E. Stein. 2005. Sustaining Fixed Rates: The Political Economy of Currency Pegs in Latin America. *Journal of Applied Economics* 8(2): 203-25.

Bodea, C. 2003. *An Empirical Evaluation of the Politics of Exchange Rates in Six East European Countries*. Paper presented at the 2003 Midwest conference, University of Rochester, March.

Bonomo, M. and M.C. Terra. 1999. *The Political Economy of Exchange Rate Policy in Brazil: 1964-1997.* IADB Working Paper R-367. Interamerican Development Bank, Washington DC.

Box-Steffensmeier, J.M. and B.S. Jones. 2004. *Event History Modeling: A Guide for Social Scientists*. Cambridge: Cambridge University Press.

Broz, J.L. 2002. Political System Transparency and Monetary Commitment Regimes. *International Organization* 56(4): 863-89.

Bussière, M. and C. Mulder. 1999. *Political Instability and Economic Vulnerability.* IMF Working Paper 99/46. International Monetary Fund, Washington DC.

Calvo, G.A. and E.G. Mendoza. 2000. Rational Contagion and the Globalization of Securities Markets. *Journal of International Economics* 51(1): 79-113.

CDP. 2004. Center on Democratic Performance—Election Result Archive. Binghamton University, New York. Access from www: < http://cdp.binghamton.edu/era/countries >.

Collins, S.M. 1996. On Becoming More Flexible: Exchange Rate Regimes in Latin America and the Caribbean. *Journal of Development Economics* 51(1): 117-38.

Cooper, R.N. 1971. Currency Devaluations in Developing Countries. In *Essays on International Finance 86*. Princeton University, Princeton, NJ.

Cox, D.R. 1972. Regression Models and Life-Tables. *Journal of Royal Statistical Society, Series B* 34: 187-220.

Cukierman, A., S. Edwards and G. Tabellini. 1992. Seigniorage and Political Instability. *American Economic Review* 82(3): 537-55.

De Haan, J. and W. Kooi. 2000. Does Central Bank Independence Really Matter? New Evidence for Developing Countries Using a New Indicator. *Journal of Banking and Finance* 24(4): 643-64.

Duttagupta, R. and I. Ötker-Robe. 2003. *Exits from Pegged Regimes: An Empirical Analysis.* IMF Working Paper 03/147. International Monetary Fund, Washington DC.

Edwards, S. 1994. *The Political Economy of Inflation and Stabilization in Developing Countries.* NBER Working Paper 4319. National Bureau of Economic Research, Cambridge, MA.

—. 1996. *The Determinants of the Choice Between Fixed and Flexible Exchange Rates.* NBER Working Paper 5756. National Bureau of Economic Research, Cambridge, MA.

Eichengreen, B., A.K. Rose and C. Wyplosz. 1995. Exchange Market Mayhem: The Antecedents and Aftermath of Speculative Attacks. *Economic Policy* 10(21): 251-97.

Frieden, J.A., P. Ghezzi and E.H. Stein. 2001. Politics and Exchange Rates: A Cross-Country Approach. In *The Currency Game—Exchange Rate Politics in Latin America*, eds: J.A. Frieden and E.H. Stein. Washington DC: John Hopkins University Press.

Giavazzi, F. and M. Pagano. 1988. The Advantage of Tying One's Hands: EMS Discipline and Central Bank Credibility. *European Economic Review* 32(5): 1055-75.

Hibbs, D. 1977. Political Parties and Macroeconomic Policy. *American Political Science Review* 71(4): 1467-87.

IMF. 2003. *International Financial Statistics.* International Monetary Fund, Washington DC.

Juhn, G. and P. Mauro. 2002. *Long Run Determinants of Exchange Rate Regimes: A Simple Sensitivity Analysis.* IMF Working Paper 104. International Monetary Fund, Washington DC.

Keefer, P. and D. Stasavage. 2003. The Limits of Delegation: Veto Players, Central Bank Independence, and the Credibility of Monetary Policy. *American Political Science Review* 93(3): 407-23.

Kiefer, N. 1988. Economic Duration Data and Hazard Functions. *Journal of Economic Literature* 26(2): 646-79.

Leblang, D.A. 2003. To Devalue or to Defend? The Political Economy of Exchange Rate Policy. *International Studies Quarterly* 47(4): 533-59.

Levy Yeyati, E. and F. Sturzenegger. 2005. Classifying Exchange Rate Regimes: Deeds versus Words. *European Economic Review* 49(6): 1603-35.

Lijphart, A. 2004. *Lijphart's Elections Archive.* University of California at San Diego, San Diego, CA. Access from : < http://dodgson.ucsd.edu/lij >.

Marshall, M. and K. Jaggers. 2002. *Polity IV Project: Political Regime Characteristics and Transitions, 1800-2002*. University of Maryland, College Park, MD.

Méon, P.G. and J.M. Rizzo. 2002. The Viability of Fixed Exchange Rate Commitments: Does Politics Matter? A Theoretical and Empirical Investigation. *Open Economies Review* 13(2): 111-32.

Milesi-Ferretti, G.M. 1995. The Disadvantages of Tying Their Hands: On the Political Economy of Policy Commitments. *Economic Journal* 105 (433): 1381-402.

Poirson, H. 2001. *How do Countries Choose Their Exchange Rate Regime?* IMF Working Paper 01/146. International Monetary Fund, Washington DC.

Popescu, M. and M. Hannavy 2004. *Political Transformation and the Electoral Process in Post-Communist Europe*. University of Essex. Access from: < www.essex.ac.uk/elections >.

Reinhart, C.M. and K.S. Rogoff. 2002. *The Modern History of Exchange Rate Regime Arrangements: A Reinterpretation.* NBER Working Paper 8963. National Bureau of Economic Research, Cambridge, MA.

Remmer, K.L. 1991. The Political Impact of Economic Crisis in Latin America in the 1980s. *American Political Science Review* 85(3): 777-800.

Rogoff, K.S. 1985. The Optimal Degree of Commitment to an Intermediate Monetary Target. *Quarterly Journal of Economics* 100(4): 1169-89.

Simmons, B.A. 1997. *Who Adjusts? Domestic Sources of Foreign Economic Policy During the Interwar Years*. 2nd edition, Princeton: Princeton University Press.

Tsebelis, G. 2002. *Veto Players—How Political Institutions Work.* Princeton: Princeton University Press.

World Bank. 2003. *World Development Indicators*. Washington DC.

Zárate, R.O. 2004. *Zárate's Political Collections*. Access from: < http://www.terra.es/personal2/monolith/home.htm >.

Notes

* The author thanks Ansgar Belke, Felix Hammermann, Hans Pitlik, and Rainer Schweickert as well as conference participants at the 2005 Annual Meeting of the European Economic Association in Amsterdam and the 2005 Annual Congress of the Swiss Society of Economics and Statistics in Zurich for very helpful comments. Jakob de Haan and Gian-Maria Milesi-Ferretti provided me with valuable data. The views expressed are my own and do not involve the responsibility of the Deutsche Bundesbank.

[1] A tolerance toward inflation is also justified because price increases improve the relative income position of the lower classes.

[2] I thank Rainer Schweickert for a useful discussion on this point.

[3] The countries included in the sample are: Algeria, Argentina, Belarus, Bolivia, Brazil, Bulgaria, Chile, Colombia, Costa Rica, Cote d' Ivoire, Croatia, Cyprus, Czech Republic, Dominican Republic, Ecuador, El Salvador, Estonia, Guatemala, Guyana, Haiti, Honduras, Jamaica, Latvia, Lebanon, Lithuania, Malaysia, Mexico, Moldova, Morocco, Nicaragua, Nigeria, Panama, Paraguay, Peru, Philippines, Poland, Republic of Korea, Romania, Russia, South Africa, Slovakia, Slovenia, Thailand, Turkey, Ukraine, Uruguay, and Venezuela.

[4] Still, political effects may continue to exist even after controlling for economic variables because, as suggested by second-generation currency crisis models, several equilibrium exchange rate values may be consistent with the same set of macroeconomic fundamentals.

[5] The following discussion on duration data models basically relies on Kiefer (1988) and Box-Steffensmeier and Jones (2004).

[6] In the present study, it expresses, e.g., the probability of a currency peg to change in the sixth year, given that it has existed for five years. By contrast, specifications in terms of a density function emphasize unconditional probabilities (e.g., the probability of a currency peg to persist exactly six years).

[7] The variable must take on non-negative values as there is no negative risk of failure.

[8] It is referred to as a partial likelihood because it makes no assumption about the baseline hazard rate at times when failures do not occur.

[9] Censoring occurs whenever a spell's full event history is unobserved. Specifically, the present dataset includes no information on exchange rate regimes for the years prior to 1975 or following the end of the observation period (post 2000). This means that we are uncertain about the beginning (left-censoring) and/or ending (right-censoring) date for some currency pegs. For right-censored data, a bias may be introduced because an exit from a currency peg in 2001 is not taken into account at all in the regression even if the instability that led to it was presumably present in the time frame under study. Previous work on exchange rate regime duration, such as Duttagupta and Ötker-Robe (2003, 10), has often simply omitted censored observations from the dataset. However, this may induce a form of case selection bias in the results because censored observations have, on

average, a longer regime persistence than uncensored spells and would thus be underrepresented in the sample.

[10] The application of the Cox method requires that time spans of exchange rate regimes can be measured exactly, meaning that no tied failures occur. In the present context, however, tied failures exist since only the yearly time interval in which the abandonment of a currency peg occurs is given. Thus, some currency pegs will share its observed duration time with other pegs. To handle this problem, all estimates use the exact partial likelihood method as an approximation. This method treats the data as discrete and is especially attractive if the number of failures in a specific time interval is large (Box-Steffensmeier and Jones 2004, 56).

[11] The pairwise correlation between these two variables is r=0.35.

[12] See also Poirson (2001) and Frieden et al. (2001) for similar empirical results.

Appendix 2-A

Table 2-A1 Data description and sources of variables

Variable	Description	Source
duration	spell length of fixed exchange rate regime	Levy Yeyati and Sturzenegger (2002)
exit	dummy variable, value equals 1 when de facto currency peg is abandoned, 0 otherwise	Levy Yeyati and Sturzenegger (2002)
elect	dummy variable for election periods, value equals 1 if election takes place in the respective period, 0 otherwise.	Lijphart (2004), Popescu and Hannavy (2004), CDP (2004)
preelect	dummy variable for pre-election periods, value equals 1 if election takes place in the following year, 0 otherwise.	Lijphart (2004), Popescu and Hannavy (2004), CDP (2004)
postelect	dummy variable for post-election periods, value equals 1 if election has taken place in the year before, 0 otherwise.	Lijphart (2004), Popescu and Hannavy (2004), CDP (2004)
left	dummy variable for partisanship, value equals 1 if government party is from ideological left, 0 otherwise.	Beck et al. (2001)
preleft	interaction variable, value equals 1 if both left and preelect equal 1, 0 otherwise	see sources for partisan and election variables
veto	deviation from average number of veto players	Keefer and Stasavage (2003)
cbi	number of turnovers in central bank governors divided by years in sample	de Haan and Kooi (1998), national central banks
polity	index variable that captures essential democratic elements, from -10 (highly autocratic) to +10 (highly democratic)	Marshall and Jaggers (2002)
democracy	index variable for democracy, from 0 (low democracy) to +10 (high democracy)	Marshall and Jaggers (2002)

govinst	5-year moving average government turnover rate	Zárate (2004)
partyinst	5-year moving average ruling party turnover rate	Zárate (2004)
debt	outstanding amount of debt owed to nonresidents by residents of an economy as percent of GDP, in logs	World Bank (2003)
gdp	gross domestic product (in billion US dollar) in logs	World Bank (2003)
open	share of exports and imports over GDP	World Bank (2003)
sdexport	standard deviation of real export growth, in logs	World Bank (2003)
capop	dummy variable, value equals 1 when capital flows are restricted	IMF (2003), Carmen Reinhart
fiscal	overall fiscal surplus as percent of GDP	World Bank (2003)
share	proportion of countries in sample with de facto fixed exchange rate regime	own calculation

Note: All variables are collected on a yearly basis. In the empirical analysis, lagged versions of macroeconomic variables are used.

CHAPTER THREE

EXCHANGE RATE CONVERGENCE BETWEEN THE EURO-CANDIDATE CURRENCIES AND THE EURO

DANIEL STAVÁREK

All New Member States (NMS) of the European Union (EU) are supposed to adopt the euro in the future. However, according to the Maastricht Treaty, the euro implementation is dependent on the fulfilment of several convergence criteria. One of the required directions of convergence is the convergence of exchange rate development. The overwhelming majority of studies dealing with this issue focus mainly on the exchange rate stability criterion, assessment of its fulfilment, and participation of the national currency in the Exchange Rate Mechanism 2 (ERM 2). Within this framework, the exchange rate volatility, equilibrium exchange rates or exchange market pressure are predominantly analysed and various practical implications for the exchange rate policy in the context of exchange rate stability criterion are provided.

Since this chapter stems from a different concept, we refer a reader interested in the above-mentioned issues to the following studies. The process of the exchange rate stability criterion assessment is comprehensively analysed in Égert and Kierzenkowski (2003). The authors come to the conclusion that although the standard fluctuation band of ERM 2 is ± 15 percent, according to the European Central Bank and European Commission, maintaining the exchange rate within the asymmetric margin of 15 percent on the appreciation side and 2.25 percent on the depreciation side for at least two years will most likely be demanded for successful fulfilment of the criterion. Volatility of the exchange rates including its asymmetric effect is estimated in e.g. Stavárek (2007a) or Fidrmuc and Horváth (2008). Some differences in the level of volatility recorded, as well as significance of the asymmetry are revealed among the NMS and candidate countries. Finally, the exchange market pressure is theoretically and empirically studied in Bielecki (2005), Poeck et al. (2007) or Stavárek (2007b). All studies point out that the most recent values of the exchange market pressure do not possess a threat for exchange rate stability and subsequent fulfilment of the respective convergence criterion.

This chapter puts emphasis on alternative approach to the convergence of the exchange rate development that has not been applied as extensively in literature. It uses exchange rates of the euro and national currency of the euro-candidate country. Both exchange rates are quoted against the third currency that is not and will not be a part of the euro area. The higher the correlation between these two exchange rates the higher the degree of convergence in the exchange rate development between the particular euro-candidate country and the euro area. However, the correlation analysis of the exchange rate development does not provide a complete picture of the convergence since the volatility of the exchange rate is not taken into account. Therefore, we apply Generalized Autoregressive Conditional Heteroscedasticity (GARCH) models to generate time series of the exchange rate volatility and carry out correlation analysis with these volatility data as well. Besides the traditional simple correlation analysis we also use a dynamic version of the analysis based on calculation of the rolling correlation coefficient.

Thus, the aim of this chapter is to estimate various alternative measures of the correlation coefficients between exchange rates of five NMS (Czech Republic, Hungary, Poland, Romania, and Slovakia) vis-à-vis US Dollar and the exchange rate of the euro vis-à-vis US Dollar (USD). Croatia, as a representative of EU-candidate countries, is also included in the analysis. Based on the results obtained, we will assess and compare the level of the achieved exchange rate development convergence.

The chapter is structured as follows. First, the exchange rate development of the analysed currencies is described along with the development and changes of the exchange rate arrangements. Next, we discuss the empirical methods applied and provide the estimation results. Finally, the main findings of the analysis are summarized.

Development of the Exchange Rate and Exchange Rate Arrangement

The indispensable part of the convergence analysis is the graphical illustration of the exchange rate development. Figure 3-1 depicts development of all seven exchange rates analysed during the period January 1999 – February 2008. The data used are on a daily basis and were drawn from the European Central Bank and national central banks databases. It is evident that Croatian kuna (HRK), Czech koruna (CZK), euro (EUR), Hungarian forint (HUF) and Slovak koruna (SKK) followed a very similar development path. The Polish zloty (PLN) witnessed a slightly different development, particularly during the period 2001 – 2003.

Figure 3-1 Exchange rate development against USD

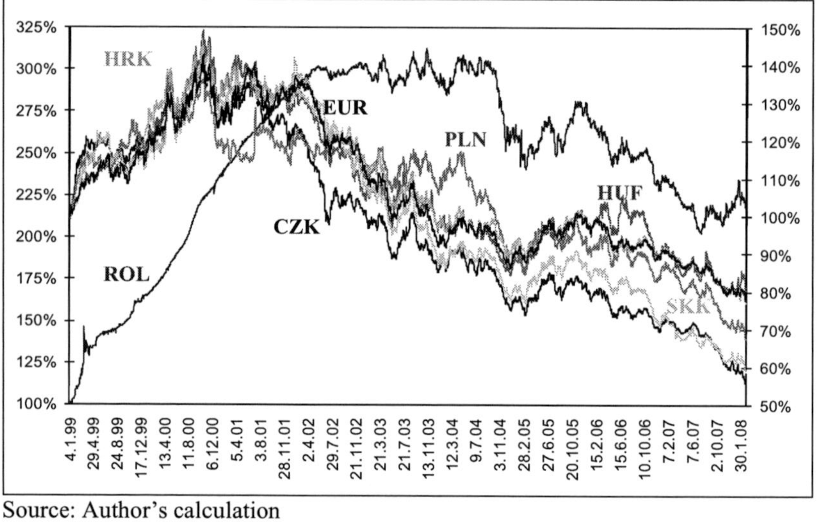

Source: Author's calculation

Note: ROL on the left axis, all other currencies on the right axis

The resembling development is reflected in one important feature – all currencies mentioned appreciated against USD during the period analysed. However, the magnitude of appreciation differs among currencies. The currency with the highest appreciation (44.13 percent) is CZK followed, with a small gap, by SKK (41.17 percent). The remaining currencies achieved substantially lower rate of appreciation, namely PLN (32.57 percent), HRK (22.96 percent), EUR (22.24 percent) and HUF (18.34 percent). However, the dataset also includes one currency with very exceptional development against USD. It is Romanian leu (ROL) and its development is presented separately in special sub-figure. ROL is the only currency with total depreciation (-121.39 percent). This can be primarily attributed to the exchange rate regime applied by the Romanian central bank until the end of 2001.

Analyzing the general picture of the exchange rate development, one can distinguish three specific sub-periods. The first sub-period is bounded by January 1999 on one side and November 2000 on the other side. During this period of time all currencies experienced depreciation against USD when exchange rates peaked at levels around 140 percent of their initial values (225 percent for ROL). The exchange rate development of all currencies was very alike at that time as the difference between the most depreciated (HUF) and least depreciated currency (PLN), ignoring ROL, was only 13.66 percentage points on 30 November 2000.

The second sub-period covers the time span from December 2000 to December 2004. This sub-period can be distinguished by a gradual process of appreciation against USD. However, some deviations from the general trend can be found. First, CZK speeded up its appreciation in July 2001 – July 2002. This widened the gap between CZK and the remaining currencies. Second, PLN did not share the common appreciation trend in January 2001 – April 2004 as PLN remained almost unchanged experiencing only some marginal fluctuations on both appreciation and depreciation side.

The third sub-period lasted for rest of the time under consideration, i.e. January 2005 – February 2008. In 2005 one can recognize a clear depreciation trend that peaked in November. Since then all currencies have been consistently appreciating against USD. However, HUF continued with its decline over the first half of 2006 reflecting the increased risks originating from unsustainable fiscal deficit and political instability. ROL also went through a wave of depreciation in August 2007 – January 2008. The prevailing appreciation development differed in pace among currencies. Whereas SKK recorded a substantial appreciation in the last quarter of 2006, CZK and PLN were appreciating remarkably over the last 8 months analysed. As a result of these developments, the gap between the most appreciated and the least appreciated currencies widened significantly during the third sub-period (15.2 percentage points on 3 January 2005 comparing with 25.8 points on 29 February 2008).

Interpretation of the correlation analysis results may be misleading if differences in exchange rate regimes are not taken into account. Therefore, next follows a review of exchange rate regimes applied in the countries analysed. Besides the regimes used over the period under consideration, we also include regimes from the preceding period aiming to provide a comprehensive picture about changes in the countries' exchange rate policies. The overview of exchange rate arrangements applied is reported in Table 3-1.

Table 3-1 Overview of the exchange rate arrangements in analysed countries

Czech Republic	
Peg to currency basket (65% DEM, 35% USD) with band ± 0.5%	05/93 – 02/96
Peg to currency basket (65% DEM, 35% USD) with band ± 7.5	02/96 – 05/97
Managed floating	05/97 –
Inflation targeting since 01/98	
Croatia	
Crawling peg	03/92 – 10/93
Tightly managed floating with reference currency	10/93 –
Hungary	
Crawling peg to currency basket (70% ECU, 30% USD) with band ± 2.25%	01/93 – 12/96
Crawling peg to currency basket (70% DEM, 30% USD) with band ± 2.25%	01/97 – 12/99
Crawling peg to EUR with band ± 2.25%	01/00 – 04/01
Crawling peg to EUR with band ± 15%	05/01 – 09/01
Peg to EUR with band ± 15%	10/01 – 02/08
Free floating	02/08 –
Inflation targeting since 08/01	
Poland	
Crawling peg to currency basket (45% USD, 35% DEM, 10% GBP, 5% FRF, 5% CHF) with band ± 1%	01/93 – 05/95
Crawling peg to currency basket (45% USD, 35% DEM, 10% GBP, 5% FRF, 5% CHF) with band ± 7%	05/95 – 02/98
Crawling peg to currency basket (45% USD, 35% DEM, 10% GBP, 5% FRF, 5% CHF) with band ± 10%	02/98 – 12/98
Crawling peg to currency basket (55% EUR, 45% USD) with band ± 15%	01/99 – 04/00
Free floating	04/00 –
Inflation targeting since 01/99	
Romania	
Tightly managed floating with USD as reference currency	01/93 – 12/01
Tightly managed floating with reference currency basket (60% EUR, 40% USD)	01/02 – 12/03
Tightly managed floating with reference currency basket (75% EUR, 25% USD)	01/04 – 12/04

Table 3-1 (cont.)

Tightly managed floating with EUR as reference currency	01/05 – 08/05
Free floating	08/05 –
Inflation targeting since 08/05	
Slovakia	
Peg to currency basket (60% DEM, 40% USD) with band ± 1.5%	01/93 – 12/96
Peg to currency basket (60% DEM, 40% USD) with band ± 7%	01/97 – 09/98
Managed floating	10/98 – 11/05
ERM 2	11/05 –
Inflation targeting since 01/05	

Source: International Monetary Fund, Frömmel and Schobert (2006), Barisitz (2007)

After gaining independence in January 1993, the Czech Republic adopted a tight peg of CZK to a basket of currencies (65 percent DEM, 35 percent USD). The initially narrow band ± 0.5 percent was widened to ± 7.5 percent in February 1996. The financial crisis that hit the Czech Republic in the first half of 1997 resulted in a shift of the exchange rate regime towards managed floating in May 1997. This arrangement has been applied since then; and in combination with inflation targeting since 1998.

After a one and half year episode with a crawling peg, Croatia has been practicing a tightly managed floating. Currently, Croatia uses EUR as the reference currency and exchange rate anchor. However, the de facto exchange rate policy of the Croatian National Bank can be characterized as a corridor of about ± 4 percent around the hypothetical central rate of 7.5 HRK/EUR (Barisitz, 2007, 85).

Hungary initially opted for a crawling peg in which HUF was pegged to the basket made up of ECU (70 percent) and USD (30 percent) and allowed to fluctuate within a narrow band ± 2.25 percent around the gradually devaluating central rate. In January 2000, the currency basket was substituted by EUR; and the bandwidth was widened to ± 15 percent in May 2001. The crawling band was abandoned in October 2001. Since then, Hungary has adopted a fixed parity regime against EUR with ± 15 percent margin along with the inflation targeting strategy. On 26 February 2008, however, National Bank of Hungary introduced free floating as the new official exchange rate arrangement.

Poland, at the initial stage of transformation process, chose a narrow crawling peg to the currency basket (45 percent USD, 35 percent DEM, 10 percent GBP, 5 percent FRF, 5 percent CHF) and applied this regime until the end of 1998. The fluctuation band was widened in three steps and the basket structure was adjusted in early 1999. In April 2000 the crawling peg was replaced by free floating that is applied concurrently with inflation targeting.

Romania used a managed floating regime for a long period of time to drive nominal depreciation of ROL. This arrangement was sometimes characterized as de facto implicit crawling band. USD was the reference currency until the end of 2001. Over the period 2002 – 2004 ROL was linked to EUR/USD basket. The EUR has been the only reference currency since early 2005. In August 2005 National Bank of Romania started with implementation of inflation targeting and loosening of the managed floating regime (Barisitz, 2007, 90).

Slovakia originally pegged SKK to the basket of DEM and USD and maintained a narrow band of ± 1.5 percent. Widening of the band in January 1997 was followed by the introduction of managed floating in October 1998. Since early 2005 managed floating was coupled with inflation targeting. In November 2005 Slovakia entered into ERM 2 as the first of the countries analysed. Two and half years later, in April 2008, the Slovak government officially asked the European Commission for assessment of the convergence criteria fulfilment.

Theoretical Concept and Literature Review

This study is based on the following assumption. If the exchange rate developments of a euro-candidate currency and EUR are highly synchronized the euro-candidate country is ready to join the euro area. We chose USD as the common reference currency because the United States are likely to stay outside the euro area and USD plays a dominant role in financial markets, official reserves holdings as well as international trade.

The level of convergence of the exchange rate development is estimated with correlation analysis employing both simple and rolling approaches. The rolling correlation is used to overcome the time invariance of the simple correlation coefficient. In order to obtain a rolling correlation we construct a 256-trading-day (one calendar year) window moving correlation coefficient. The correlation analysis is applied on two kinds of time series – exchange rate daily returns and estimated conditional volatility.

The daily returns are calculated in a standardized way:

$$Y_t^j = \left[\log(S_t^j) - \log(S_{t-1}^j)\right] \cdot 100 \tag{3.1}$$

where Y^j is the exchange rate daily return of the of currency j, S^j is the exchange rate of currency j at time t or $t-1$, respectively.

The conditional variance time series are generated by estimation of GARCH (1,1) model. Subsequently, their daily changes are used in the correlation analysis of the exchange rate volatility. We apply the following GARCH model specification:

$$\Delta s_{jt}^D = \mu_j + \xi_{jt}, \tag{3.2}$$

$$\sigma_{jt}^2 = \gamma_{j1} + \gamma_{j2}\xi_{jt-1}^2 + \gamma_{j3}\sigma_{jt-1}^2 + \omega_{jt} \tag{3.3}$$

where s_{jt}^D denotes the log exchange rate of the currency j vis-à-vis the Dollar in the time t. Besides the constant term, the mean equation (3.2) does not include any other explanatory variable. The constant term μ_j shows the average rate of depreciation or appreciation. The error term, ξ_{jt}, of the mean equation (3.2) is assumed to have a time varying conditional variance, σ^2, specified by equation (3.3). Equation (3.3) comprises the ARCH term, ξ_{jt-1}, that reflects the impacts of news from previous periods that affect exchange rate volatility, and the GARCH term, σ^2_{jt-1} that measures the impact of the forecast variance from previous periods on volatility.

The long-term similarity of the exchange rate development of two currencies vis-à-vis the reference currency may reflect the fact that both currencies are affected by similar factors. Likewise, convergence of the exchange volatility implies that shocks on exchange rates are accommodated symmetrically, i.e. in a similar direction and intensity. Hence, a concurrent achievement of high correlation in exchange rate development and exchange rate volatility may be interpreted as a sign of sufficient symmetry and readiness of the candidate country for joining the euro area and adoption of the single currency.

This approach to investigation of the exchange rate convergence has not been applied extensively so far in the literature. Komárková and Komárek (2007) used the static and time-varying correlation analysis on weekly nominal exchange rate data of four central European countries (Czech Republic, Hungary, Poland, Slovakia) over the period 1995 – 2Q 2006. They came to the conclusion that CZK is the currency most synchronized with EUR/USD currency pair. On the other hand, PLN reported the lowest correlation coefficients over the whole period of estimation. The authors also point out that convergence of the exchange rate development has been increasing since the countries analysed joined the EU in May 2004. Kang et al. (2002) followed the same approach in their analysis; however, they focused on Korean and Japanese exchange rates.

Since the traditional correlation analysis assumes linearity between two variables some researchers argue that it is not the most accurate technique for estimation of the exchange rate convergence. Thus, some alternative procedures have been introduced and applied in the literature. For instance, Arguilar and Hördahl (1998) propose construction of a time-varying correlation coefficient based on estimation of a bivariate GARCH model. The authors investigate this way a likelihood of 11 euro area candidate countries to join the euro area from the start.

Babetskaia-Kukharchuk et al. (2008) use a bivariate version of the Baba-Engle-Kraf-Kroner GARCH model to calculate dynamic correlation coefficients of four central European currencies (CZK, HUF, PLN, SKK) with EUR. Employing daily nominal exchange rates from January 1994 to October 2005 they find evidence of convergence in exchange rate volatilities. The highest correlation coefficients were obtained for SKK, followed, with a marginal gap, by CZK and HUF. The convergence of PLN remained slow over the entire period analysed.

Some studies such as Aguilar and Hördahl (1998), Castrén and Mazzota (2005) or Nikkinen et al. (2006) use data on OTC currency option prices to obtain implied exchange rate volatility and calculate implied correlation coefficients.

Empirical Results

Before we proceed with presentation of the correlation analysis results, it is worthwhile to clarify the interpretation of the results. The correlation coefficient indicates strength and direction of a linear relationship between two variables and may gain values from minus one to one. The correlation is 1 in the case of an increasing linear relationship, -1 in the case of a decreasing linear relationship, and some value in between in all other cases implying the degree of the relationship. The closer the coefficient is to either of the extremes, the stronger the correlation between the variables.

From the NMS and EU candidate countries' point of view, it is desirable to have the development and volatility of the national currency perfectly correlated with EUR. Therefore, we interpret a highly positive correlation coefficient as signal of readiness for the euro adoption. Similarly, the increasing coefficient documents a greater likelihood of the euro area membership. However, it must be stated that convergence of the exchange rate development and volatility is not the only indicator that shall be used in making the decision on joining the euro area. See Angeloni et al. (2007) or Darvas and Szapáry (2008) for discussion on a variety of other suitable convergence indicators.

The first part of the correlation analysis is focused on convergence of the exchange rate development. Therefore, we calculated daily returns according to equation (3.1) for all exchange rate time series. We use exchange rates in direct quotes, i.e. number of domestic currency's units for one USD. In order to compare a trend development of the daily returns of the euro-candidate currencies and the euro we applied Hodrick-Prescott (HP) filter. Unfiltered as well HP filtered time series are graphically presented in Figure 3-2.

Even this simple graphical analysis indicates that development of some euro-candidate currencies is not synchronized with EUR over certain periods. Above all, we can mention the following currencies and episodes: CZK in 2002 and 2007 – 2008 HUF in 2003 and 2006, PLN in 2001 – 2002, ROL in 2007 – 2008 or SKK in 2006 – 2007. It clearly evident that, due to exchange rate regime applied, the exchange rate development of HRK is the most harmonized with the development of EUR. As far as the daily returns' volatility is concerned, none of the currencies analyzed shows extraordinary figures.

Figure 3-2 Daily returns of exchange rates vis-à-vis USD

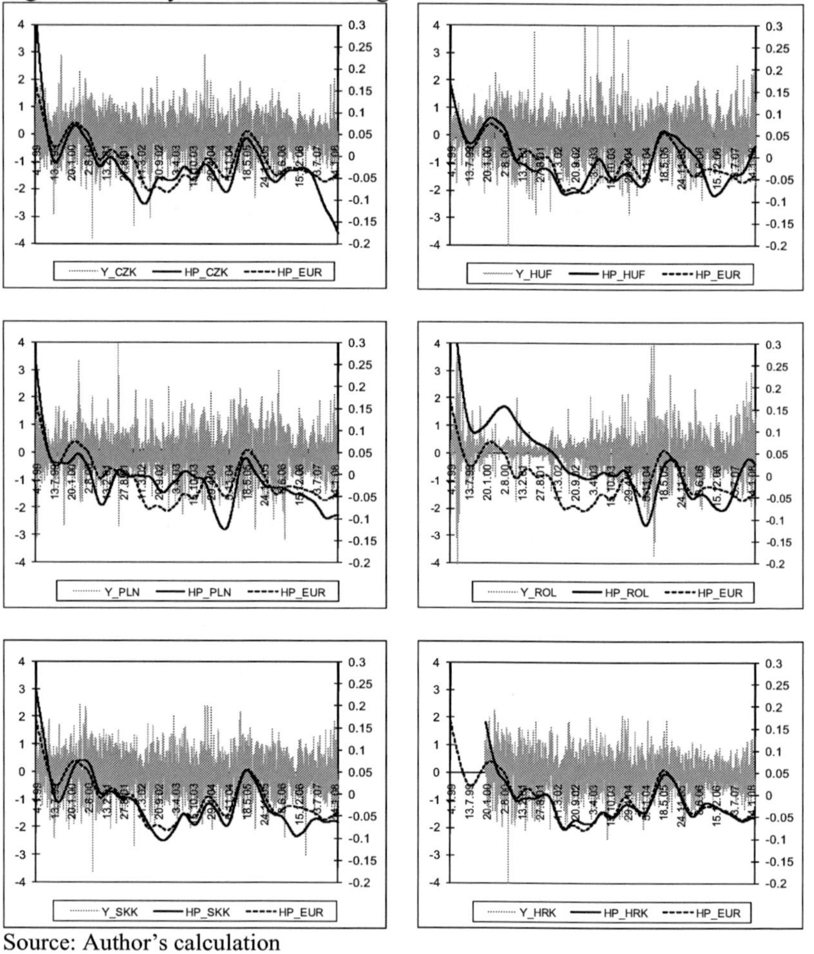

Source: Author's calculation

Note: HP indicates Hodrick-Prescott filter, HP series on the right axis

The second type of time series we used in the correlation analysis is conditional volatility generated by GARCH models estimation. Volatility of all exchange rates is depicted in Figure 3-3. For better comparison, volatility of each of the NMS national currencies is presented along with volatility of EUR/USD pair.

Figure 3-3 Conditional volatility estimated by GARCH model

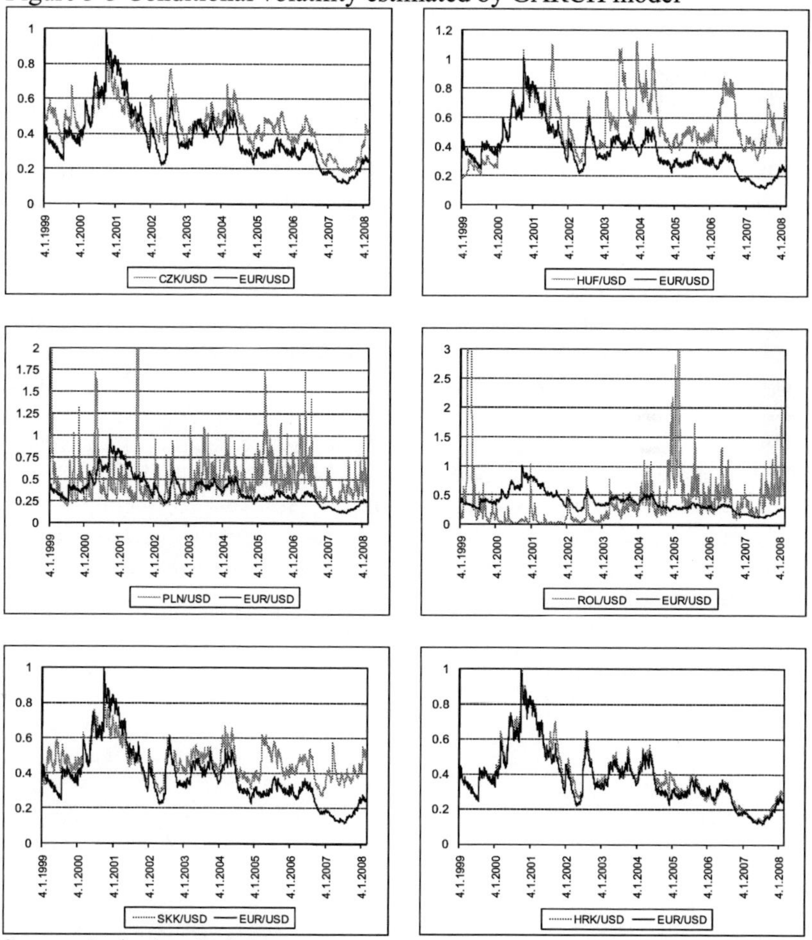

Source: Author's calculation

In general, the volatility of EUR/USD exchange rate is lower than the volatility of the euro-candidate currencies' exchange rates over the whole period of nine years and two months. The only exemption is June 2000 – June 2001, i.e. a turbulent period when waves of depreciation of EUR (euro-candidate currencies) against USD were often followed by an appreciation and vice versa. However, substantial differences in volatility can also be found among euro-candidate currencies. For instance, volatility of PLN exchange rate was usually twice as high as volatility of CZK or SKK. The volatility of ROL during the second half of the period analysed even exceeded the PLN level.

Similarly with daily returns, HRK is the currency most harmonized with EUR. Volatilities of both currencies' exchange rates against USD are almost identical. One can reveal a high degree of convergence in the case of CZK and SKK. Volatility of HUF/USD exchange rate diverged from the EUR/USD development path in the second half of the period analysed. However, the most remarkable differences in magnitude and fluctuations of volatility can be observed on PLN and ROL.

We start correlation analysis with the computation of a set of regular static correlation coefficients covering sub-periods of one year (the most recent sub-period is extended by two months to February 2008) as well as the entire period.

As Table 3-2 shows, correlation coefficients calculated of daily returns time series are higher than volatility-based coefficients. This is the case for all currencies and years. Even very strong development correlation (above 0.85) goes frequently hand in hand with substantially lower volatility correlation (e.g. CZK in 2006, SKK in 2005 and 2006 or PLN in 2007) in the recent years.

Table 3-2 Correlation analysis of national currencies' exchange rates with EUR/USD

	1999		2000		2001	
	returns	**volatility**	**returns**	**volatility**	**returns**	**volatility**
CZK	0.7705	0.7416	0.9445	0.9135	0.9085	0.6927
HUF	0.8375	0.7773	0.9933	0.9829	0.7904	0.5353
PLN	0.3465	0.4083	0.5123	0.1880	0.3397	0.0626
ROL	0.0453	0.0433	0.0554	-0.0205	0.1247	-0.0326
SKK	0.8458	0.7367	0.9413	0.9190	0.9511	0.8623
HRK	---	---	0.9926	0.9894	0.9054	0.8280
	2002		**2003**		**2004**	
	returns	**volatility**	**returns**	**volatility**	**returns**	**volatility**
CZK	0.7453	0.7020	0.8817	0.7104	0.8864	0.8483
HUF	0.8645	0.8041	0.7005	0.3195	0.8495	0.7694
PLN	0.3993	0.1668	0.6436	0.3771	0.8049	0.6212
ROL	0.2000	0.0971	0.8174	0.6556	0.7394	0.6805
SKK	0.8722	0.7794	0.9275	0.8960	0.9676	0.9339
HRK	0.9611	0.9273	0.9455	0.9119	0.9221	0.8643
	2005		**2006**		**2007 – 02/2008**	
	returns	**volatility**	**returns**	**volatility**	**returns**	**volatility**
CZK	0.8710	0.7594	0.9037	0.7341	0.8063	0.6774
HUF	0.8631	0.7612	0.6920	0.5151	0.7511	0.5577
PLN	0.6975	0.6166	0.7435	0.5094	0.8325	0.6464
ROL	0.5854	0.5424	0.8257	0.6793	0.6392	0.4840
SKK	0.8424	0.6680	0.8768	0.7442	0.7912	0.4854
HRK	0.9537	0.9051	0.9691	0.9654	0.9681	0.9322
	1999 – 02/2008					
	returns	**returns**				
CZK	0.8626	0.8626				
HUF	0.8068	0.8068				
PLN	0.5680	0.5680				
ROL	0.3840	0.3840				
SKK	0.8944	0.8944				
HRK	0.9528	0.9528				

Source: Author's calculation

This kind of disharmony may be explained by the fact that although the mentioned euro-candidate currencies and euro are influenced by similar factors (high development correlation) the final effect is not always of similar direction and intensity. One can also reveal that each currency analysed tends to have its own correlation development pattern. While there are currencies with a remarkable growth of correlation coefficient over the estimated period (ROL, PLN), other currencies experienced a drop in correlation (HUF, SKK) or stagnation with only marginal changes in both directions (HRK). Hence, the standings of the most correlated currencies in the most recent sub-period (2007 – February 2008) is as follows: HRK, PLN, CZK, SKK, HUF, ROL (in terms of daily returns) and HRK, CZK, PLN, HUF, SKK, ROL (in terms of volatility).

Despite fundamental differences we may underline some development episodes that were shared in common by all currencies. The correlation of volatility decreased on all currencies in 2001. It can be attributed to effect of terrorist attacks on financial markets and persisting uncertainty after that. By contrast, 2000 was the year when correlation of development increased on all currencies. As it is evident from Figure 3-1 and Figure 3-3, 2000 can be characterized as the year of a considerable USD appreciation against all other currencies and the year of increasing exchange rate volatility. Moreover, it is worthwhile to point out one more interesting episode that occurred in 2004 when ten NMS joined the EU. The correlation between all NMS currencies analysed and the euro increased remarkably that year as compared with 2003 figures. It is interesting that neither ROL nor HRK shared this development trend. Correlation coefficients from the most recent sub-period do not support the hypothesis of increasing exchange rate convergence between euro-candidate countries and the euro. Correlation of most of currencies shrank in 2007-2008 (except for HUF and PLN) to levels that cannot be considered as a zone of sufficient convergence.

The traditional correlation analysis suffers from inherent lack of dynamics and lack of continuity. Therefore, in order to investigate dynamics of the correlation over time, we calculated rolling correlation coefficients. The length of the rolling window is one year. Thus, each rolling coefficient is based on data from the particular day of observation and 255 preceding trading days. Development of this consecutive measure of exchange rate convergence is graphically presented in Figure 3-4.

The results suggest that correlation of daily returns and correlation of volatility experienced very similar development as the increase (decrease) of the former is usually accompanied by a change of the latter in the same direction. However, the daily returns coefficients of all currencies exceeded the coefficient reporting the exchange rate volatility convergence. The gap between the two correlation coefficients was not constant but varied over the period of estimation. Occurrences of insignificant differences (e.g. HUF and SKK in 2000, CZK in 2001) were followed by circumstances when the daily returns coefficient was twice as high as the volatility coefficient (e.g. HUF in 2003 and first half of 2007, SKK in 2007 – 2008).

Such a disharmony emerged from substantial fluctuations in development of the volatility correlation coefficients. Almost all drops and increases in correlation were more rapid and intensive in the case of volatility correlation. The only exception was PLN whose volatility correlation with EUR was nearly as smooth as the daily returns correlation. PLN is the currency of the largest economy among NMS. Therefore, shocks and other impulses may be absorbed into exchange rate development in a more delicate way as compared with other currencies from the region.

The results also provide evidence how the exchange rate regime applied may affect exchange rate convergence. Croatia was using very tightly managed floating of HRK with EUR as the reference currency over the whole period. Subsequently, the correlation of exchange rate development never decreased below 0.85 (0.93 in two last years) and the correlation of volatility never dropped under 0.8 (0.9 in two last years). Therefore, we can consider exchange rate convergence of HRK with EUR as almost absolute. On the other hand, the exchange rate arrangement used in Romania in 1999-2002 contributed crucially to the correlation oscillating around zero level and documenting virtually no convergence.

As far as the level of achieved convergence is considered, we can distinguish several sub-periods characterized by different levels of correlation as well as different standings of the most converged currencies. For instance, CZK, HUF and SKK recorded very high correlation coefficients of daily returns in 2000 and the first half of 2001. Most likely, such a development benefited from finalization of the treaties of EU accession. None of NMS negotiated the opt-out clause and thus, the euro adoption in those countries has been set as an unavoidable political and economic goal for the future.

Figure 3-4 Rolling correlation coefficients

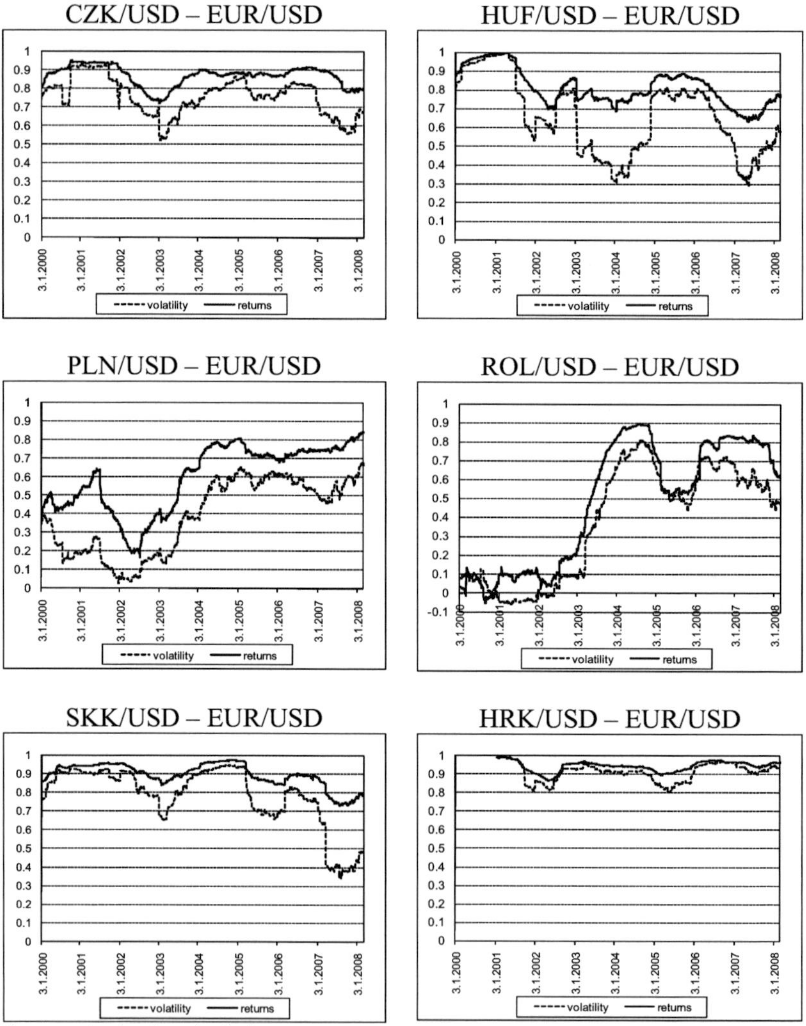

Source: Author's calculation

The correlation of HUF began to fall first in July 2001 followed by CZK and SKK in December 2001. In July 2001, SKK became the currency most correlated with EUR and kept this position until May 2005. Development of the SKK correlation coefficient was almost perfectly paired with CZK as the gap remained very stable at 0.05. The coefficients of CZK, HUF and SKK converged to level 0.87 and persisted practically unchanged for next 10 months. After very heterogeneous development in the last year we ended up (besides HRK) with PLN as the most converged currency (correlation coefficient on 29 February 2008 was 0.8450) followed by CZK (0.8059), SKK (0.7937), HUF (0.7629) and ROL (0.6142). The leading position of PLN documents a great progress in convergence that has been achieved since PLN was the least converged NMS currency until September 2006. The worst result was recorded in July 2002 when the correlation coefficient was only 0.1661.

The correlation of exchange rate volatility went through a similar development, however the coefficients gained lower values and differences among currencies were more noticeable. At the end of the period analysed (neglecting HRK with correlation coefficient 0.9364), CZK and PLN turned out to be the most synchronized currencies in terms of the exchange rate volatility. The respective coefficients were 0.6778 and 0.6718. The remaining standings were as follows: HUF (0.5793), SKK (0.4838) and ROL (0.4736). We believe that a long-persisting correlation above 0.85 may serve as an appropriate indicator of sufficient exchange rate convergence. However, as the results presented suggest, none of the NMS currencies achieved such a level of convergence in the most recent period of time. For the worse, the analysis revealed that almost all currencies experienced a decline of convergence over the last year. This kind of development is not favourable mainly for Slovakia as SKK is supposed to be replaced by EUR on 1 January 2009.

The next issue that requires an in-depth analysis is the relationship between exchange convergence and process of the European economic and monetary integration. The accession treaties that were discussed above resulted in enlargement of the EU on 1 May 2004 that comprised ten NMS including Czech Republic, Hungary, Poland and Slovakia. We notice a clear trend of increasing convergence from March 2003 when all negotiations about conditions of entry had been concluded and all NMS were finalizing preparations for the EU membership. The trend of growing convergence continued after the day of enlargement and principally CZK and HUF recorded significant gains in volatility convergence. A wave of rapid appreciation in the second half of 2004 prevented PLN from more intensive volatility convergence. On the other hand, HRK and ROL, currencies that did not participate in the EU enlargement in 2004, experienced a substantial drop of the correlation over the immediate post-enlargement period. An extensive increase of ROL convergence occurred approximately one year before admission of Romania to the EU. However, the day of entry was followed by a steady decline of both types of the correlation.

We also can investigate impacts of the SKK entry into ERM 2 and revaluation of its central parity on the convergence. Both events took place unexpectedly and surprised participants in the foreign exchange market. SKK entered into ERM 2 on 25 November 2005 and one can identify only mediocre instant impact. However, as the post-entry period gains larger share in the one-year rolling correlation window there is evidence of increasing convergence. Hence, it can be deduced that the entry into ERM 2 was perceived by financial markets as a firm commitment of the Slovak government to fulfil all convergence criteria and adopt EUR as soon as possible. On the contrary, several months later SKK speeded up its appreciation against EUR as well as USD and the actual market exchange rate departed remarkably from the central parity. This kind of development was reflected in a decrease of correlation. The official reaction to the excessive appreciation came out on 19 March 2007 in the form of a revaluation of the ERM 2 central parity. Consequently, a significant drop in convergence occurred immediately. This shift of the central parity brought along uncertainty to the foreign exchange market since it might cause some troubles with fulfilment of the exchange rate stability convergence criterion.

Conclusion

In this chapter, we analysed exchange rate convergence of the euro-candidate currencies with EUR against USD. We constructed static as well as rolling correlation coefficients which provide evidence of achieved level of convergence in terms of exchange rate development and volatility. The higher the correlation is between national euro-candidate currency and EUR, the higher the exchange rate convergence. Apparently, a long-lasting high degree of convergence with a clearly stable or increasing trend is the most plausible scenario.

With empirical results obtained, we may conclude that the convergence of exchange rate development surpassed the convergence of volatility on all currencies and over the entire period of estimation. It is also evident that a tightly managed floating with EUR as the reference currency leads automatically to a more stable and robust correlation. We did not find any progress in convergence of the NMS currencies since their entry to the EU. The most remarkable upturns of convergence were recorded during the pre-EU-entry period. On the contrary, after the EU entry convergence of all NMS currencies, except for PLN, decreased. We witnessed a more significant decline in the case of volatility convergence.

Although some of the recent values of correlation coefficients are solid and demonstrate a fair synchronization, none of them (besides HRK) are so high as to allow us to consider the level of convergence as sufficient. The underlying shocks are still not fully symmetric which results in a lower convergence of the exchange rate volatility. This conclusion supports strategies of the Czech Republic, Hungary and Poland to postpone the day of entry into ERM 2. The findings also provide evidence that the euro adoption in Slovakia, expected on 1 January 2009, is seen as premature from the exchange rate convergence point of view.

References

Aguilar, J. and P. Hördahl. 1998. Exchange rates and currency options as EMU indicators. *Sveriges Riksbank Quarterly Review* 2: 58-81.

Angeloni, I., M. Flad and F. Mongelli. 2007. Monetary Integration of the New EU Member States: What Sets the Pace of Euro Adoption. *Journal of Common Market Studies* 45(2): 367-409.

Babetskaia-Kukharchuk, O., I. Babetskii and J. Podpiera. 2008. Convergence in exchange rates: market's view on CE-4 joining EMU. *Applied Economics Letters* 15(5): 385-90.

Barisitz, S. 2007. Exchange Rate Arrangements and Monetary Policy in Southeastern Europe: An Update (2004-2007). *OeNB Focus on European Economic Integration* 2: 78-99.

Bielecki, S. 2005. Exchange market pressure and domestic credit evidence from Poland. *The Poznan University of Economics Review* 5(1): 20-36.

Castrén, O. and S. Mazzotta. 2005. *Foreign exchange rate option and returns based correlation forecasts evaluation and two applications.* ECB Working paper 447. European Central Bank, Frankfurt am Main.

Darvas, Z. and G. Szapáry. 2008. *Euro area enlargement and euro adoption strategies.* European Economy - Economic Papers 304. European Commission, Brussels.

Égert, B. and R. Kierzenkowski. 2003. *Asymmetric Fluctuation Bands in ERM and ERM-II: Lessons from the Past and Future Challenges for EU Acceding Countries.* William Davidson Institute Working Paper 597. University of Michigan, Ann Arbor, MI.

Fidrmuc, J. and R. Horváth. 2008. Volatility of exchange rates in selected new EU members: Evidence from daily data. *Economic Systems* 32(1): 103-18.

Frömmel, M. and F. Schobert. 2006. Exchange rate regimes in Central and East European countries: Deeds vs. words. *Journal of Comparative Economics* 34(3): 467-83.

Kang, S., Y. Wang and D.R. Yoon. 2002. *Exchange rate co-movements and business cycle synchronization between Japan and Korea.* Research Paper 40. ADB Institute, Tokyo.

Komárková, Z. and L. Komárek. 2007. Integration of the Foreign Exchange Markets of the Selected EU New Member States. *Politická ekonomie* 55(3): 315-33.

Nikkinen, J, P. Sahlström and S. Vähämaa. 2006. Implied volatility linkages among major European currencies. *Journal of International Financial Markets, Institutions and Money* 16(2): 87-103.

Poeck van, A., J. Vanneste and M. Veiner. 2007. Exchange Rate Regimes and Exchange Market Pressure in the New EU Member States. *Journal of Common Market Studies* 45(2): 459-85.

Stavárek, D. 2007a. On Asymmetry of Exchange Rate Volatility in New EU Member and Candidate Countries. *International Journal of Economic Perspectives* 1(2): 74-82.

—. 2007b. Estimation of the Exchange Market Pressure in the EU4 Countries: A Model-Dependent Approach. *Investment Management and Financial Innovations* 4(3): 80-94.

Acknowledgement

The research is due to the support provided by GAČR (Czech Science Foundation – Grantová Agentura České Republiky) under the project no. 402/08/0067 "Financial integration of New EU Member States with the Eurozone". The support is greatly acknowledged.

CHAPTER FOUR

DEPENDENCY MODELS FOR A SMALL EXCHANGE RATE SENSITIVE PORTFOLIO

TOMÁŠ TICHÝ

The main focus of this chapter is to present the simplest approaches to the dependency modelling of subordinated Lévy models and apply them in order to estimate the probability distribution of returns of a small portfolio sensitive to the evolution of exchange rates. We start with the motivation for the use of advanced stochastic processes within the market risk modelling. Next, we briefly review several basic facts that lie behind the theory of subordinated Lévy models, namely *the Variance gamma model* and *the Normal inverse Gaussian model*. After that, several ways to model the dependency among particular sources of randomness are proposed. Finally, the ability of selected models to fit the probability distribution of a small exchange rate sensitive portfolio is examined. We study mainly the measures of the overall risk (left quantiles, VaR) and higher moments of the distribution (skewness and kurtosis).

Market Risk Modelling and Measuring

An important part of market risk management of financial institutions is to estimate a short-term change in the portfolio value at a prespecified probability level, $\Delta V(\alpha, \Delta t)$. Regulatory authorities generally require a financial institution to measure a worst-case ten-day loss with a significance of 1%, $\Delta V(0.01,10)$, though the calculation is commonly based on a one-day risk multiplied by the square root of a given time length, $\sqrt{10}\Delta V(0.01,1)$. Hence, there is a 99 percent confidence that a loss we can incur will not be higher than a quantity generally referred to as the Value at Risk (*VaR*).

Major financial institutions keep large portfolios of various financial instruments. Although the central limit theorem and the law of large numbers provide us with a justification to apply a model based on the normality of log-returns, i.e. to ignore one-side fat tails, observations of fatal market crashes during last decades indicate that the assumption of the normality of returns can lead to serious mistakes even for a large and well-diversified portfolio.

Alternative one-dimensional models capturing both the empirically observed skewness and kurtosis are formulated either as various extensions of Gaussian distribution (Pareto or Student distribution, potentially also skewed, see Jondeau et al., 2006) or as a mixture of distinct distributions. More importantly, several authors have formulated also various subordinated processes assigned to the general Lévy family of stochastic processes during last decades (see e.g. Cont and Tankov, 2004 or Schoutens, 2003 for a comprehensive review).

As opposed to simple extensions of the Gaussian distribution, efficient modelling of dependency for subordinated Lévy processes is still an open question. Generally, it is not sufficient to correlate particular building blocks of the overall process, but it is necessary to model the dependency in one step. Hence, the application of the theory of copula functions seems to be inevitable. Notwithstanding, it is not always the case. There exist circumstances under which a simplified dependency model can provide us with a demanded result. In this study we therefore focus on the ability of several simplified approaches to model the short-term returns of a relatively small exchange rate sensitive portfolio.

Subordinated Lévy Models

The processes that belong to the general Lévy-type models family can be characterized by independent and stationary increments. Another typical feature is the stochastic continuity – the probability that a jump will occur within a particular time interval τ is zero.

Formal Definition[1]

Suppose a probability distribution that is infinitely divisible. Then, a stochastic process $\{X(t), t \in [0,T]\}$ is a Lévy process on [0,T], if (for $\tau \geq 0$):

1. it starts at zero: $X(0) = 0$,
2. its increments are independent: $X(t+\tau) - X(t)$ does not depend on $X(s)$, $s \leq t$,
3. its increments are stationary distributed: $X(t+\tau) - X(t) = X(\tau)$, in other words, it depends only on τ,

4. it is stochastically continuous: $\lim_{\tau \to 0} \Pr[X(t) > \varepsilon] = 0$ for $\varepsilon > 0$. Note that for many Lévy models, an infinite intensity of possibly very small jumps is a very important feature (see also property 4).

Generally, it is more feasible to define the Lévy process through the characteristic function. The cumulant of the characteristic function $\Phi(u) = \ln \phi(u)$ is denoted as a characteristic exponent and fulfils the Lévy-Khintchin formula:

$$\phi(u) = i\gamma u - \tfrac{1}{2}\sigma^2 u^2 + \int_{-\infty}^{\infty} \left[\exp(iux) - 1 - iuxI_{|x|<1}\right]\nu(dx). \tag{4.1}$$

Here, I_A is the indicator function (it gives one, if A holds and zero otherwise), $\gamma \in R$, $\sigma^2 \geq 0$ and ν is a measure on $R \setminus \{0\}$ with

$$\int_{-\infty}^{\infty} \inf[1, x^2]\nu(dx) = \int_{-\infty}^{\infty} (1 \wedge x^2)\nu(dx) < \infty. \tag{4.2}$$

For a given infinitely divisible distribution, we can define a triplet of Lévy characteristics,

$$\{\lambda, \sigma, \nu\}.$$

The former two define the drift of the process (deterministic part) and its diffusion. The latter is a Lévy measure. If it can be formulated as $\nu(dx) = u(x)dx$, it is a Lévy density. It is similarly to the probability density, with the exception that it need not be integrable and zero at origin.

Geometric Brownian Motion

A very special type of Lévy models is the *Geometric Brownian motion* (GBM), since its increments are always continuous. Although the model is a standard and very popular tool of financial practitioners, it has several drawbacks arising from the fact that it is based on normal distribution (returns are symmetrically distributed with no excess kurtosis).

The GBM,

$$S_{t+dt}^{(P)} = S_t \exp\left[\left(\mu - \tfrac{\sigma^2}{2}\right)dt + \sigma\sqrt{dt}\,\varepsilon\right], \tag{4.3}$$

is a solution to the following stochastic differential equation (SDE):

$$\frac{dS^{(P)}}{S} = \mu dt + \sigma dZ \ . \tag{4.4}$$

Here, μ is the long term average return of S, σ is its volatility, both per annum, and dZ_t is an increment of a Wiener process: $dZ_t = \varepsilon\sqrt{dt}$, where ε is taken from the standard normal distribution, $\varepsilon \in N[0,1]$. Finally, note that (P) indicates the model that is defined under the real world measure.[2]

Since in this text we focus solely on the returns of financial assets or a portfolio of them, but not the value, we can restrict ourselves to SDE (4.4) or its alternatives.

Subordinated Lévy Models

Many Lévy models commonly applied in finance are formulated as a (geometric) Brownian motion driven by a particular intrinsic process (*a subordinator*). From an economic point of view, such processes can be understood as a GBM within a random business time – it depends on the economic activity and arrival of new information.

Denoting $Z(t;\sigma,\mu)$ as a Wiener process in dependency on time t with parameters $\mu = 1$ and $\sigma = \sqrt{dt}$, we can define a Brownian motion $X(t;\theta,\vartheta)$ with drift θ and volatility ϑ driven by another Lévy process $l(t)$ with a unit mean and a variance specified by ν very simply – we replace t by $l(t)$. Thus:

$$X(t) = \theta l(dt) + \vartheta Z(l_{dt}) = \theta l(dt) + \vartheta\varepsilon\sqrt{l(dt)} \ . \tag{4.5}$$

This relation can be interpreted in such a way that the increment of X within an infinitesimal time interval dt is of normal distribution with mean $\theta l(dt)$ and variance $\vartheta^2 l(dt)$. The mean of the driving process $l(dt)$ should be dt and its variance specified by ν will determine the *fat tails*. In turn, the mean of the overall process controls the asymmetry. Finally, the formula to get the return of asset S is:

$$\frac{dS^{(P)}}{S} = \mu dt + \theta[l(dt) - dt] + \vartheta\varepsilon\sqrt{l(dt)} \ . \tag{4.6}$$

Note that we deduce dt in (4.6) in order to get the expected return μdt in average.

Very useful subordinators are *a gamma process* from gamma distribution, $l(t) \equiv g(t;\nu)$, leading to *the variance gamma model* (VG), and *an inverse Gaussian process* from inverse Gaussian distribution, $l(t) \equiv I(t;\nu)$, leading to *the normal inverse Gaussian model* (NIG).[3] In both cases, ν describes the variance of the subordinator. Formulas to fit the first four moments of VG and NIG models are depicted in Table 4.1.

Table 4-1 The first four moments of VG and NIG models

Moments	**VG**	**NIG**
Mean	θ	θ
Variance	$\vartheta^2 + \nu\theta^2$	$\vartheta^2 + \nu\theta^2$
Skewness	$\theta\nu\left(3\vartheta^2 + 2\nu\theta^2\right)\left(\vartheta^2 + \nu\theta^2\right)^{-3/2}$	$3\theta\nu\left(\vartheta^2 + \nu\theta^2\right)^{-1/2}$
Kurtosis	$3\left(1 + 2\nu - \dfrac{\nu\vartheta^4}{\left(\vartheta^2 + \nu\theta^2\right)^2}\right)$	$3\left(\dfrac{\theta^2\nu(1+5\nu) + \vartheta^2(1+\nu)}{\vartheta^2 + \nu\theta^2}\right)$

Dependency Models

In order to get a true picture of the evolution of a group of financial assets, the dependency must be taken into account. A common, even not ideal tool to express the dependency among particular components of the portfolio risk is the covariance (correlation) matrix. Consider two subordinated Lévy processes as in (4.5), X_1 and X_2. In this case, we get the covariance:

$$\operatorname{cov}(X_1, X_2) = \theta_1\theta_2 \operatorname{cov}(l_1, l_2) + \vartheta_1\vartheta_2 E\left[\sqrt{l_1 l_2}\right]E[\varepsilon_1\varepsilon_2], \tag{4.7}$$

which gives us the coefficient of linear correlation as follows:

$$\begin{aligned}\operatorname{cor}(X_1, X_2) &= \frac{\operatorname{cov}(X_1, X_2)}{\operatorname{var}(X_1)\operatorname{var}(X_2)} \\ &= \frac{\theta_1\theta_2 \operatorname{cov}(l_1, l_2) + \vartheta_1\vartheta_2 E\left[\sqrt{l_1 l_2}\right]E[\varepsilon_1\varepsilon_2]}{\sqrt{\vartheta_1^2 + \nu_1\theta_1^2}\sqrt{\vartheta_2^2 + \nu_2\theta_2^2}}.\end{aligned} \tag{4.8}$$

Cholesky Decomposition

The Cholesky decomposition is a popular tool of dependency modelling, although it is applicable only for special distributions. Generally, it allows us to transform a vector of independent Gaussian variables into a vector of dependent ones. It is based on the fact that the covariance (correlation) matrix Σ (R) can be decomposed into a product of triangular matrices A, $\Sigma = A \cdot A^T$. However, since the subordinated Lévy models consist of two distinct (and independent) processes, it is useless if we are not equipped with other tools.

Composite Models

Following the definition of a subordinated Lévy process (4.5), several models can be distinguished due to the dependency among particular subordinators and/or the Gaussian part. Besides that, we can assume a unique subordinator – each information arrival drives all asset prices we consider.

Model 1

Suppose that we have only one gamma process and that the standard normal variables ε are independent. In such a case, the correlation formula (4.8) can be rewritten as follows:

$$\operatorname{cor}(X_1, X_2) = \frac{\theta_1 \theta_2 \nu}{\sqrt{\vartheta_1^2 + \nu\theta_1^2}\sqrt{\vartheta_2^2 + \nu\theta_2^2}}, \tag{4.9}$$

since $\nu_1 \equiv \nu_2$ and $E[\varepsilon_1 \varepsilon_2] = 0$. At the first sight, it might be surprising that even if we have independent Wiener processes, the correlation might be non-zero. However, we should be aware of the fact that the subordinators are identical so that the jumps arise at the same moments in time. Only these events create the dependency.

In order to fit the model parameters to the empirically obtained data, we should proceed in accordance with the formulas in Table 4.1 to calculate the second to fourth moment of the distribution (variance, skewness and kurtosis) and due to (4.9) to fit also the correlation, if it is feasible. However, we should respect the fact that only one parameter of the subordinator variance ν is available – compare to n parameters of drift, θ, and volatility, ϑ. Moreover, the parameterisation should be done so that also the correlation formula will hold. Considering two distinct assets, we have seven equations but only five parameters.[4]

Model 2

Let us suppose that there is only one gamma process but, in contrast to Model 1, the standard normal variables ε are dependent. This feature gives us the following formula to get the correlation between two subordinated Lévy processes:

$$\operatorname{cor}(X_1, X_2) = \frac{\theta_1\theta_2\nu + \vartheta_1\vartheta_2\rho_{12}}{\sqrt{\vartheta_1^2 + \nu\theta_1^2}\sqrt{\vartheta_2^2 + \nu\theta_2^2}}. \quad (4.10)$$

Here, parameter $\rho_{1,2}$ indicates the dependency of Wiener processes or, in other words, the coefficient of linear correlation of standard normal variables. This allows us to apply the Cholesky decomposition in order to model the dependency structure of Wiener processes. Since these variables are of unit variance and of zero mean, ρ should clearly have no effect on variance, skewness or kurtosis. Comparing with Model 1, we have one parameter more for each pair of processes (the correlation of Wiener components ρ).

A significant disadvantage of both models, Model 1 and Model 2, which is usually inconsistent with market observations, is that the jumps (price changes) arrive at identical moments for all assets. Thus, it cannot happen that the price of one asset moves and the prices of others remain at the same level. This problem can be eliminated applying the following approach.

Model 3

Let us assume the VG process. Due to the well-known properties of the gamma distribution, we can decompose the gamma variable Y as follows:

$$Y = G + I, \quad G \in G[a/\nu, \nu], \quad I \in G[(1-a)/\nu, \nu] \quad \Rightarrow Y \in G[1/\nu, \nu],$$

where $G[x, y]$ denotes the gamma distribution with mean x and variance y. Hence, the arrival of information is decomposed into information of general nature, G, affecting all assets, and idiosyncratic events, typical only for a particular asset, I. This gives us the following formulation of the correlation formula:

$$\operatorname{cor}(X_1, X_2) = a\frac{\theta_1\theta_2\nu}{\sqrt{\vartheta_1^2 + \nu\theta_1^2}\sqrt{\vartheta_2^2 + \nu\theta_2^2}}. \tag{4.11}$$

Model 4

This approach connects the overall distribution directly. A very efficient way is to utilize a suitable copula function.[5] The copula functions are a very useful tool for dependency modelling. It is a projection of the dependency among particular distribution functions into [0,1],

$$C:[0,1]^n \to [0,1] \text{ on } R^n,\ n \in \{2,3,...\}. \tag{4.12}$$

In fact, it can be regarded as a multidimensional distribution function with marginals in the form of a standardized uniform distribution.

For simplicity assume once again two potentially dependent random variables X and Y with marginal distribution functions F_X, F_Y and joint distribution function $F_{X,Y}$. Then, following the Sklar's theorem:

$$F_{X,Y}(x,y) = C(F_X(x), F_Y(y)). \tag{4.13}$$

If both F_X and F_Y are continuous then copula function C is unique. Sklar's theorem implies also an inverse relation,

$$C(u,v) = F_{X,Y}\left(F_X^{-1}(u), F_Y^{-1}(v)\right). \tag{4.14}$$

Formulation (9.14) above should be understood such that the joint distribution function gives us two distinct pieces of information: (i) the marginal distributions of random variables, (ii) a dependency function of distributions. Hence, while the former is given by $F_X(x)$ and $F_Y(y)$, a copula function specifies the dependency, nothing less, nothing more. That is, only when we put both these information together, we have sufficient knowledge about the pair of random variables X, Y.

Data Set Description

The dataset we collected for this study comprises of daily effective exchange rates for the euro (EUR), British pound (GBP), Slovak koruna (SKK), and US dollar (USD) with respect to the Czech koruna (CZK) as published by the Czech National Bank, i.e. market quotes at 2 p.m. The term that we monitored started on 1 January 2000. The last quotes were taken on 31 December 2007. Thus, the length of this series of log-returns is 2,014 observations. For each exchange rate, basic descriptive statistics – mean, variance, standard deviation, skewness, and kurtosis – of daily log-returns (per annum, if applicable) were evaluated, see Table 4-2. In Appendix 4-A we provide the charts of both daily exchange rates and daily log-returns evolution.

Table 4-2 Basic descriptive statistics for daily log-returns of selected exchange rates (p.a., if applicable)

Parameter	EUR	GBP	SKK	USD
Mean	–0.0378	–0.0578	–0.0090	–0.0849
Variance	0.0028	0.0067	0.0034	0.0112
Standard dev.	0.0525	0.0817	0.0580	0.1055
Skewness	–0.2970	–0.4110	0.0646	–0.1220
Kurtosis	7.4320	5.3200	7.6180	4.0470

Source: Author's calculations

It is apparent that the mean (drift over the whole length) varies substantially between –1 percent (SKK) and –9 percent (USD). The standard deviation of two exchange rates is around 5 percent (SKK, EUR); the other two are close to 8 percent (GBP) and 10 percent (USD), respectively. Except for the SKK rate, the skewness is significantly negative. We have observed the highest one for GBP (–0.411). By contrast, the highest kurtosis can be observed for the EUR and SKK rates (7.5). From these four exchange rates, only the distribution of USD returns slightly resembles the Gaussian one. However, when testing if the distribution can be regarded to be Gaussian following the tests of Jarque-Bera type, the hypothesis of normality must be strongly rejected for all exchange rates.

In our research, we focus first of all on dependency modelling – we therefore provide also the correlation matrix for exchange rate returns

(4.15). Note that the components of the correlation matrix express the coefficient of linear correlation among particular pairs of vectors of daily log-returns over eight years period. It is apparent that the highest dependency is documented for the (EUR-SKK) pair, while the (SKK-USD) pair is relatively independent.[6]

$$R=\begin{pmatrix} 1.00 & 0.54 & 0.61 & 0.40 \\ 0.54 & 1.00 & 0.37 & 0.65 \\ 0.61 & 0.37 & 1.00 & 0.22 \\ 0.40 & 0.65 & 0.22 & 1.00 \end{pmatrix}. \quad (4.15)$$

Exchange Rate Sensitive Portfolio

In this section two selected dependency models are analysed. First, we examine the VG and NIG models independently. After that, we proceed to the modelling of returns of several portfolios based on Model 1 and Model 2.

Independent Modelling

The following Tables 4-3 and 4-4 give us parameters of VG and NIG models, respectively, when fitted independently to observed data. It is apparent that particular parameters are very close for both models. Next, due to relatively low θ's, ϑ is very close to the standard deviation of the time series. Moreover, the parameter of variance of the subordinator is very close for EUR and SKK, the two exchange rates with the highest correlation. By contrast, the highest distance of ν is apparent for SKK and USD – the exchange rates with the lowest correlation.

Table 4-3 Parameters for independent VG models

Parameter	EUR	GBP	SKK	USD
θ	–0.0002	–0.0010	0.0001	–0.0008
ϑ	0.0033	0.0051	0.0037	0.0067
ν	1.4578	0.7354	1.5384	0.3458

Source: Author's estimation

Table 4-4 Parameters for independent NIG models

Parameter	EUR	GBP	SKK	USD
θ	–0.0002	–0.0010	0.0001	–0.0008
ϑ	0.0033	0.0051	0.0037	0.0067
ν	1.4383	0.6979	1.5374	0.3425

Source: Author's estimation

Composite models

In this subsection we will analyse the power of Model 1 and Model 2 to give us a true picture of the probability distribution of portfolio returns and compare it with the standard model (GBM).

Since the crucial point is the level of ν, the parameter of variance of the subordinator, we choose two distinct portfolios with the composition as follows. Portfolio Π1 consists of EUR and SKK with equal weights, Π1 = {0.5, 0, 0.5, 0}. Similarly, portfolio Π2 consists only of SKK and USD, Π2 = {0.5, 0, 0.5, 0}. Hence, the exchange rate pair with the highest correlation comprises portfolio Π1, while the pair with the lowest correlation gives us portfolio Π2.

The first step is to refit the parameters of both models to VG and NIG processes (we apply RMSE criterion with equal weights). The results are apparent from Table 4-5. It is evident that both models, Model 1 and Model 2, give us identical parameters for VG model (except the correlation of Wiener component, since it is not included into Model 1). The same is true for NIG model – we have therefore included only Model 2 into the table.

Table 4-5 Refitted parameters for portfolio Π1

Parameter	Model 1 (VG)		Model 2 (VG)		Model 2 (NIG)	
	EUR	SKK	EUR	SKK	EUR	SKK
θ	–0.0002	–0.0001	–0.0002	–0.0001	–0.0002	–0.0001
ϑ	0.0033	0.0037	0.0033	0.0037	0.0033	0.0037
ν	1.5003		1.5003		1.4951	
ρ	—		0.6190		0.6189	

Source: Author's estimation

A very interesting conclusion is that the refitted parameter ν is somewhere between the values documented in Table 4-3 – it is closer to the exchange rate with higher variance (SKK). Concerning the parameter of correlation among Wiener components, it is not very far from the relevant component of the correlation matrix.

Next, we use the parameters of tables 4-2 and 4-5 to run the Monte Carlo simulation of exchange rates returns and calculate a return of the portfolio over 1 day. We assume k = 100,000 independent realizations of random evolution. The results are shown in Table 4-6 – we calculate the mean, variance, skewness, kurtosis and also *VaR* considering three various significances: $\alpha = 5$ percent, $\alpha = 1$ percent, and $\alpha = 0.1$ percent.

It is apparent that only the mean of the returns is fitted well by all models. The standard model (GBM) works very well also considering the variance. By contrast, the higher moments are totally inconsistent. It also implies that the true values of further left quantiles cannot be reached by this model – assuming $\alpha = 0.05$, the risk is slightly overestimated, but going further to the left, the model starts to be seriously underestimating.

Next, each subordinated Lévy model fit kurtosis very well. This fact implies a significant improvement when calculating the probability of high losses. However, since models VG1 and NIG1 cannot fit correlation between particular components, the variance of the overall portfolio is underestimated – the effect of diversification is higher than it should be. Clearly, it results into loosing the power to fit the left quantiles. The only shortage of VG2 and NIG2 models is underestimation of the portfolio skewness. This, in turn, implies that the left tails are not as fat as they should be.

The fitting of the overall probability distribution is depicted in Appendix 4-B. We provide there the Gaussian kernel estimation of the log-density function[7] (empirical data are depicted by thick grey line) and compare it with the distribution of the portfolio returns obtained by Monte Carlo simulation assuming GBM (thin black), VG2 (dashed black), and NIG2 (grey thin). The empirical distribution indicates that only left tails are substantial – both VG1 and NIG models fit this feature very well.

Table 4-6 Selected parameters of returns – portfolio Π1

Parameter	Emp.	GBM	VG1	VG2	NIG1	NIG2
*Mean**	–0.937	–0.964	–0.953	–0.980	–0.942	–0.888
*Variance***	9.882	9.872	6.151	9.903	6.146	9.917
Skewness	–0.382	–0.000	–0.105	–0.067	–0.107	–0.054
Kurtosis	7.406	2.999	7.491	7.519	7.482	7.397
VaR (95%)*	50.78	52.52	41.41	52.18	41.40	52.20
VaR (99%)*	87.54	74.26	73.86	93.03	73.90	92.43
VaR (99.9%)*	174.16	97.95	121.89	153.32	121.4	151.52

Source: Author's estimation
Note: * is multiplied by 10^4 and ** is multiplied by 10^6

In order to obtain the probability distribution of portfolio Π2, we proceed similarly to the case of portfolio Π2. This time, however, the correlation of both exchange rates is very low and, more importantly, we cannot assume that the exchange rates are sensitive to the arrival of the same information – the parameters of subordinator variances, ν's, are totally different when fitted independently. In Table 4-7 we provide mutually fitted parameters, though considering unequal weights might give us better results.

Table 4-7 Refitted parameters for portfolio Π2

Parameter	Model 1 (VG)		Model 2 (VG)		Model 2 (NIG)	
	SKK	USD	SKK	USD	SKK	USD
θ	0.0045	–0.0002	0.0011	0.0002	0.0038	–0.0003
ϑ	0.0006	0.0067	0.0004	0.0062	0.0026	0.0066
ν	0.64		0.65		0.47	
ρ	—		0.422		0.387	

Source: Author's estimation

The results of simulation are depicted in Table 4-8. Apparently, this portfolio is more risky than Π2. Concerning the standard model (GBM), the conclusions are identical to portfolio Π1 – it works well only for the mean, variance and VaR (95 percent). The most interesting result concerning subordinated models is that each model (VG1 and NIG1, VG2 and NIG2) performs differently. Some of them perform very poorly also for the variance, the skewness is significantly positive, while it should be negative. The reason might be that to get identical ν for both processes, other measures (skewness, variance) had to be disregarded. Finally, there is no clear advantage of subordinated models over the standard GBM.

Table 4-8 Selected parameters of returns – portfolio Π2

Parameter	Emp.	GBM	VG1	VG2	NIG1	NIG2
*Mean**	–1.879	–1.786	–1.865	–1.889	–1.882	–1.969
*Variance***	17.23	17.23	14.35	10.46	14.33	17.65
Skewness	–0.294	–0.001	1.047	0.386	0.627	0.558
Kurtosis	5.005	3.011	5.738	5.056	4.663	4.607
VaR (95%)*	71.74	70.09	52.47	51.60	57.17	64.03
VaR (99%)*	115.31	98.47	76.08	80.73	84.66	95.88
VaR (99.9%)*	216.54	130.27	109.01	121.01	121.46	137.74

Source: Author's estimation
Note: * is multiplied by 10^4 and ** is multiplied by 10^6

We provide the log-densities of the overall probability distribution also for this portfolio in Appendix 4-B. This time, however, neither VG1 nor NIG differs significantly from GBM concerning the fitting of the left tail.

Backtesting

Validation is an integral part of any model. In order to assess the strength of particular models as a risk measurement tool, we examine one-day *VaR*'s for each day between 1 January 2001 and 31 December 2007. To calculate these risk measures we run Monte Carlo simulation following the models examined above (GBM, VG1, VG2, NIG1, NIG2). The inputs are set on the basis of data observed during 250 business days preceding the day on which we calculate the *VaR*. Next, it is compared with a loss incurred on a given day.

Since the period of seven years gives us about 1,700 observations, the real loss should not be higher than *VaR* on more than 85 days (5 percent significance), 17 days (1 percent significance), and 2 days (0.1 percent significance), respectively. This procedure is usually referred to as the backtesting and the days on which the loss exceeds VaR are known as exceptions.

The results are depicted in Table 4-9. On this basis we can say that both advanced models, VG2 and NIG2, work very well – the number of exceptions is very close to the assumption. Next, the GBM is acceptable only for higher significances. Surprisingly, VG1 and NIG1 are very poor for α = 5 percent. By contrast, when we decrease α significantly, both models will overperform GBM substantially.

Table 4-9 Number of exceptions over 2001-2007, Π1

Parameter	Assum.	GBM	VG1	VG2	NIG1	NIG2
VaR (95%)	85	85	131	82	134	83
VaR (99%)	17	33	30	15	32	15
VaR (99.9%)	2	13	7	2	7	2

Source: Author's estimation

Conclusion

In this chapter we have discussed the possible advantages of simple dependency models for subordinated Lévy processes in risk modelling. First, we suggest several simple dependency models with the potential to fit also the higher moments of the distribution, the skewness and kurtosis.

We have examined selected models on the basis of the VG and NIG model using a dataset comprising four exchange rate quotes over the last eight years. We have chosen two distinct portfolios, consisting either of two highly dependent exchange rates (EUR, SKK) or relatively independent ones (SKK, USD).

It was documented that simplified models, which we called here VG2 and NIG 2, provide us with very good results, concerning both the fitting of the overall distribution (mainly left tails) and the risk measuring procedure (on the basis of backtesting).

References

Applebaum, D. 2004. *Lévy Processes and Stochastic Calculus*. Cambridge: Cambridge University Press.

Barndorf-Nielsen, O.E. 1995. *Normal Inverse Gausian Distributions and the Modeling of Stock Returns*. Research Report No. 300. Department of Theoretical Statistics, Aarhus University.

—. 1998. Processes of Normal Inverse Gaussian Type. *Finance and Stochastics.* 2(1): 41-68.

Bertoin, J. 1998. *Lévy Processes*. Cambridge: Cambridge University Press.

Carr, P., H. Geman, D.B. Madan and M. Yor. 2002. The Fine Structure of Asset Returns: An Empirical Investigation. *Journal of Business* 75(2): 305-32.

—. 2003. Stochastic Volatility for Lévy Processes. *Mathematical Finance* 13(3): 345-82.

Cherubini, U., E. Luciano and W. Vecchiato. 2004. *Copula Methods in Finance*. Wiley.

Cont, R. and P. Tankov. 2004. *Financial Modelling with Jump Processes.* Chapman &Hall/CRC Press.

Eberlein, E. and U. Keller. 1995. Hyperbolic Distributions in Finance. *Bernoulli* 1(3): 281-99.

Jondeau, E., S.H. Poon and M. Rockinger. 2006. *Financial Modeling under Non-Gaussian Distributions*. Springer Verlag.

Luciano, E. and W. Schoutens. 2006. Multivariate Jump-Driven Financial Asset Model. *Quantitative finance* 6(5): 385-402.

Madan, D.B. and F. Milne. 1991. Option Pricing with VG Martingale Components. *Mathematical Finance* 1(4): 39-56.

Madan, D.B. and E.E. Seneta. 1990. The VG Model for Share Market Returns, *Journal of Business* 63(4): 511-24.

Madan, D.B., P. Carr and E.C. Chang. 1998. The Variance Gamma Process and Option Pricing. *European Finance Review* 2(1): 79-105.

Nelsen, R.B. 2006. *An Introduction to Copulas*. 2nd ed. Springer.

Rank, J. (ed). 2007. *Copulas. From Theory to Application in Finance.* Risk books.

Schoutens, W. 2003. *Lévy Processes in Finance*. Wiley.

Tichý, T. 2008. Alternative dependency measures and a small portfolio. In *Proceeding of Mathematical Methods of Economics*. Liberec: Technical University Liberec.

Acknowledgement

The research is due to the support provided by GAČR (Czech Science Foundation – Grantová agentura České republiky) under the project No. 402/08/1237. The support is greatly acknowledged.

Notes

[1] For more on the theory of Lévy models see e.g. Bertoin (1998) or Applebaum (2004).

[2] The real world measure is suitable for risk assessment. By contrast, to price a financial derivative the real world drift μ must be replaced by the risk neutral one – the riskless rate r.

[3] For more details on Variance gamma model, see e.g. Madan and Seneta (1990) – for a symmetric case, Madan and Milne (1991), and Madan et al. (1998) for an asymmetric case. Similarly, Normal inverse Gaussian model is as per Barndorff-Nielsen (1995) and (1998). Its generalisation, the Hyperbolic model, was introduced in Eberlein and Keller (1995). Further models can be found in Schoutens (2003) or Cont and Tankov (2004).

[4] In general, we have $3n + 1$ equations and $2n + 1$ parameters.

[5] The most general reference for the theory of copula functions is Nelsen (2004), while Rank (2007) and Cherubini et al. (2004) target mainly on the application issues in finance.

[6] In a related research (see Tichý, 2008), it was showed on the same series of data that a linear correlation for a moving one-year time window is very unstable. In fact, for particular subintervals it gives both zero dependency and almost perfect dependency. Moreover, alternative dependency measures (e.g. Kendall tau, Spearman rho) provide approximately the same curves.

[7] We use a log-density function in order to emphasise the fat tails.

Appendix 4-A

Figure 4-A1 Daily evolution of exchange rates

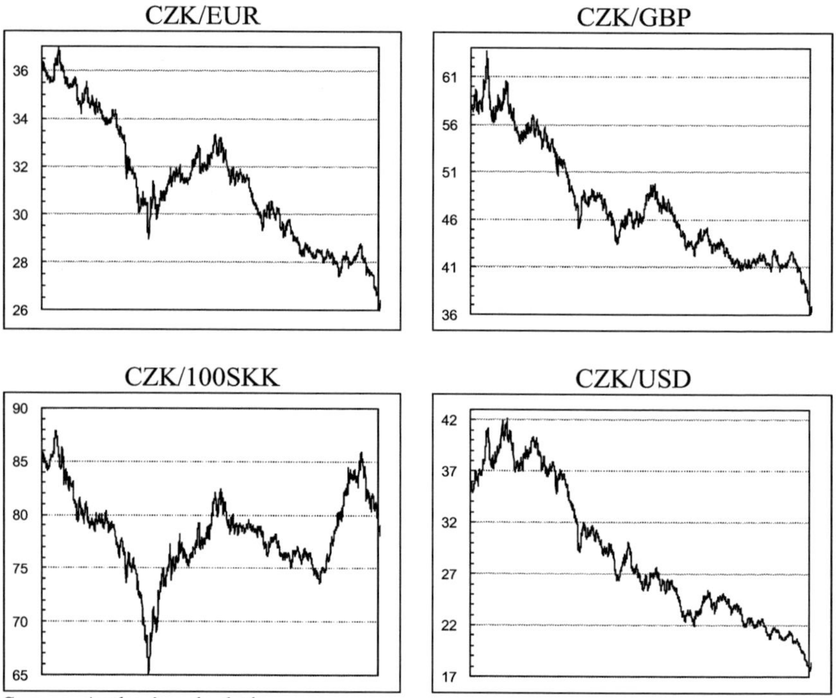

Source: Author's calculations

Figure 4-A2 Daily log-returns of exchange rates

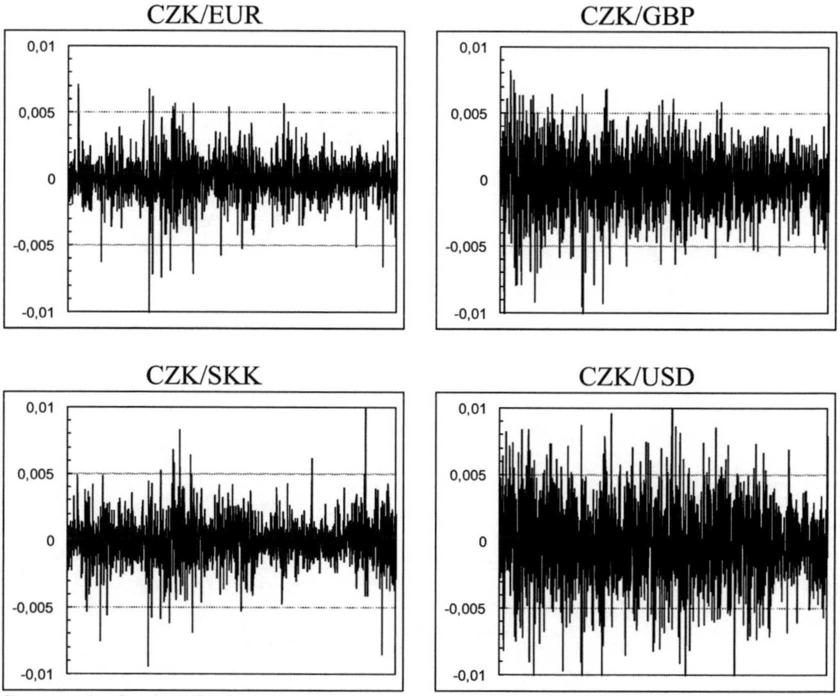

Source: Author's calculations

Appendix 4-B

Figure 4-B1 Log-densities for Π1

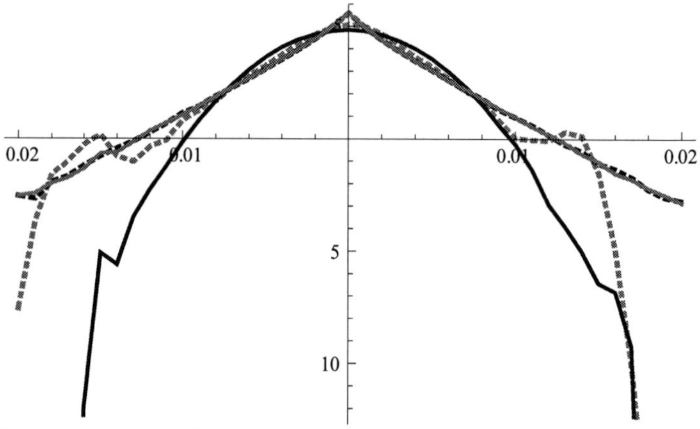

Source: Author's estimation

Figure 4-B2 Log-densities for Π2

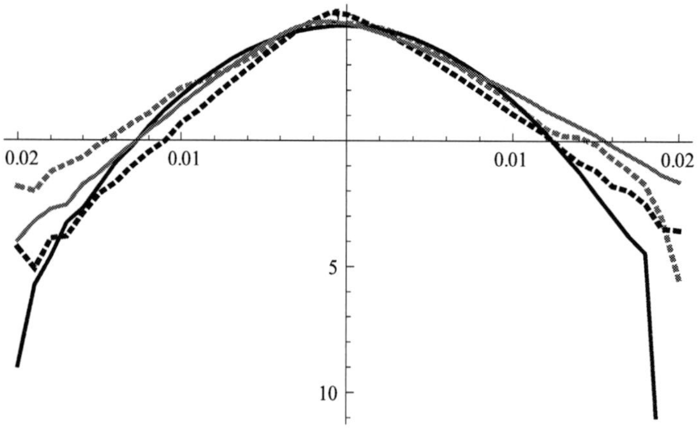

Source: Author's estimation

Note: In both charts we provide empirical log-density (dashed grey line) and compare it with the results obtained by Monte Carlo simulation assuming GBM (solid black), VG2 (dashed black), and NIG2 (solid grey).

CHAPTER FIVE

THE EUROPEAN BOND MARKETS LEADERSHIP: EVIDENCE FROM A REGIME SWITCHING EXAMINATION FRAMEWORK

DIMITRIS GEORGOUTSOS
AND PETROS M. MIGIAKIS

The economic environment of the 21st century is dominated, according to numerous papers, by the globalisation process, which is strongly enhanced compared to recent decades and is often compared to the past financial integration process at the end of the 19th century. For a more thorough discussion of the inter-temporal globalisation processes see among others Bordo et al. (1998) and Lothian (2000, 2001). As a result, the European integration process has been on its way since the World War II. Especially following the elimination of national divergences in the implementation of monetary policy along with the implementation of the monetary union, European financial markets reportedly share increasing degrees of financial integration. However, several issues still remain to be answered in a robust way for the European integration process. In this frame, we investigate the strength of the linkages of the European bond markets aiming at finding dominant characteristics for some of the government bonds of the system.

Previous works have reported divergent views on the dominant role of the German Bund for the ten-year benchmark sector of the European bond markets. Based on this framework we report evidence shedding light on the dominance in the European bond markets. Specifically, allowing for the dominant characteristics to vary, the results of our analysis indicate that although the German bonds have significant causal effects towards the rest of the EMU's government bonds, underlying thus their dominant position in the European bond markets sector, the effects of the French bonds on the rest of the European government bonds should not be ignored when assessing the dominance issue. Specifically, we provide evidence in the direction that the German dominance is disrupted and replaced by dominance of the French bonds, in periods of increased French inflation, formulating thus expectations on rising interest rates.

In order to perform our investigation we adopt regime switching structures of the underlying relations, thus allowing for changing structures of interactions among the European bond markets. Specifically, we apply the Markov Switching examination framework introduced by Hamilton (1989) and adjusted for multi-variable systems by Krolzig (1997). Additionally we report initial results for the linear formulation of the short-run adjustment mechanism of the cointegration framework (Engle and Granger, 1987; Johansen, 1988, 1992; Johansen and Juselius, 1992, 1994) in order to highlight the improvement of the results brought about by the regime switching framework. All in all, finding strong interactions in the European bond markets, we provide results that bridge two divergent stances on the dominance in European bond markets.

The rest of this chapter is organised as follows. First, we report relevant previous research findings. Subsequently, we describe the empirical framework and presents and discuss the results. Finally, the findings summary and concluding remarks are provided.

Literature Review

The interactions between international bond markets has been the subject of investigation in recently published papers, rendering thus an increased interest in the further examination of the issue. Indicatively, Yang (2006) examines the interactions among five markets, namely those of the United States, Germany, Japan, United Kingdom and Canada, and fails to report significant long run cointegration relations while describing the causal patterns of the interrelations. Weber (2006) examines the convergence of the UK interest rates, both short and long term, towards either the European or the US rates. His findings show a slightly greater convergence towards the European rates. Finally, Kim et al. (2006) examine the financial integration process of the international bond market, among which some of the European markets and those of the US and UK can be found, aiming at highlighting the volatility spillover effects among the markets. Their results indicate that integration has advanced in pace with European monetary unification, however the risk contained in the markets has followed different patterns in Europe and internationally, in the former case diminishing while in the later increasing.

The European bond markets have been the focus of the attention of research work with regard to the effects the European Economic and Monetary Union (EMU) has had on them, both prior to and following the introduction of the euro. The significant convergence of European government bond markets has been reported in various works that describe the state of integration of the relevant financial sector. Among others Codogno et al. (2003), Dunne et al. (2002), Pagano and von Thadden (2004), Baele et al. (2004), report increased financial integration in the European bond markets. In the empirical literature examining European bond markets the German dominance hypothesis is common ground for the results exploited by researchers, e.g. Baum and Barkoulas (2006). However, contradicting evidence has been reported indicating that this opinion is not unambiguous. Specifically, Dunne et al. (2002) investigate the dominance hypothesis in the European bond markets providing evidence that the German Bunds represent the main outflux or flow of causal interactions towards the European bond markets. However, the researchers question the dominance of the relevant bonds as their evidence also leaves room for dominant roles of the French and Italian bonds. On the other hand, Kiehlborn and Mietzner (2005) report that the German bonds are the dominant factor of the European bond markets.

The investigation framework of the combination of cointegration analysis and causal relations is the most used methodology for assessing issues of financial integration. Haug et al. (2000) report that complete convergence can be established from the outcome of a single common stochastic trend left outside the cointegration space. As the investigation of financial integration is the starting point of our analysis, we also adopt the relevant criterion for the full integration. In a similar early work Centeno and Mello (1999) investigate parity relations in the short-term side of the yield curve among various European money markets. Additionally, they investigate causal effects stemming from the German rates in relation to the rest of the European Monetary System's markets. The reported evidence indicates exogeneity of the German rates and endogeneity of the rest of the system's variables, thus indirectly leading to dominant characteristics of the German rates in the system.

Methodological Framework Used for the Assessment of Interactions

Our dataset is comprised of monthly yields of government bonds with a term to maturity of ten years of the countries of the euro area – namely Austria, Belgium, Finland, France, Germany, Greece, Ireland, Italy,

Netherlands, Portugal and Spain. Specifically, we have chosen the ten year issues of the aforementioned markets in order to examine the long term benchmark sector of the bond markets of the countries referred to above. The time period investigated in the present chapter covers a time span of approximately nine years, specifically January 1997 – January 2006. We do not divide a priori the system between the pre-euro and the post-euro eras as this is performed in a more accurate way by the structural methodology implemented.

Financial time series are well known for encompassing stochastic characteristics. As a result, cointegration techniques are necessary in order to assess the interactions among the European bond markets. Specifically, interest rates are known to have I(1) characteristics (however, unit root and stationarity properties are examined before entering the main investigation through Dickey and Fuller, 1979 and Kwiatkowski et al., 1992). Additionally, since cointegration analysis has seen extensive application in recent years by financial researchers, we opt to limit ourselves to a brief discussion in this section.

We adopt the cointegration analysis techniques introduced in a bilateral framework by Engle and Granger (1987), and in a multivariate concept by Johansen (1988), further advanced by Johansen (1992), Johansen and Juselius (1992, 1994) and Gregory and Hansen (1996). As a result, our examination depends on revealing the existence of significant long-run equilibria among the bond yields examined, rank of the cointegration space, decomposition of the long-run relations and hypothesis testing.

$$\begin{aligned} &\Delta X_t = \Pi X_{t-1} + \sum_{j=1}^{n}\sum_{l=1}^{k-1} \Gamma_{ji} \Delta X_{j\,t-l} + U_t, \\ &t = 1,2,\ldots, T \\ &U_t \sim NID(0,\Sigma) \end{aligned} \qquad (5.1)$$

The representation of I(1) time series with cointegration characteristics is given by relation (5.1) in which Γ_{ji} and Π represent matrices of p x p rank. Matrix Π represents the matrix containing the cointegration relations of the system and Γ_{ji} is the matrix of the coefficients of the lagged variables in each of the equations of the system. The concept of the multivariate cointegration analysis for I(1) variables is based on the elimination of the stochastic trends, of non-stationary variables. If all the stochastic trends are eliminated ($r = p$) the time series is stationary, while if no linear combination can be found ($r = 0$), no cointegration relation exists among the system's variables, indicating that each separate time series is driven by a separate stochastic trend. In all intermediate occasions between no linear combination and stationarity, the time series is driven by several linear combinations and stochastic trends ($0 < r < p$). Consequently, our analysis will begin with the determination of the number of linear combinations, or else cointegration vectors, that exist in the system.

The representation of the cointegration space is given by $\Pi = \alpha\beta$, where α, β are vectors of rank p x r representing the short run adjusting relations and the long run equilibrium formulating relations respectively, while a restricted constant is contained in the cointegration space. Following equation (5.1) the cointegration space $\Pi = \alpha\beta$ is decomposed into its long run equilibrium relations and their short run dynamics. Specifically, β represents the eigenvector(s) or else the cointegration vector(s) of the system while vector α contains the coefficients consisting of the adjustment mechanisms towards the long run relations. For the long run we analyse the cointegration vectors into their components, while for the short run we examine the significance of the adjustment mechanisms towards the long run equilibria.

Additionally, we examine the hypotheses of long run exclusion from the cointegration vectors' formulation (Engle et al., 1983; Johansen, 1992). The tests are used as indications of significant influence by the markets examined in the long run equilibria. The formula of the hypothesis testing of restricted cointegration vectors' coefficients is presented in Johansen (1992). In the decomposition of the cointegration space the examination of the significance of the long run coefficients is the equivalent of testing for long run exclusion. Specifically, the test for long run exclusion examines the hypothesis $H_0 : \beta = 0$.

Next we examine the decomposition of the cointegration space following the tests formed by Johansen and Juselius (1994). As we do not presuppose that the underlying long run relations are stable over time we examine the regime switching properties of the relations in order to identify structural breaks that might have occurred in the time period examined. Naturally, we expect significant breaks to be evident in the time of the adoption of the common monetary policy framework. In order to count for possible structural breaks in the long run relations we apply the Gregory and Hansen (1996) methodology. Specifically by adopting Gregory and Hansen's methodology the structural breaks of the system can be identified. The structural breaks can stem either from shifts of the level (model C), or the trend (model C/T), while in the case both the components of the cointegrating relation exhibit shifts in their structures the examination considered is that of a fullbreak (model C/S). Relation (5.2) reports the relevant examination.

$$C_{1,t} = \mu_1 + \mu_2 v_{t\tau} + \alpha_{1_1}^T C_{2,t} + \alpha_2^T C_{2,t} v_{t\tau} + e_t \qquad (5.2)$$
$$t = 1, \ldots, n$$

In (5.2) the coefficients C represent the components of the long run relations of the cointegration space, while μ represents the vector's constant, α^T represents the coefficients of the components respectively, $v_{t\tau}$ the unobserved state variable and e_t the error term. Gregory and Hansen use the Philipps and Perron's Z statistic for the residual of the earlier relation's regression, in order to specify regime shifts. Although Gregory and Hansen tests indicate the structural formulation focusing on the stationarity of the cointegrating relations the same examination can be significant for declaring structural reformulation even if the stationarity characteristics are already confirmed by the cointegration tests. Trenkler (2005) and Lütkepohl, Saikkonen and Trenkler (2004), discuss the effects of ignoring regime shifts in cointegration relations.

Subsequently, we examine the short run decomposition. Following Engle et al. (1983) and Johansen (1992), we estimate the hypothesis of the weak exogeneity, that is, the hypothesis that the short run coefficients are not significant for the deterministic process. The weak exogeneity is our main proxy for evaluating the effects of the cointegration space in the underlying markets in a linear formulation. As in the case of the long run relations the weak exogeneity hypothesis examines the significance of the short run adjustment coefficients. Specifically through the illustration of the cointegrating system given by Johansen (1988) and Johansen and Juselius (1992) we examine the null hypothesis $H_0 : \alpha = 0$, in order to accept or reject the significant adjustment of the system's variables towards the long run common equilibria.

Next we examine the causal relations among the European bond markets. However, the investigation framework we adopt is again of a non-linear formulation in order to capture changing patterns in the causal relations of the European bond markets. Thus following the methodology described by Krolzig (1996, 1997) we examine the short run pricing effects of the system for the presence of Markov regime switching characteristics. The following equation (5.3) illustrates the Markov Switching – Vector Error Correction Model (MS-VECM) we estimate for the short run structure.

$$\Delta X_t = \sum_{r=1}^{n-p} \alpha_r(s) VEC_{r\,t-1} + \sum_{j=1}^{n} \sum_{i=1}^{k-1} \Gamma(s)_{j_i} \Delta X_{j_{t-i}} + U_t,$$
$$t = 1,2,\ldots, T \qquad (5.3)$$
$$U_t \sim NID\ (0, \Sigma(s))$$

Specifically, we relax the assumption of linearity in the relations illustrated by the VECM and introduce a regime switching variable S_t that follows a Markov chain in the transitional procedure of its probabilities leading to a similar categorization of the system between two regimes. Thus, we permit the system's short run causal effects to differentiate according to their structural state, in order to capture alterations in the structure of the causal relations throughout the period we examine. As a result, the regime switching framework will indicate different patterns potentially leading to different dominance characteristics in the European bond markets.

Empirical Analysis of the Interactions and Leader-Follower Relations in the European Bond Markets

In order to define the underlying structure of the examination framework we need firstly to determine the lags that need to be imposed in the underlying cointegrating Vector Autoregressive System (VAR). We rely on two main criteria in order to define the appropriate lags to be imposed, the information criteria and the autocorrelation tests. Table 5-1 presents the results and, as reported, the lower lag structure is indicated to contain more informational value than the four lags. However, between the two and three lags we chose to impose three lags in order to avoid autocorrelation characteristics that are indicated to remain in the system's relation in the case of two lags.

Table 5-1 Specification of the lag structure

	2 lags	3 lags	4 lags
Hanan-Quinn	-59.876	-59.362	-58.639
Schwartz	-56.742	-54.401	-51.829
LM(1)	186.44 (0.00)	154.04 (0.02)	115.46 (0.62)
LM(4)	140.12 (0.11)	134.16 (0.19)	148.60 (0.04)

Source: Authors' calculations
Note: p-values in parenthesis

Next, we turn to the examination of the stationarity characteristics of the system's variables in order to specify the integration rank. The tests we follow are both the traditional Dickey and Fuller's (1979) unit root test and the Kwiatkowski et al. (1992) stationarity test. Table 5-2 reports the relevant results.

Table 5-2 Unit root and stationarity tests

	Levels				**1st Differences**			
	l=0		**l=5**		**l=0**		**l=5**	
	D-F	***KPSS***	***D-F***	***KPSS***	***D-F***	***KPSS***	***D-F***	***KPSS***
Austria	-1.09	1.071	-1.81	0.207	-10.1	0.065	-3.89	0.056
Belgium	-1.16	1.031	-1.69	0.201	-9.91	0.062	-4.07	0.056
Finland	-1.35	0.889	-1.80	0.177	-10.4	0.065	-4.24	0.067
France	-1.33	0.969	-1.75	0.192	-9.73	0.058	-4.22	0.054
Germany	-1.41	0.778	-2.01	0.156	-10.2	0.057	-4.27	0.053
Greece	-1.34	0.786	-1.44	0.159	-10.9	0.050	-4.06	0.051
Ireland	-1.62	0.706	-2.21	0.139	-10.2	0.073	-4.20	0.064
Italy	-2.31	0.627	-2.77	0.124	-9.51	0.122	-3.57	0.100
Nether-lands	-1.20	1.001	-1.72	0.198	-10.4	0.055	-4.22	0.053
Portugal	-1.74	0.781	-2.00	0.152	-6.07	0.103	-5.24	0.083
Spain	-1.69	0.713	-2.16	0.140	-9.89	0.111	-3.79	0.094

Source: Authors' estimation

Note: Critical Values D-F: l=0: 1%= -3.491, 5%=-2.888, 10%=-2.581, l=5: 1%= -3.494, 5%=-2.889, 10%=-2.585, KPSS: 10%=0.119, 5%= 0.146, 1%= 0.216

The results of the unit root and stationarity tests unambiguously indicate that the time series we use are I(1). As a result we examine the system for cointegration relations according to Johansen's trace tests. Table 5-3 reports the results of the tests.

Table 5-3 Cointegration rank tests

	p = 11	p = 10	p = 9	p = 8	p = 7	p = 6
λ_{Trace}^{*}	291.4	244.15	202.92	165.58	131.70	102.14
λ_{max}^{*}	69.74	63.57	57.42	52.00	46.45	40.30
	p = 5	p = 4	p = 3	p = 2	p = 1	
λ_{Trace}^{*}	76.07	53.12	34.91	19.96	9.24	
λ_{max}^{*}	34.40	28.14	22.00	15.67	9.24	
	r < 1	r < 2	r < 3	r < 4	r < 5	r < 6
λ_{Trace}^{*}	475.05	338.55	246.27	182.73	133.48	94.92
λ_{max}^{*}	136.50	92.28	63.54	49.24	38.56	35.67
	r < 7	r < 8	r < 9	r < 10	r < 11	
λ_{Trace}^{*}	59.25	37.15	21.43	9.87	1.94	
λ_{max}^{*}	22.10	15.72	11.56	7.93	1.94	

Source: Authors' estimation

Note: The critical values of the trace and max eigenvalue statistics as reported in Osterwald-Lennum (1992), and are indicated * for a confidence interval of 95%, p stands for the number of stochastic trends left outside the cointegration space.

As reported in Table 5-3 the hypothesis that the number of cointegration vectors is smaller than the proxy is consistently rejected until the specification of five cointegration vectors. As a result, six stochastic trends are left outside the cointegration space. This initial result points in the direction of partial elimination of the unrestricted stochastic trends of the system. Specifically, following the Haug et al. (2000) criterion of full integration, the later case is rejected by the cointegration rank tests. However, this result indicates significant convergence of the European bond markets, in line with current empirical literature dealing with the issue of financial integration of the European bond markets. However, more illustrative on the focus of this chapter are the results of the long run equilibrium relations and the short run dynamics.

The Long Run Decomposition

The decomposition of the cointegration vectors reflects the long run relations that reflect the equilibrium relations of the European bond markets. In order to specify the respective relations we first examine the exclusion of the system's variables from the cointegration vectors' long run decomposition as described in the section discussing the methodological aspects. Table 5-4 reports the results.

As indicated by these results, not all the government bonds examined participate significantly in the specification of the system's long run equilibria. Specifically Greece, Italy and Spain are reported to be excluded from the long run structure of the cointegration space. This finding signifies differentiation in the degree of financial integration of the euro area's bond markets, and additionally leads to the extraction of an initial result of leader-follower characteristics in the European bond markets. Evidently, the markets found to be excluded from the cointegration space decomposition are high-yielders and thus follow developments caused by other dominant bonds, in a declining rates' environment.

Table 5-4 Long run exclusion tests

$H_0 : \beta i = 0$	**$X^2(5)$**	**p-value**
Austria	15.88	0.01
Belgium	12.83	0.03
Finland	11.76	0.04
France	65.67	0.00
Germany	32.60	0.00
Greece	7.19	0.21
Ireland	17.11	0.00
Italy	7.37	0.19
Netherlands	23.80	0.00
Portugal	28.14	0.00
Spain	5.13	0.40
Constant	4.62	0.46

Source: Authors' estimation

In order to specify robust stationary long run relations that make up the cointegration space we identify relations among the system's bonds that explain in a significant fashion the long run equilibria incorporated in the system. Table 5-5 contains the hypotheses we used in order to specify the relations incorporated in the cointegration vectors. Specifically adopting the results of the long run exclusion tests, we specified the cointegration space, using rolling techniques. We concluded in a significant approximation of the long run stationary equilibria in line with the long run exclusion tests' results. Table 5-5, presents the hypotheses we tested in the upper bound and the numerical results of the eigenvectors of the cointegration space, in the lower cells.

Table 5-5 Specification of the cointegration space

	$X^2(3)$	p-value
$H_0 : \beta_i = (\beta_{Bel}, \beta_{Fin}, \beta_{Gre}, \beta_{Ita}, \beta_{Por}, \beta_{Spa}, \beta_{Cons}) = 0$	7.888	0.05
$H_0 : \beta_i = (\beta_{Gre}, \beta_{Ita}, \beta_{Spa}, \beta_{Cons}) = 0$		
$H_0 : \beta_i = (\beta_{Fin}, \beta_{Gre}, \beta_{Por}, \beta_{Cons}) = 0$		
$H_0 : \beta_i = (\beta_{Aus}, \beta_{Gre}, \beta_{Ire}) = 0$		
$H_0 : \beta_i = (\beta_{Gre}, \beta_{Ita}, \beta_{Por}, \beta_{Spa}) = 0$		
$H_0 : \{\beta_i = 0\} \cap \{\beta_j = 0\} \cap ... \cap \{\beta_z = 0\} \; i, j..., z \in \{1,2,...n\}$		

Source: Authors' calculations

Additionally, we investigate the cointegration space for structural differentiation during the period examined. The Johansen tests confirm existence of cointegration in the system as reported earlier, thus we do not need to run tests for structural breaks in order to properly evaluate, what would have been, underestimated cointegrating relations, according to Lutkepohl et al. (2004). However in order to exploit the full informational capacity of the system we examine its structural identification through time. Specifically, using the Gregory and Hansen (1996) technique, we have identified several structural breaks in the cointegration vectors of the system. Table 5-6 reports the results.

As presented in Table 5-6, excepting the first vector, almost all the significant structural breaks of the system are concentrated around the period of the implementation of the monetary union in Europe. The first vector contains variables capturing the bond market behaviour of Germany, France, Austria, Ireland and Netherlands, specified as the markets for which there are unambiguous results of strong effects on the cointegration space, reported by the tests of long run exclusion. As a result, these findings confirm that the underlying structure of the relation remains stable regardless of the developments in the meantime period. Additionally, the tests provide useful insight on the causes of the structural differentiations, as in most cases both the trending factors and the constant of the cointegration vectors are found to produce the reported breaks.

Table 5-6 Gregory and Hansen's structural breaks tests for the cointegration space

	C/S: $y_{1t} = f(*, \mu(s_t), \alpha(s_t))$
VEC_1	-8.400 (2002:03)
VEC_2	-9.640 (1999:03)
VEC_3	-12.455 (1998:08)
VEC_4	-7.961 (1998:08)
VEC_5	-10.821 (1998:09)

Source: Authors' estimation
Note: critical values: -6.51 (1%), -6.0 (5%)

All in all, we have specified robust cointegrating relations in the system of the European bond markets, as expected, indicating the enhanced integration characteristics of the system. However, the limitations of the integration are evident, complying with the examination framework of Haug et al. (2000). Specifically, apart from the limited elimination of the stochastic trends of the system exogeneity characteristics indicate the formulation of groups according to the degree of strength of the interactions among the markets; a result in line with divergent economic conjunctions in the European countries. However, the structural differentiation of the cointegration space occurring around the implementation of the common monetary policy framework underlines the importance of this development for the European financial integration process. As a result, the decomposition of the long run relations among the European bond markets we have described formulates an efficient framework for the examination of the causality and adjustment characteristics in the system.

The Short Run Dynamics

Based on the decomposition of the cointegration space, standing as a significant approximation of the long run equilibria, we analyse the causality relations in the European bond markets. Following von Hagen and Fratianni (1990) we accept dominant characteristics of a market in case it causes at least a significant proportion of the system's markets and simultaneously is not caused by the system, indicating exogeneity characteristics. Intuitively we would expect that the results should indicate dominance of either the German or the French bonds.

Initially, we examine the weak exogeneity characteristics of the system's variables in a linear fashion. Specifically, we estimate significance of the adjustment mechanisms of the European bonds we examine in relation to the long run equilibrium relations as captured by the cointegration vectors. Table 5-7 contains the results of the relevant tests.

Table 5-7 Linear weak exogeneity tests

$H_0 : \beta i = 0$	$X^2(5)$	p-value
Austria	5.71	0.32
Belgium	3.13	0.68
Finland	3.10	0.68
France	6.47	0.26
Germany	2.04	0.84
Greece	2.54	0.77
Ireland	5.29	0.38
Italy	5.26	0.39
Netherlands	4.29	0.51
Portugal	15.19	0.01
Spain	7.79	0.17
Constant	5.71	0.32

Source: Authors' estimation

Specifically, as expected, the French and the German bonds are indicated to be exogenous in their short run behaviour, confirming their leader characteristics. This result is in line with expectations, however the same does not hold for the rest of the system's variables. Specifically, the government bond of Portugal alone is indicated to absorb the short run deviations and converge towards the long run equilibrium relations. However, these results are reversed by the examination of the system's short run dynamics in a non-linear fashion.

Table 5-8 reports the results of the examination of the regime switching mechanism in the short run relations of the system, indicating that under all criteria the regime switching examination framework enhances the informational value of the system. Additionally, Table 5-9 presents the description of the two regimes found to formulate the structure of the system under the non-linear approach. Specifically, as indicated, the two regimes are practically equivalent as regards length. However, Regime 1 is indicated to be slightly more persistent than the second regime, as its stability concentrates double the probabilities of the transition to the second regime. On the other hand, the second regime is indicated to be more "transitional" as the pass-through to the first regime is almost equivalent to its stability. All in all, the results confirm the regime switching mechanism's significance and indicate a slight prevalence of the first regime.

Table 5-8 Validation of the regime switching mechanisms

	AIC	Log Likelihood
Linear structure	-29.723	1964.21
Regime switching structure	-31.192	2418.79
LR – Linearity test	909.158	
	X^2 (374) (0.00)	X^2 (376) (0.00)

Source: Authors' estimation
Note: p-values in parentheses

Table 5-9 Descriptive statistics of the two regimes

	Transition probs.		Duration	Number	Regime
	Regime 1	Regime 2	(months)	of obser.	probs.
Regime 1	0.641	0.358	2.79	59	0.552
Regime 2	0.442	0.557	2.26	48	0.447

Source: Authors' calculations

Tables 5-10a and 5-10b present the causal interactions among the system's bond markets. Evidently their decomposition reveals two different patterns on the leadership characteristics in the European bond markets' system, in line with the confirmation of the regime switching mechanism. Specifically, in the first regime the German bond is indicated to have significant causality effects towards the rest of the system's markets, although with the exceptions of Finland, Greece and Italy. On the other hand, in the second regime the outcome concerning dominance characteristics of the Bund is reversed, indicating that the French bond is the most significant causal factor, among the European bond markets. Specifically, the French bond is indicated to align with the criteria of von Hagen and Fratianni (1990) on the dominance characteristics, for the time period the second regime holds. Additionally this finding is in line with the results reported by Dunne et al. (2002), stating that the French bond has important benchmark characteristics. As a result, the first finding of the regime switching structure of the system indicates that there exists evidence of a diarchy in the European bond markets. However, there are several points that should be highlighted.

Table 5-10a Causality tests among European bond markets under Regime 1

	AT	BE	FI	FR	DE	GR	IE	IT	NT	PT	ES	ECT_1	ECT_2	ECT_3	ECT_4	ECT_5
AT	-	-	-	-	-	13.66 (0.00)	-	-	8.730 (0.01)	12.83 (0.00)	6.310 (0.04)	-	-	-	4.233 (0.04)	-
BE	5.994 (0.05)	-	-	5.613 (0.06)	16.17 (0.00)	-	-	-	10.18 (0.01)	12.31 (0.00)	6.128 (0.05)	-	-	-	3.378 (0.07)	-
FI	-	-	-	-	-	-	-	-	-	-	-	-	-	-	-	-
FR	6.848 (0.03)	-	-	9.087 (0.01)	9.416 (0.01)	-	-	-	9.087 (0.01)	9.332 (0.01)	-	14.62 (0.00)	-	-	3.641 (0.06)	-
DE	6.313 (0.04)	-	-	5.947 (0.05)	12.20 (0.00)	-	-	-	6.976 (0.03)	10.28 (0.01)	4.578 (0.10)	2.874 (0.09)	-	-	3.613 (0.06)	-
GR	-	-	-	4.815 (0.09)	-	-	-	-	-	-	-	-	-	5.061 (0.02)	-	4.137 (0.04)
IE	-	-	-	-	5.897 (0.05)	-	-	-	-	5.285 (0.07)	6.677 (0.04)	-	-	-	-	-
NT	-	-	-	-	-	-	-	-	-	-	5.976 (0.05)	-	-	-	-	-
PT	-	-	-	-	7.14 (0.03)	-	-	-	4.853 (0.09)	4.908 (0.09)	-	-	-	-	-	-
ES	-	-	-	-	10.10 (0.01)	-	-	-	7.190 (0.03)	9.715 (0.01)	5.650 (0.06)	-	6.528 (0.01)	-	-	-

Source: Authors' estimation

Note: T-statistics in parentheses

Table 5-10b Causality tests among European bond markets under Regime 2

	AT	BE	FI	FR	DE	GR	IE	IT	NT	PT	ES	ECT_1	ECT_2	ECT_3	ECT_4	ECT_5
AT	-	-	-	10.37 (0.01)	-	-	-	-	-	-	7.509 (0.02)	-	-	-	-	3.120 (0.07)
BE	-	-	-	7.124 (0.03)	-	-	5.452 (0.07)	-	-	-	10.13 (0.01)	-	-	-	-	-
FI	-	-	-	7.882 (0.02)	-	-	5.011 (0.08)	-	-	-	10.18 (0.01)	-	-	-	-	-
FR	-	-	-	-	-	-	-	-	-	-	5.475 (0.06)	-	-	-	-	-
DE	-	-	-	5.770 (0.06)	-	-	-	-	-	-	5.344 (0.07)	-	-	-	-	-
GR	-	-	-	12.27 (0.00)	-	-	-	6.723 (0.03)	-	-	8.663 (0.01)	-	-	-	-	-
IE	-	-	-	8.846 (0.01)	-	-	-	4.980 (0.08)	-	-	5.970 (0.05)	-	-	-	-	-
NT	-	-	-	7.499 (0.02)	-	-	4.961 (0.08)	-	-	-	10.17 (0.01)	-	-	-	-	-
PT	-	-	-	6.227 (0.04)	-	-	7.156 (0.03)	-	-	-	7.444 (0.02)	-	3.874 (0.05)	-	-	-
ES	-	9.425 (0.01)	6.000 (0.05)	6.396 (0.04)	-	-	-	-	-	-	5.409 (0.07)	-	-	-	6.449 (0.01)	-

Source: Authors' estimation

Note: T-statistics in parentheses

Figure 5-1 Regime characterisation of the time span

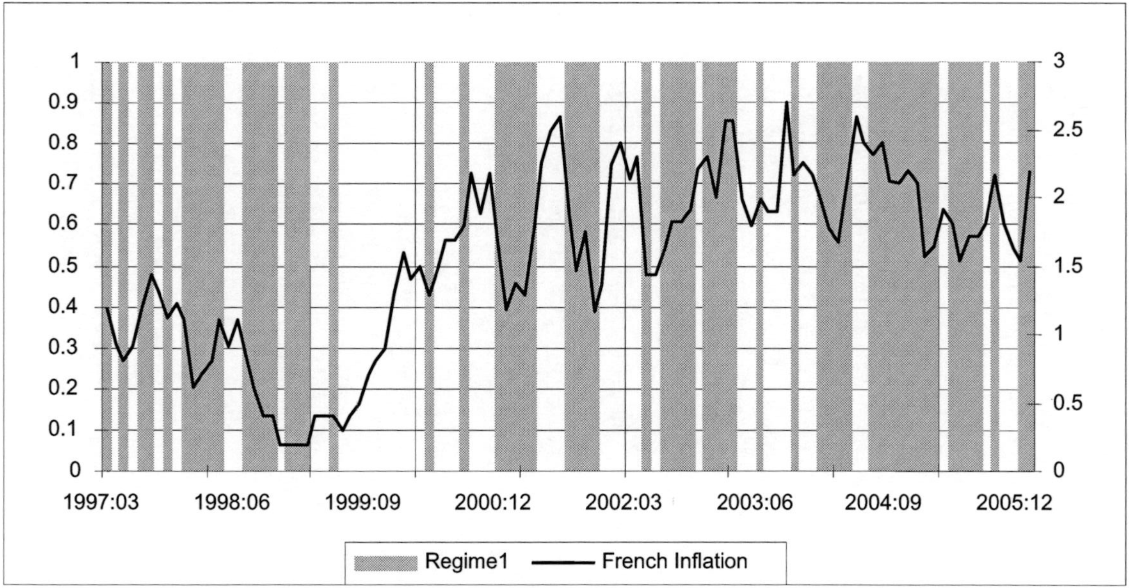

Source: Authors’ calculations

Overall, the two regimes differ substantially in the causal relations they contain. The first regime reports significant adjustment mechanisms, in contrast with the linear structure's weak exogeneity tests and significant causality relations among some of the system's bond markets. The adjustment mechanisms found to be significant in the first regime indicate the improvement of the examination framework brought about by the adoption of a regime switching approach and highlight the significant adjustment towards long run equilibria indicating increased convergence characteristics, in line with the increased integration characteristics of the long run structure.

Additionally, significant relations among the system's markets are in line with the increased interactions described by the rest of the regime's findings. The second regime, characterised by the dominant features of the French bond, contains few significant adjustment mechanisms, and very few other causality patterns are found to be significant. However, the Spanish bond's variable is indicated to have significant causality effects on the rest of the system's markets. Thus the two regimes describe two different statuses in the European bond markets, with regard to the interactions of the system's variables. Figure 5-1 illustrates the specific characterization of the time span we examine according to the prevailing regime.

As indicated in Figure 5-1 the first regime covers to a large degree the period prior to the monetary unification and the period after 2002. Accordingly, the second regime prevails in the period in between, approximately the time span 1999-2002. These results are indications of the significant convergence of the European economies, as a whole, for the period prior to the introduction of the common currency and in line with previous research stating the dominance of the German economy in the time period before the introduction of the euro. With regard to the benchmark status of the German bond, support is found on the prevalence of the first regime, in which the causal relations indicate German leadership. However, following implementation of the common monetary policy framework, a shift is indicated, lasting until 2002, resulting in greater significance of the French bonds. Overall, the conclusion should not be other than a diarchy in the European bond markets, although the leadership of the German bond is related to the prevalent regime, in which it occurs that more significant interactions and adjustment mechanisms exist. However, the benchmark status in the European bond markets is indicated not to be a case of permanent characteristic, but rather a time-variant, state shared between the ten year government bonds of Germany and France.

Subsequently, a most important step of our analysis is to justify in economic reasoning the transitional process among the two regimes we have found. As a result we have regressed the binary variable of the regimes against several economic variables, such as the short-term rate's monthly changes or the German inflation, in order to explain the regime switching effects, rendering thus logic in the transition mechanism. Table 5-11 presents the results of the Logit regression.

Table 5-11 Regime switching justification

Transition variable	t-statistic	p-value
$\Delta_m r_{Ger}^{3m}$	-1.253	(0.210)
$\Delta_m r_{Fr}^{3m}$	-1.241	(0.214)
$\Delta_m (r_{Ger}^{10y}, r_{Ger}^{3m})$	0.289	(0.772)
$\Delta_m (r_{Fr}^{10y}, r_{Fr}^{3m})$	0.259	(0.795)
$\Delta_m inf_{Ger}$	-0.271	(0.786)
$\Delta_m inf_{Fr}$	-2.324	(0.020)
$\Delta_m (inf_{Ger}, inf_{Fr})$	-1.019	(0.308)
$\Delta_m IndProd_{Ger}$	-0.849	(0.395)
$\Delta_m IndProd_{Fr}$	-0.612	(0.539)
$\Delta_m (IndProd_{Ger}, IndProd_{Fr})$	0.426	(0.669)

Source: Authors' estimation

Note: Δ_m monthly change, $r_{country}^{maturity}$ interest rate, $inf_{country}$ inflation, $IndProd_{country}$ industrial production index

As reported in Table 5-11, among the variables we have examined, the monthly changes of the French inflation are indicated to have significant explanatory power with regard to the transition mechanism between the two regimes. As the regression's dependent variable was the Regime 1, the results indicate that a significant increase of the French inflation leads to transition from Regime 1 (German leadership) to Regime 2 (French leadership). Consequently, we interpret this finding as resulting from the formulation of expectations for interest rates rises because of the movements of French inflation, subsequently resulting in more close monitoring of the French yield curve from participants on the bond markets. Additionally, this effect offers a well-supported explanation on the dominant features of the French bond in Regime 2, as they are indicated to stem from specific economic developments. As the basic point of reference of the present chapter, we add that the explanation of the transitional mechanism by the French inflation's monthly changes, combined with the causality patterns we have reported, indicate that the benchmark status in the European bond markets is held by the German Bund, although, in line with reported research, the French bonds play an equally important role, intensified under proper economic conjunction. These findings are in line with economic reasoning and indicate investors' rationality. Additionally, they offer a bridge between two different strands of the empirical literature dealing with the issue of benchmark status in the European bond markets.

Conclusion

All in all, we argue that the issue of the benchmark status in the European bond markets is subject to economic and market conditions, underlying market participants' rationality. Having described the strongly integrated framework in which the European government bonds are priced, we have established an efficient reflection of the leadership in the financial markets under investigation. The regime switching framework we have used supports the evidence of the long run structure, indicating strong interactions while reversing ambiguous linear structure results on the adjustment mechanisms' significance. Additionally, it provides the appropriate investigation platform in order to capture the shifts of the benchmark status between the German and the French bonds.

This effect is indicated to be an important characteristic of the European bond markets' interactions, which are characterised by a strongly integrated framework. French inflation's monthly changes are indicated to explain the transition between the German-dominated and the French-dominated regime. As a result, this chapter offers compliance with existing literature, which until now reported divergent views on the benchmark status. The overall outcome indicates that a diarchy should be stated as the prevailing state, with the German Bund holding the leadership while the French bond is the main source of causality in the market's directions under specific economic conditions.

References

Baele, D., A. Ferrando, P. Hordahl, E. Krylova and C. Monnet. 2004. *Measuring Financial Integration In the Euro Area.* ECB Occasional Paper Series no 14. European Central Bank, Frankfurt am Main.

Baum, C. and J. Barkoulas. 2006. Dynamics of Intra-EMS Interest Rate Linkages. *Journal of Money, Credit and Banking* 38(2): 469-82.

Bordo, M., B. Eichengreen and J. Kim. 1998. *Was There an Early Period of Financial Integration Comparable to Today?* NBER Working Paper

Series no. 6738. National Bureau of Economic Research, Cambridge, MA.

Centeno, M. and A.S. Mello. 1999. How Integrated are the Money Market and the Bank Loans Market within the European Union? *Journal of International Money and Finance* 18(1): 75-106.

Codogno, L., C. Favero and A. Missale. 2003 Yield Spreads on EMU Government Bonds. *Economic Policy* 18(37): 503-32.

Dickey, D.A. and W.A. Fuller. 1979. Distribution of the estimates for autoregressive time series with a unit root. *Journal of the American Statistical Association* 74(366): 427-31.

Dunne, P., M. Moore and R. Portes. 2002. *Defining Benchmark Status: An Application Using Euro-Area Bonds.* NBER Working Paper Series no. 9087. National Bureau of Economic Research, Cambridge, MA.

Engle, R.F. and C.W. Granger. 1987. Co-Integration and Error Correction: Representation, Estimation And Testing. *Econometrica* 55(2): 251-76.

Engle, R.F., D. Hendry and J.F. Richard. 1983. Exogeneity. *Econometrica* 51(2): 277-304.

Gregory, A.W. and B.E. Hansen. 1996. Residual-based tests for cointegration in models with regime shifts. *Journal of Econometrics* 70(1): 99-126.

Hagen, von J. and M. Fratianni. 1990. German dominance in the EMS: evidence from interest rates. *Journal of International Money and Finance* 9(4): 358-75.

Hamilton, J.D. 1989. A New Approach to the Economic Analysis of Nonstationary Time Series and the Business Cycle. *Econometrica* 57(2): 357-84.

Haug, A., J. MacKinnon and L. Michelis. 2000. European Monetary Union: A Cointegration Analysis. *Journal of International Money and Finance* 19(3): 419-32.

Johansen, S. 1988. Statistical Analysis of Cointegrating Vectors. *Journal of Economic Dynamics and Control* 12(2-3): 231-54.

—. 1992. Weak Exogeneity and cointegration in U.K. money. *Journal of Policy Modeling* 14(3): 313-34.

Johansen, S. and K. Juselius. 1992. Testing Structural Hypothesis in a Multivariate Cointegration Analysis of the PPP and UIP for UK. *Journal of Econometrics* 53(1-3): 211-44.

Johansen S. and Juselius K. 1994. Identification of the Long-Run and the Short-Run Structure. An Application to the ISLM Model. *Journal of Econometrics* 63(1): 7-36.

Kiehlborn, T. and M. Mietzner. 2005. *EU Financial Integration: Is There a 'Core Europe'? Evidence from a Cluster Based Approach.* Working

Paper no. 130. Series in Accounting and Finance. Johann Wolfgang Goethe-Universität, Frankfurt am Main.

Kim, S.J., B. Lucey and E. Wu. 2006. Dynamics of Bond Market Integration Between Established and Accession EU Countries. *Journal of International Financial Markets, Institutions and Money* 16(1): 41-56.

Krolzig, H.M. 1996. *Statistical Analysis of Cointegrated VAR Process with Markovian Regime Shifts*. SFB 373 Discussion Paper 25/1996. Humboldt Universität, Berlin.

—. 1997. *Markov Switching Vector Autoregressions. Modelling Statistical Inference and Application to Business Cycle Analysis.* Springer Verlag.

Kwiatkowski, D., P. C. B. Phillips, P. Schmidt and Y. Shin. 1992. Testing the Null Hypothesis of Stationarity against the Alternative of a Unit Root: How Sure Are We That Economic Time Series Have a Unit Root? *Journal of Econometrics* 54(1-3): 159-78.

Lothian, J. 2000. Capital Market Integration and Exchange-Rate Regimes in Historical Perspective. *Research in Banking and Finance* 1.

—. 2001. Financial Integration over the Past Three Centuries. *Bancaria* 9.

Lutkepohl, H., P. Saikkonen and C. Trenkler. 2004. Testing for the Cointegrating Rank of a VAR Process with Level Shift at Unknown Time. *Econometrica* 72(2): 647-62.

Osterwald-Lennum, M. 1992. A Note with Fractiles of the Asymptotic Distribution of the Maximum Likelihood Cointegration Rank Test Statistics: Four Cases. *Oxford Bulletin of Economics and Statistics* 54(4): 461-72.

Pagano, M. and L. von Thadden. 2004. The European Bond Markets Under EMU. *Oxford Review of Economic Policy* 20(4): 531-54.

Trenkler, C. 2005. The Effects of Ignoring Level Shifts on Systems Cointegration Tests. *Allgemeines Statistisches Archiv* 89(3): 281-301.

Yang, J. 2006. International Bond Markets Linkages: A Structural VAR Analysis. *Journal of International Financial Markets, Institutions and Money* 15(1): 39-54.

Weber, E. 2006. *British Interest Rate Convergence Between the US and Europe: A Recursive Cointegration Analysis.* SFB Discussion Paper Series no 649. Humboldt Universität, Berlin.

CHAPTER SIX

YIELD CURVE REACTION TO MACROECONOMIC NEWS IN EUROPE: DISENTANGLING THE US INFLUENCE

MARIE BRIÈRE AND FLORIAN IELPO

On the financial markets it is of primary importance to understand what makes interest rates vary during a trading day. Insofar as interest rates are very heavily dependent on economic fundamentals, it is particularly important to analyse how the arrival of new information about these fundamentals is incorporated into prices. One way to detect which data are considered the most important for the markets is to measure the short term impact of announcements through their surprise effect.

The impact of news about the economy and monetary policy has already been closely studied in the United States (Ederington and Lee, 1993; Fleming and Remolona, 1997; Balduzzi et al., 2001; Piazzesi, 2005 to name a few). In Europe however, given the ECB's relative youth and the shallow historic depth of the European data available to date, these studies remain few and relatively recent (Ehrmann and Fratzscher, 2002; Goldberg and Leonard, 2003; Andersson et al., 2006). These papers highlight the fact that the European market's peculiar feature is that it is subject to complex influences: it is impacted not only by European but also American news, by national economic figures and by aggregated statistics of the European Central Bank (ECB).

As a result, one key difficulty in Europe arises from the fact that it is absolutely crucial to bear in mind the influence of US interest rates on European ones. According to Ehrmann and Fratzscher (2002), Goldberg and Leonard (2003), this influence can be due to several factors: (i) the integration of financial markets and contagion effects; (ii) the real macroeconomic integration of the two zones; (iii) the common perception among markets that the US is the engine of world growth; and (iv) the status of "leading indicators" enjoyed by US figures compared with their European equivalents.

The methodology used by the above authors to capture the American influence is to include both European and American economic announcements in the regression used to explain European interest rates. Although this methodology is a relatively simple way to take account of American influence, it has the drawback of ignoring part of the information. Notably, the US yield curve changes even in the absence of any economic announcements in the US[1], and these changes in the American curve certainly exert an influence on European rates. This partial omission of information is harmful and, as we will see below, can create biases when estimating the impact of economic announcements in Europe. This suggests that it would be a useful improvement to show the influence of the entire American yield curve on European rates, and not merely of announcements in the US alone.

Bernanke and Boivin (2003) demonstrated that in a "data-rich" economic environment, it is optimal to take account of a maximum of available information, rather than concentrate on a small number of variables, even those chosen to be the most relevant. They propose to use the Stock and Watson (2002) method of dimension reduction schemes, akin to traditional Principal Component Analysis, as a way to extract key information from large databases.

We adopt a similar approach in this chapter, but we apply it to a different type of problem. The influence of American interest rates on the European curve passes through multiple channels and cannot be modelled on a simple basis. For instance, European 10-year yields are not influenced only by their US counterparts but by the entire American yield curve, starting with short rates and monetary policy (Diebold et al., 2006; Driessen et al., 2003). One prerequisite is therefore to manage to synthesise all the information coming from day-to-day changes in the entire American yield curve, using a restricted number of factors[2] that can subsequently be incorporated into our regression on each maturity of European interest rates.

This chapter contributes to the existing literature in several ways. First, it proposes an original methodology that makes it possible to separate, within day-to-day changes in European rates, the impact due to European economic announcements from the influence of the American yield curve. This allows us to measure the impact of announcements more rigorously by limiting the bias caused by the omission of variables. A second contribution is to measure the impact of announcements on the entire swap curve. Whereas many studies focus on a single maturity to demonstrate the impact of news, it is particularly worthwhile to understand how the shape of the entire curve changes and which maturities are most sensitive to the arrival of one piece of information or another. As demonstrated by Fleming and Remolona (1999) and Guégan and Ielpo (2007) for American rates, announcements do not necessarily have the same impact on short rates as on long rates. To our knowledge, no study to date has focused this analysis on Europe.

We examine the impact of 18 macroeconomic and monetary policy announcements on the European swap curve (maturities ranging from 3 months to 30 years) between January 2000 and July 2007, integrating the influence of American swap rates through the three first factors extracted from a Principal Component Analysis (PCA). Our empirical results highlight the importance of taking the American yield curve into account in measuring the impact of announcements in Europe. For some of the major announcements, the results in fact differ appreciably, depending on whether this influence is integrated or not.

Our findings show that only a handful of the 18 announcements have an impact on the entire yield curve, namely activity and sentiment indicators, chiefly in Germany, and European M3 money supply. ECB policy rate announcements affect only the very short segment of the curve. Unsurprisingly, we find little influence from the job figures, a result already documented in the existing literature. For price indicators, we demonstrate that the inflation figures have a relatively weak surprise effect on European interest rates, whereas the M3 money supply has a substantial impact. The latter result fits in with the crucial role of this indicator for the ECB. Our results contrast however with those previously obtained, and most of the differences appear to be due to our more exhaustive integration of the American influence.

For each announcement, we then highlight the shape of the reaction of the entire yield curve. We see very clearly that for most economic announcements, intermediate maturities concentrate the most striking reactions. The short end of the curve (less than one year) or the very long end (more than 15 years) generally shows a much weaker reaction, causing a hump shape in the curve. This clearly reveals investors' expectations of the monetary authorities' reaction to economic news. Finally we provide a hierarchy of the economic figures that have the strongest impact on the 16 maturities, showing that the determining factors are different for the short and long end of the curve.

This chapter is organised as follows. First, we describe the data and methodology used. Next, we present the empirical results obtained. Lastly, some concluding remarks are drawn.

Data and Methodology

This section presents our methodology and the associated dataset. We first discuss our motivations, before presenting the methodology used to capture the euro bond market reaction to macroeconomic news. Finally, we detail the dataset used in the study.

Announcements and Surprises in a Data-Rich Environment

Several US macroeconomic announcements are known to impact the euro yield curve (Ehrmann and Fratzscher, 2002). Moreover, euro rates display a very high correlation with US rates. Therefore, neglecting the US component when analysing variations in euro rates will naturally lead to problems of omitted variables.[3] The difficulty in treating US information comes from its nature: at present there is an abundance of news on the US market, not all of it quantitative.

Empirical studies such as Balduzzi et al. (2001) and Guégan and Ielpo (2007) present evidence that the number of economic news items that actually impact on the US yield curve can be substantial. Moreover, important US news is not limited to economic figures, but also extends to many other types of intelligence, some of which cannot be reduced to figures, such as central bankers' speeches (Brière, 2006). Thus, the real number of US economic news items to be considered when disentangling US influence from euro rates can be too large to be taken properly into account. To a great extent, US rates can be understood as a summary of the news that is important to the market. Nonetheless, the US yield curve is made up of a large number of maturities: choosing those that best account for US yield curve movements can be tricky. Thus, we are confronted with a "data-rich" environment: the number of possible explanatory variables can be larger than the number of observations itself, given the length of the euro rate dataset.

Situations of this kind can be treated with factor-based methods, such as Principal Component Analysis (PCA), as presented in Stock and Watson (2002). For example, when trying to find the factors that actually explain the variations of the Federal Reserve's target rate, Bernanke and Boivin (2003) proposed using a few factors obtained from a PCA to summarize the huge amount of economic information with which monetary policy makers are confronted. Here, we argue that methods of this kind are particularly suited to our problem. PCA has been applied to interest rates in many papers following the seminal work of Litterman and

Scheinkman (1991), which first underlined the existence of three main factors driving most yield curve movements.[4]

Thus, we propose to take into account the US component in euro rate movements using the first three factors of a PCA analysis of the corresponding US rates and introducing them as explanatory variables of euro rates into the usual linear model used to measure the surprise impact. This way, we are likely to capture most of the US influence on the European yield curve, without using an excessive number of explanatory variables that could quickly undermine the robustness of the estimations.

General Methodology

We propose to estimate a version of the Balduzzi et al. (2001) model, refined and augmented with the US yield curve factors obtained with a PCA performed over a daily yield curve dataset.

Suppose we observe J types of macroeconomic announcements (on a monthly or quarterly basis). For each announcement $j = 1,\dots,J$, there is a consensus forecast given by the median of an economist's survey (further details are given below in the next section). Let $F_{i,t}$ be this forecast at time t for the announcement j and $G_{j,t}$ be the realized announcement. We define the surprise j at time t as:

$$S_{j,t} = \frac{G_{j,t} - F_{j,t}}{\sigma_j}, \tag{6.1}$$

where σ_j is defined as the standard error of the economic surprises calculated on the whole sample.[5] This scaling procedure enables us to compare the results between surprises (Balduzzi et al., 2001; Andersson et al., 2006).

Surprises are used as explanatory factors of the daily variation of rates for a given maturity. Let $R^{EU}_{t,\tau}$ be the daily closing swap rate of maturity τ on date t. Then, the linear model presented in Balduzzi et al. (2001) can be stated as follows:

$$R^{EU}_{t,\tau} - R^{EU}_{t-1,\tau} = \alpha + \sum_{j=1}^{J} \beta_{j,\tau} 1_{j,t} S_{j,t} + \varepsilon_{t,\tau}, \tag{6.2}$$

where $1_{j,t} = 1$ if the surprise j is released on date t and 0 if not. For a given τ, $\varepsilon_{t,\tau}$ is a Gaussian white noise.

We can improve this standard model by adding dummy variables to capture daily effects. After running different tests, we elected to use a single "Friday effect", which is highly significant (see Table 6-5). The second modification made to the canonical model of Balduzzi et al. (2001) consisted in taking into account the very high autocorrelation identified in the time series of daily variations in swap rates. This was done by adding their lagged increment to the standard linear model, which thus becomes:

$$R_{t,\tau}^{EU} - R_{t-1,\tau}^{EU} = \alpha + \sum_{j=1}^{J} \beta_{j,\tau} 1_{j,t} S_{j,t} + \gamma_{j,\tau} 1_{friday,t} + \rho_{j,\tau}(R_{t-1,\tau}^{EU} - R_{t-2,\tau}^{EU}) + \varepsilon_{t,\tau}, \quad (6.3)$$

with $1_{friday,t} = 1$ if t is a Friday and 0 otherwise.

Finally, we propose to add to this model the factors $f_{i,t}$, $i = 1,2,3$, obtained from the PCA performed on US rates. Let ΔR^{US} be the matrix of the daily variations in interest rates for each of the US maturities available, i.e.:

$$\Delta R^{US} = \left\lfloor R_{t,\tau}^{US} - R_{t-1,\tau}^{US} \right\rfloor. \qquad \forall t,\tau$$

Let C be the correlation matrix associated with the series in ΔR^{US}. Given that C meets the standard conditions for the Spectral Theorem to apply, it can be decomposed as:

$$C = D\Lambda D$$

where $\Lambda = diag(\lambda_1,...,\lambda_p)$ the ordered eigenvalues matrix, when C has rank p, and D is the matrix whose columns contain the associated eigenvectors. We recall that the PCA factors are composed as:

$$f_i = \Delta R^{US} D_i$$

where D_i is the ith column of the matrix D . $f_i = (f_{i,1}\ f_{i,2}\ ...\ f_{i,n})'$, for a sample of size n, where $f_{i,t}$ is the value at time t for the ith factor. For further details on PCA, see Tsay (2002).

With these settings in mind, the model specified in equation (6.3) can be augmented the following way:

$$R_{t,\tau}^{EU} - R_{t-1,\tau}^{EU} = \alpha + \sum_{j=1}^{J} \beta_{j,\tau} 1_{j,t} S_{j,t} + \gamma_{j,\tau} 1_{friday,t} + \rho_{j,\tau}(R_{t-1,\tau}^{EU} - R_{t-2,\tau}^{EU}) + \sum_{i=1}^{3} \delta_i f_{i,t} + \varepsilon_{t,\tau}. \quad (6.4)$$

Thus the three factors f_i summarise the information in the US yield curve and are the same for all the maturities in the European curve. As we will now show, these three factors, i.e. the level, slope and curvature of the American curve, have a major impact on almost all the maturities in the European curve.

As the interest rate datasets usually display a form of autoregressive variance (Ehrmann and Fratzscher, 2002), we thus allow $\varepsilon_{t,\tau}$ to follow a GARCH(1,1) process, making it possible to account for heteroscedasticity in our dataset. Our model can be consistently estimated by Generalized Least Squares, thus taking into consideration non-spherical innovations. According to the Zellner theorem, whose assumptions are satisfied here, this is equivalent to estimating these equations either simultaneously or maturity by maturity. We have opted for the second approach because it is numerically easier to implement.

Data

The US rate dataset contains daily swap rates with maturities ranging from 1 to 30 years used to compute the PCA factors. Our sample period covers the period 2 January 2000 – 30 July 2007, including each business day. Table 6-1 presents descriptive statistics of the daily changes in US swap rates, for selected maturities.

Table 6-1 Summary statistics for daily variations of US swap rates

	Min	Max	Mean	Std. Dev.
1 year	-0.480	0.360	-6.44E-05	3.94E-02
2 years	-0.395	0.286	-2.16E-04	4.90E-02
3 years	-0.318	0.303	-2.13E-04	5.22E-02
4 years	-0.280	0.306	-1.95E-04	5.25E-02
5 years	-0.275	0.311	-1.77E-04	5.36E-02
6 years	-0.252	0.293	-1.64E-04	5.28E-02
7 years	-0.251	0.291	-1.49E-04	5.21E-02
8 years	-0.248	0.290	-1.39E-04	5.12E-02
9 years	-0.253	0.277	-1.29E-04	5.14E-02
10 years	-0.259	0.282	-1.20E-04	5.09E-02
15 years	-0.251	0.270	-1.26E-04	4.92E-02
20 years	-0.252	0.277	-1.34E-04	4.70E-02
30 years	-0.248	0.297	-1.35E-04	4.48E-02

Source: Authors' calculations

The euro swap rate dataset is constructed in the same way, including daily swap rates for the same maturities. To these rates, we add cash Euribor rates for maturities of 3 months, 6 months and 9 months to take into account the very short end of the yield curve. Table 6-2 presents summary statistics for selected maturities of the daily changes in euro rates.

Table 6-2 Summary statistics for daily variations of euro swap rates

	Min	Max	Mean	Std. Dev.
3 months	-0.358	0.159	4.36E-04	1.48E-02
6 months	-0.266	0.177	3.77E-04	1.69E-02
9 months	-0.211	0.187	3.17E-04	2.11E-02
1 year	-0.123	0.142	2.14E-04	2.44E-02
2 years	-0.145	0.196	8.55E-06	3.36E-02
3 years	-0.154	0.360	-1.16E-04	3.63E-02
4 years	-0.215	0.207	-2.10E-04	3.69E-02
5 years	-0.216	0.210	-2.65E-04	3.68E-02
6 years	-0.205	0.207	-3.14E-04	3.60E-02
7 years	-0.144	0.202	-3.48E-04	3.42E-02
8 years	-0.147	0.200	-3.79E-04	3.36E-02
9 years	-0.155	0.202	-4.00E-04	3.32E-02
10 years	-0.150	0.197	-4.14E-04	3.28E-02
15 years	-0.157	0.184	-4.66E-04	3.25E-02
20 years	-0.164	0.178	-4.77E-04	3.19E-02
30 years	-0.163	0.189	-4.89E-04	3.14E-02

Source: Authors' calculations

It should be noted that in the US and Europe, the change in long rates is negative on average during the period under review because, on the whole, they have declined. For short rates with maturities under three years, the results differ between the two zones: they have declined on average in the US but not in Europe. The reason for this is monetary policy differences, with the Fed cutting its interest rates much more sharply than the ECB during the period 2000-2004.

Table 6-3 presents the list of macroeconomic releases used as explanatory variables in the linear model specified by equation (6.4). These figures are obtained from the Bloomberg calendar presented in detail in Guégan and Ielpo (2007). This calendar presents the economic figures that are known to be monitored by financial market participants. It includes the release dates of the news, along with the Bloomberg consensus forecast and the economic figure finally released. Table 6-4 provides descriptive statistics on surprises. As discussed in Guégan and Ielpo (2007), we use the *actual release* figure, as opposed to the *revised* figure: most economic news is first announced on a crude basis by the statistics agencies, then refined during the following announcements. This data vintage problem is particularly important when estimating reaction functions as presented in equation (6.4): market participants are known to react to the first release.

Table 6-3 List of announcements investigated

Activity and employment	**Prices**	**Sentiment and surveys**	**Monetary policy**
Unemployment EC	Money Supply M3 EC	IFO Business Expectations GE	Target Rate EC
Unemployment GE	CPI EC	ZEW Expectations GE	
GDP EC	CPI Flash EC	Consumer confidence EC	
GDP GE	CPI GE	INSEE Confidence FR	
Retail Sales EC	PPI GE		
Retail Sales GE			
Industrial production GE			
Manufacturing orders GE			

Note: EC for euro area, GE for German and FR for French announcements

Table 6-4 Descriptive statistics on announcement surprises

	Min	**Max**	**Mean**	**Median**	**St. Dev.**
Activity and employment					
Unemployment EC	-0.2	0.4	-0.04	-0.1	0.13
Unemployment GE	-102.5	89	-4.47	-3	32.91
GDP EC	-0.2	0.1	-0.03	-0.1	0.13
GDP GE	-0.3	0.5	-0.04	-0.1	0.20
Retail sales EC	-1.7	3.1	-0.08	-0.2	0.72
Retail sales GE	-3.9	4.6	-0.42	-0.4	1.68
Industrial production GE	-3.2	2.5	-0.24	-0.2	1.40
Manufacturing orders GE	-4.8	6.7	0.22	0.3	2.44

Table 6-4 (cont.)

Prices					
M3 EC	-0.7	1.1	0.17	0.2	0.41
CPI EC	-0.3	0.2	0.00	0	0.13
CPI flash EC	-0.2	0.3	0.01	0.1	0.13
CPI GE	-0.9	0.4	0.00	0.1	0.24
PPI GE	-0.6	0.8	0.07	0.1	0.29
Sentiment and surveys					
IFO Business expectations GE	-2	3.8	0.31	0.3	1.32
ZEW Expectations GE	-21.6	20.6	-1.18	-1.15	8.42
Consumer confidence EC	-2	4	0.33	1	1.64
INSEE Confidence FR	-8	7	-0.42	-1	2.93
Monetary policy					
Target rate EC	-0.5	0.25	-0.05	0.25	0.35

Source: Authors' calculations

Results

European Figures impacting fixed-income markets

For each of the 16 interest-rate maturities, we carried out the regressions presented in the previous section. Table 6-5 recapitulates the impact of our 18 economic announcements on three key maturities in the yield curve: 2, 5 and 10 rates, with and without introducing the three American factors to the regressions.

Table 6-5 Influence of the announcements on 2, 5 and 10 year euro swap rates

	2 year rate		5 year rate		10 year rate		Number of maturities impacted	
Variable	**Without US**	**With US**	**Without US**	**With US**	**Without US**	**With US**	**Without US**	**With US**
Activity and employment								
Unemployment EC	0.0057 (0.11)	0.004 (0.11)	0.0063 (0.12)	0.0046 (0.10)	0.0047 (0.19)	0.0033 (0.17)	0/16	0/16
Unemployment GE	-0.003 (0.39)	-0.0022 (0.36)	-5.00E-04 (0.90)	-1.00E-04 (0.97)	-0.0013 (0.70)	-0.0012 (0.62)	0/16	0/16
GDP EC	0.0025 (0.70)	-0.001 (0.82)	-9.00E-04 (0.90)	-0.0012 (0.81)	-0.0023 (0.72)	-5.00E-04 (0.91)	0/16	0/16
GDP GE	0.0028 (0.65)	0.0032 (0.45)	0.0048 (0.47)	0.0049 (0.30)	0.0033 (0.58)	0.0031 (0.45)	0/16	0/16
Retail Sales EC	-0.0023 (0.53)	0.0021 (0.42)	-0.0039 (0.34)	4.00E-04 (0.89)	-0.0018 (0.62)	0.0019 (0.45)	0/16	0/16
Retail Sales GE	0.0085** (0.02)	0.0057** (0.02)	0.0099*** (0.01)	0.0061** (0.02)	0.0105*** (0.00)	0.0068*** (0.00)	15/16	15/16
Industrial Production GE	-0.001 (0.78)	-4.00E-04 (0.87)	-2.00E-04 (0.96)	-7.00E-04 (0.8)	-5.00E-04 (0.88)	-0.0015 (0.51)	0/16	0/16
Manufacturing Orders GE	0.0021 (0.55)	8.00E-04 (0.74)	0.0055 (0.15)	0.0039 (0.15)	0.0071** (0.04)	0.0057*** (0.01)	4/16	7/16
Prices								
M3 EC	-0.0018 (0.64)	0.0081*** (0.00)	-0.0042 (0.33)	0.0055* (0.07)	-0.0025 (0.52)	0.0053* (0.05)	0/16	9/16

Table 6-5 (cont.)

CPI EC	0.0055 (0.15)	0.0037 (0.15)	0.0074** (0.07)	0.0044 (0.13)	0.0068** (0.07)	0.0036 (0.15)	3/16	0/16
CPI flash EC	0.0032 (0.46)	0.0027 (0.37)	0.0033 (0.49)	0.003 (0.36)	0.0027 (0.53)	0.0025 (0.39)	0/16	0/16
CPI GE	0.0066 (0.13)	0.0037 (0.22)	0.0065 (0.18)	0.0028 (0.41)	0.006 (0.16)	0.0023 (0.44)	0/16	0/16
PPI GE	-0.001 (0.78)	-2.00E-04 (0.93)	0.0022 (0.56)	0.0026 (0.34)	0.0018 (0.60)	0.002 (0.40)	0/16	0/16
Sentiment and surveys								
IFO Business expectations	0.0146*** (0.00)	0.0135*** (0.00)	0.018*** (0.00)	0.0165*** (0.00)	0.0158*** (0.00)	0.0143*** (0.00)	14/16	14/16
ZEW Expectations	0.0134*** (0.00)	0.0081*** (0.00)	0.0142*** (0.00)	0.0081*** (0.01)	0.0121*** (0.00)	0.0063*** (0.02)	13/16	12/16
Consumer confidence EC	-0.0016 (0.72)	-0.005 (0.11)	0.0012 (0.81)	-0.004 (0.24)	0.001 (0.82)	-0.0044 (0.14)	0/16	2/16
INSEE Confidence FR	0.0029 (0.42)	0.0024 (0.34)	0.005 (0.21)	0.0035 (0.21)	0.0083** (0.02)	0.0062** (0.01)	4/16	5/16
Monetary policy								
Target rate EC	0.0034 (0.37)	0.0016 (0.54)	0.0043 (0.31)	0.0018 (0.53)	0.0017 (0.65)	-0.0007 (0.79)	0/16	0/16
Week effects								
Friday	-0.0042** (0.02)	-0.1346*** (0.00)	-0.0036* (0.07)	-0.1533*** (0.00)	-0.0032* (0.08)	-0.1394*** (0.00)	2/16	16/16

Table 6-5 (cont.)

US yield curve factors								
Factor 1	---	-0.005 (0.48)	---	-0.0036*** (0.00)	---	-0.0512*** (0.00)	---	11/16
Factor 2	---	0.086*** (0.00)	---	0.0268* (0.06)	---	-0.0254** (0.05)	---	11/16
Factor 3	---	-0.166*** (0.00)	---	-0.035 (0.19)	---	-0.0473** (0.04)	---	11/16
Diagnostic tests								
R^2	0.03	0.55	0.03	0.54	0.03	0.55	--	--
Box Pierce Test	0.93	0.69	0.95	0.55	0.98	0.39	--	--

Source: Authors' estimation

Note: ***,**,* significant up to respective thresholds of 1%, 5% and 10%, (p-values) in brackets. "Number of maturities impacted" is the number of significant coefficient at the 5% level over the 16 regressions.

Our first observation is that the introduction of the three first PCA factors extracted from the American yield curve in the regression changes the impact of European announcements, a sign that the omission of these variables generates a true bias. It also reduces the standard error of our coefficients.[6] The impact of European CPI diminishes when we introduce the American factors: it becomes non significant for most of the maturities. For the M3 money supply figure, the difference is even more striking, since for nine of the yield maturities, the coefficient goes from being non significant (and negative) without counting the American influence to significant when this influence is factored in. The same applies to the European consumer confidence reading, which becomes significant for three maturities, whereas beforehand it was not. We note that the amplitude of the impact is twice as great for the ZEW when the American influence is factored in.

In all, six announcements significantly impact the entire European yield curve[7] (5 percent threshold): two activity figures (German manufacturing orders and retail sales), a price indicator (the M3 money supply) and three "sentiment" indicators (IFO and ZEW in Germany, and INSEE's measure of consumer confidence in France).

If we compare our results with those of the existing literature (Ehrmann and Fratzscher, 2002; Goldberg and Leonard, 2003; Andersson et al., 2006) we once again find a strong influence from "economic sentiment" figures (ZEW and IFO most of all), plus a very restricted number of activity indicators.[8] In our study, however, we note a much more significant influence of German retail sales. This may be due to the fact that the period we are studying is slightly more recent, when the weakness of German domestic demand was a genuine market worry. We also find little influence of the job indicators, as noted by Andersson et al. (2006), mainly due to the markets' prior knowledge of German pre-scheduled releases.

Among the national sentiment figures, the German ones have the greatest impact. The IFO and ZEW indicators have an impact on the entire yield curve whereas French consumer confidence impacts the long end of the curve only. German statistics play a much greater role than the aggregated European data, for two main reasons: first, the German economy's very important role within the European Union in the eyes of the markets; and second, the aggregated European statistics are always published later than national statistics, adding only a small amount of additional information when they come out.

The main difference between our results and existing studies has to do with the price indicators. Previous studies highlighted the markets' weak reaction to announcements of the M3 money supply, though this is one of the ECB's pillars. Our results are different, showing that taking account of the American yield curve influence changes this result. It highlights a real impact of the M3 money supply on rates, a much more important one than that of the inflation indicators themselves. This result is in line with the importance of this indicator for the ECB, stressed in most central bankers' speeches, and the testimony of investors on this subject. The weak influence of euro and national inflation figures, even if the CPI is one of the explicit targets of the ECB, is probably due to the fact that euro inflation is pretty well anticipated by economists and markets (moreover for European figures they know prior releases of German and Italian data).

Table 6-6 presents the figures which have a significant impact on rates for eight maturities (3 and 6 month, 2, 5, 10, 15, 20 and 30 years) in the curve. We note the significant figures above the 10 percent thresholds. Announcements have been classified by the size of their market impact on yields.

It is worth noting that the determining factors are different for the short and long end of the curve. For virtually all maturities from the 5-year rate, the four most important indicators for the markets are the Germany's IFO, ZEW, retail sales and manufacturing orders. Note that France's INSEE consumer confidence figures have virtually a weak impact only on long rates (between 7 and 20 years). A set of different figures appear for short term rates (less than 5 years), namely the money supply and the German retail sales. Target rates have a weakly significant impact only on the very short end of the curve (3-month rate).

Comparison with results obtained in the US in recent years (Fleming and Remolona, 1999; Balduzzi et al., 2001; Piazzesi, 2005; Guégan and Ielpo, 2007) highlight differences and similarities with the American economy. Activity and economic sentiment indicators take on very great importance in both zones, while (for the reason mentioned above) employment indicators, though very important within the US, have no impact in Europe. Another key difference is the fact that, inflation figures have barely any impact in Europe over the period under study, whereas they are of crucial importance in the US. They appear to have been replaced in Europe by the money supply, an indicator which the Federal Reserve does not explicitly monitor.

Table 6-6 Classification of the most important figures for selected maturities of euro rates

Rank	3M	6M	2Y	5Y
1	Target Rate EC*	Retail sales GE***	IFO Business Expect. GE***	IFO Business Expect. GE***
2	Manufacturing Orders GE*	IFO Business Expect. GE*	M3 EC***	ZEW Expect. GE***
3	---	M3 EC**	ZEW Expect. GE***	Retail sales GE**
4	---	---	Retail sales GE**	M3 EC*
5	---	---	---	Unemployment EC*
Rank	**10Y**	**15Y**	**20Y**	**30Y**
1	IFO Business Expect. GE***	IFO Business Expect. GE***	IFO Business Expect. GE***	IFO Business Expect. GE***
2	Retail sales GE***	Retail sales GE**	Retail sales GE***	Retail sales GE**
3	ZEW Expect. GE**	ZEW Expect. GE**	ZEW Expect. GE**	Manufacturing Orders GE**
4	INSEE confidence FR**	Manufacturing Orders GE**	Manufacturing Orders GE**	ZEW Expect. GE*
5	Manufacturing Orders GE**	INSEE Confidence FR*	INSEE Confidence FR*	M3 EC*
6	M3 EC**	M3 EC*	CPI EC*	---
7	---	---	Unemployment EC*	---

Source: Authors' estimation
Note: ***,**,* significant up to respective thresholds of 1%, 5% and 10%.

Distortion of the Yield Curve by Announcements

For each figure which exerts a significant impact on European interest rates the above Figure 6-1 shows the shape taken by the reaction of yield curves. Each graph synthesises the results of our 16 regression analyses by maturity. We represent in grey the impact of European economic figures measured on a "trivial" basis (i.e. without taking account of the American influence), and in black this same impact, taking account of the three factors from the US yield curve. Dotted lines each time indicate the 95 percent confidence interval.

The most striking stylised feature, already noted in the US by Fleming and Remolona (1999), as well as Guégan and Ielpo (2007), is the hump-shaped reaction of rates to most economic announcements. Intermediate maturities concentrate the strongest reactions. This shape is highly revealing of market participants' expectations of the monetary authorities' reactions to economic news. They do not expect the authorities to react at once (accounting for the weak impact on the very short end of the curve), but they think that this reaction to take the form of a gradual cycle of rises or cuts in target rates. Finally, a stronger than anticipated economic announcement leads to a steepening of the short end of the curve, then a flattening on longer-end maturities.

Figure 6-1 Impact of significant announcements on the entire euro swap curve

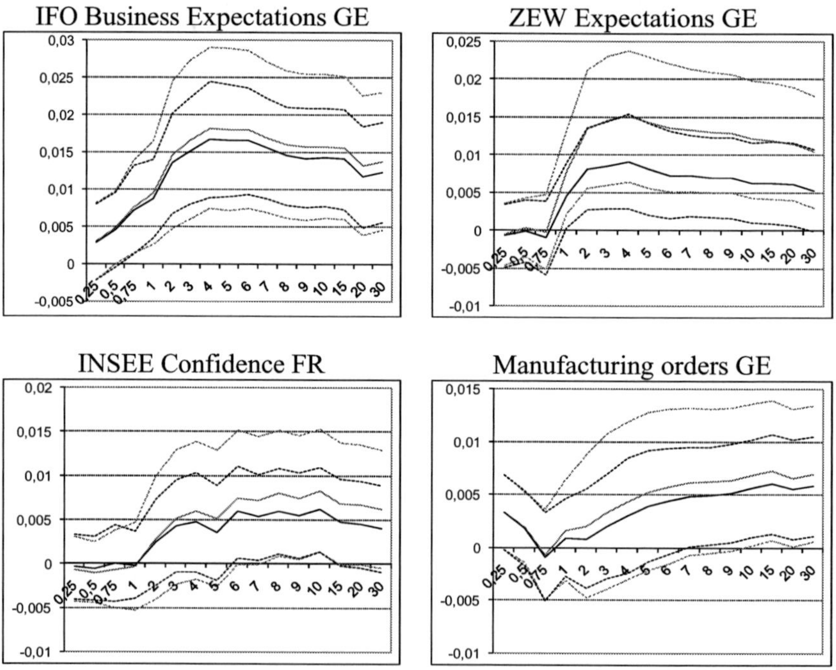

Figure 6-1 (cont.)

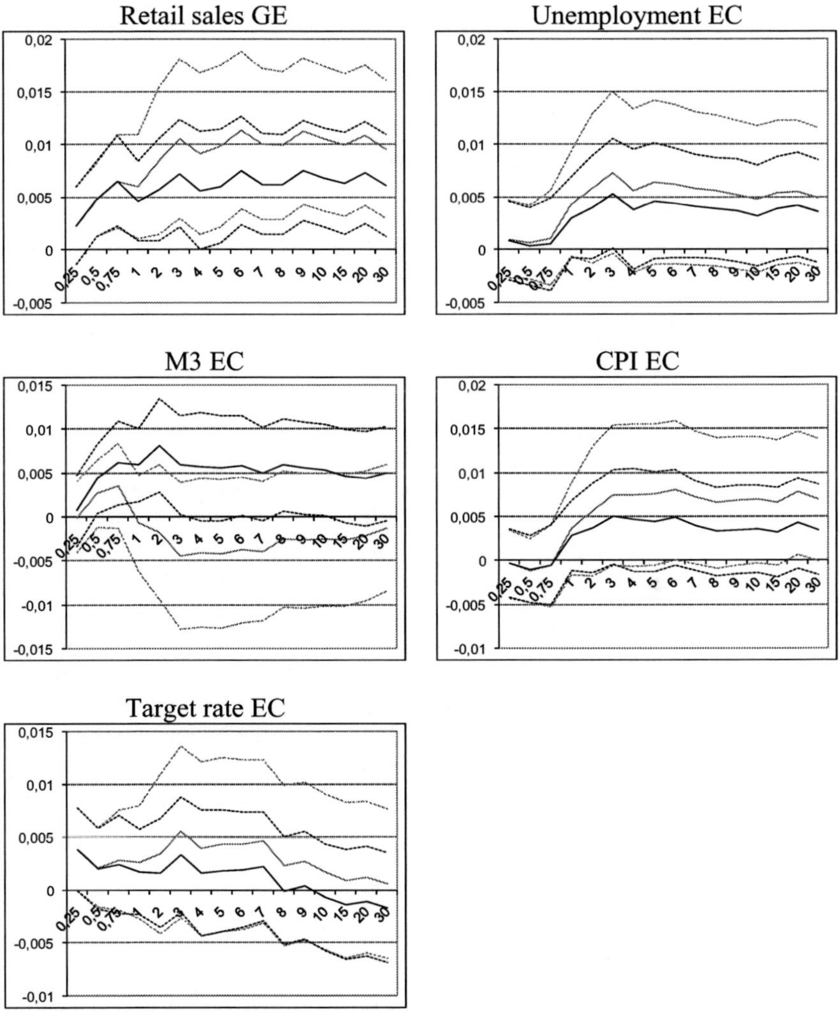

Source: Authors' estimation

Note: Black lines denote that US influence is taken into account; grey lines denote impacts without US influence. Dashed lines represent confidence intervals

Announcements of target rates have the particular feature of influencing yields only in the very short term: their impact extents only to the 3 month rates, and this reaction's shape slopes downwards with rate maturities, becoming insignificant. All in all, a target rate increase will lead to a flatter yield curve.

It is very striking to analyse this impact, which underpins the idea that the long end of the curve's reaction to news about monetary policy depends considerably on the markets' view of how credibly the monetary authorities are fighting inflation. In an environment where the authorities enjoy credibility, a rise in target rates can have no impact on long term rates (currently the case in Europe) provided the markets anticipate that the effects of this decision will be to lower anticipations of long-term inflation. It can even push down long rates, as was noticed in the US. This is the well known "paradox" in monetary policy announcements highlighted by Carlstrom (1995), since he demonstrated that a rise in short rates can lead to a fall in long rates, or at least in long rates which are relatively inert to changes in short rates.

Figure 6-2 shows the regression coefficients for the three factors obtained on the American yield curve using PCA. Figure 6-A1 in Appendix 6-A presents the three standard factors themselves, which account for distortions in the yield curve: parallel shift (Factor 1), steepening (2) and changes in the curvature of the yield curve (3).

Interestingly, the American yield curve factors produce fairly similar effects in the US and in Europe. An increase in the level factor causes yields to fall in both regions. Unlike in the US, however, the impact in Europe is not uniform since long yields are affected more than short yields. It should be noted that the first US factor has virtually no impact on very short-term maturities. The short ends of the US and euro curves remain independent, and this is easily understandable since they mostly react to their own monetary policies. The slope and curvature factors are very similar in both zones: if the US curve steepens or changes in curvature, a similar movement, albeit weaker, occurs in Europe.

Figure 6-2 Impact of the three PCA-based factors across the entire curve

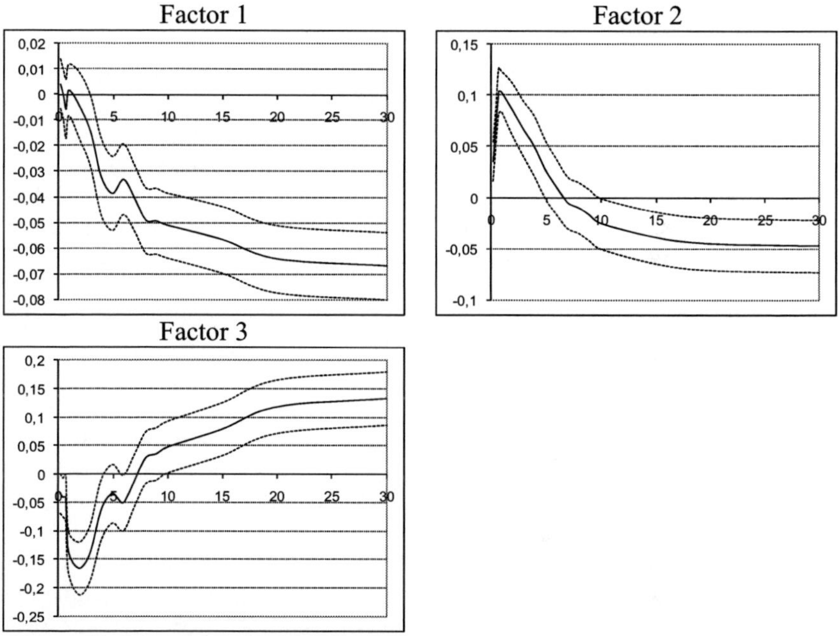

Source: Authors' estimation
Note: Dashed lines represent confidence intervals.

Conclusion

We have examined the impact of 18 macroeconomic and monetary policy announcements on the European swap curve (maturities of between 3 months and 30 years) for the period from January 2000 to July 2007. And we have presented an original methodology allowing the influence of the American swap curve to be integrated using the first three factors arising from a PCA.

This chapter makes it possible to measure the importance the European financial markets have given to news about the ECB since its creation, and to analyse which economic figures they find most important. Compared with the existing literature, which still provides little information about the euro area, our chapter presents the usefulness of focusing on the entire European curve and to examine it over a relatively long period of time, which has not been done to date.

Our empirical results underscore the importance of taking into account the influence of the American yield curve to measure the impact of announcements in Europe. For some statistics, we obtain different results by factoring in this impact. Our methodology has the advantage of taking into account the American influence as exhaustively as possible, unlike previous papers which restricted themselves to integrating the effects of American macroeconomic announcements on European rates.

Only a very few European economic figures influence the yield curve in Europe. We note the very important impact of German economic sentiment and activity figures, which the markets view as more important than the European aggregate statistics. Two results contrast with those obtained in the existing literature: the weak impact of inflation figures and the strong influence of the M3 money supply. As noted in the US, the curve's reaction is hump shaped, with the most significant reactions concentrated in intermediate maturities. This shape is highly revealing of market participants' expectations of the monetary authorities' reactions to economic news. Participants tend to anticipate a reaction by the authorities in the medium term, assuming that a change in the economic environment will lead them to make a gradual cycle of rises or cuts in their target rates, which will not take effect immediately.

One clear limitation of this work is to take an overall view of the period under study. In fact, the influence of economic news on the markets varies by cycle period (Guégan and Ielpo, 2007) or the market's perception of central banks' priorities (Kearney, 2002), as demonstrated by a still small number of studies carried out in the US. The influence of the American factor is doubtless not uniform, as suggested by the results of Ehrmann and Fratzscher (2002). It would therefore be particularly worthwhile to refine our analysis by distinguishing different phases, or to study the changes in impact coefficients year on year, in order to detect any changes in the markets' interest for each piece of news.

References

Andersson, M., L.J. Hansen and S. Sebestyen. 2006. *Which News Moves the Euro Area Bond Market?* ECB Working Paper No 631. European Central Bank, Frankfurt am Main.

Bai, J. and S. Ng. 2002. Determining the Number of Factors in Approximate Factor Models. *Econometrica* 70(1): 191-221.

Balduzzi, P., E.J. Elton and T.C. Green. 2001. Economic News and Bond Prices: Evidence from the US Treasury Market. *Journal of Financial and Quantitative Analysis* 36(4): 523-43.

Bernanke, B.S. and J. Boivin. 2003. Monetary Policy in a Data-Rich Environment. *Journal of Monetary Economics* 50(3): 525-46.

Brière, M. 2006. *Market Reactions to Central Bank Communication Policies: Reading Interest Rate Options Smiles.* Solvay Business School Working Paper, 06-009.

Carlstrom, C.T. 1995. A Monetary Policy Paradox. *Economic Commentary*. Federal Reserve Bank of Cleveland, August.

Diebold, F.X., C. Li and V.Z. Yue. 2006. *Global Yield Curve Dynamics and Interactions: A Generalized Nelson-Siegel Approach.* University of Pennsylvania Working Paper 74. University of Pennsylvania, Philadelphia.

Driessen, J., B. Melenberg and T. Nijman. 2003. Common Factors in International Bond Returns. *Journal of International Money and Finance* 22(5): 629-56.

Ederington, L.H. and J.H. Lee. 1993. How Markets Process Information: News Releases and Volatility. *Journal of Finance* 48(4): 1161-91.

Ehrmann, M. and M. Fratzscher. 2002. *Interdependence between the Euro Area and the US: What Role for EMU?* ECB Working Paper No 200. European Central Bank, Frankfurt am Main.

Fleming, M.J. and E.M. Remolona. 1997. What Moves the Bond Market? *Federal Reserve Bank of New York Economic Policy Review* December: 31-50.

—. 1999. *The Term Structure of Announcement Effects.* BIS Working Paper No 71. Bank for International Settlement, Basel.

Goldberg, L.S. and D. Leonard. 2003. What Moves Sovereign Bond Markets? The Effects of Economic News on US and German Bond Yields. *Current Issues in Economics and Finance* 9(9).

Guégan, D. and F. Ielpo. 2007. *Further Evidence on the Impact of Economic News on Interest Rates.* Centre d'Economie de la Sorbonne Working Paper 2007-03.

Kearney A.A. 2002. The Changing Impact of Employment Announcements on Interest Rates. *Journal of Economics and Business* 54(4): 415-29.

Litterman, R. and J. Scheinkman. 1991. Common Factors Affecting Bond Returns. *Journal of Fixed Income* 1(1): 54-61.

Piazzesi, M. 2005. Bond Yields and the Federal Reserve. *Journal of Political Economy* 113(2): 311-44.

Stock, J.H. and M.W. Watson. 2002. Macroeconomic Forecasting using Diffusion Indexes. *Journal of Business and Economic Statistics* 20(2): 147-62.

Tsay, R.S. 2002. *Analysis of Financial Time Series*. Wiley.

Notes

[1] This may be caused by the fact that many other factors besides the economic data and announcements of base rates are likely to influence US yield curves, starting for instance with the speeches of central bankers, or changes in the prices of other assets.

[2] In order to avoid the "dimensionality curse".

[3] This can strongly compromise the estimation results, as it leads to bias within the Generalized Least Square estimates and a loss of estimation efficiency.

[4] On the consistency of the PCA factors, see Bai and Ng (2002).

[5] By normalising the surprise effect at each date, using the standard deviation of the surprises computed across the entire sample, we implicitly assume the conditional variance of the surprises to be constant (an assumption satisfied empirically on our sample for most economic announcements).

[6] This is easily visible in the Figure 6-1. Indeed, variable omission leads to greater variance of our estimators.

[7] We consider that the announcement affects the entire yield curve if at least five maturities are significantly impacted at 5 percent.

[8] Note that Ehrmann and Fratzscher (2002) studied the impact of announcements on monetary rates (ranging from 1 to 12 months), Goldberg and Leonard (2003) examined the rates of German treasury bonds of between 2 and 10 years, and Andersson et al. (2006) looked at the German 10 year future contract.

Appendix 6-A

Figure 6-A1 Results of PCA Analysis of US yield curve daily variations

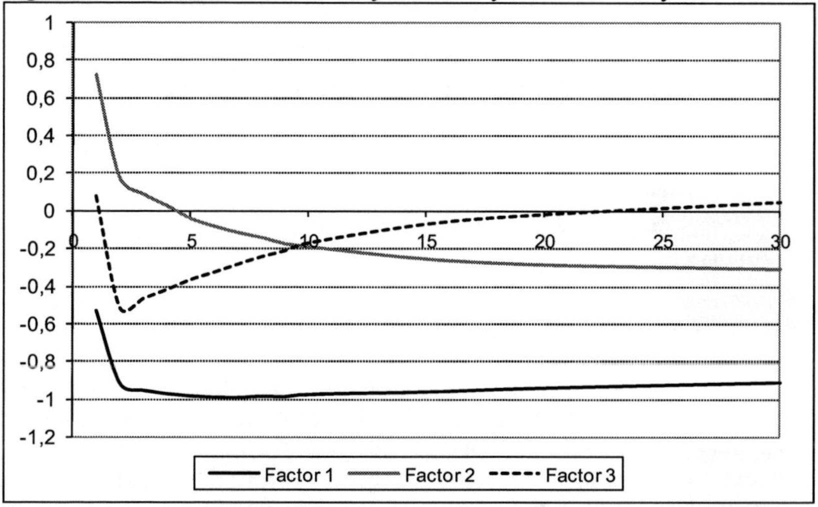

Source: Authors' estimation

CHAPTER SEVEN

STOCK MARKET VOLATILITY IN THE CZECH REPUBLIC, CROATIA AND SELECTED EU MEMBER STATES

LUMÍR KULHÁNEK

In this chapter, first, we take notice of the development of the stock markets in the Czech Republic and Croatia. Subsequently, a comparison of stock market volatility are made with the development of the stock markets in three selected countries of the European Union (France, Germany, United Kingdom), where only France and Germany are part of the euro area. Both main quantitative characteristics of the development of stock market indices are analysed (monthly returns and risk), as well as the correlation of returns and changes in the correlation of returns among particular countries. Finally, based on comparisons of monthly stock markets returns and risks in the Czech Republic, Croatia and selected developed European Union (EU) Member States in examined period from January 1997 to February 2007 we discuss characteristics which are typical for the emerging markets.

Stock Markets Development in Analysed Countries

At present, we are witnesses of the integration process of the national financial markets towards the worldwide, global financial market. Investors tend not to make a distinction between national and foreign financial instruments; banks operate in the worldwide area. For these reasons, the motives for international investing are examined along with advantages and disadvantages regarding the strategy of international investing on the stock markets. With reference to this fact, it is necessary to pay attention to the development of the emerging stock markets. There are a great number of reasons for this research. Among the main ones can be ranked the fact that globalization tendencies lead to the integration of the closed economies into the international capital flows, capital markets have arisen in the transforming economies and the extension of activities of the private investors have taken place.

The increase in demand for cross-border investment stocks within the euro area brings about considerable changes in the market structures, both on exchange-traded markets and in brokerage industry. These changes occur not only in the euro area market structures, but rather on a EU level. In this chapter we will take notice of the development of two European emerging stock markets (Czech and Croatian stock markets) in comparison with development of three European developed stock markets (French, German and British stock markets) in the period from 1997 to 2007.

Description of the Data Used

The analysis of the stock markets development and their international comparison are made by applying monthly national equity indices. For the Czech Republic is used index PX (PX50 until March 2006). Index PX is a price index of blue chip issues traded on the Prague Stock Exchange weighted by the market capitalization. Index base is updated periodically; weight of any individual issuer is limited to 25 percent of index capitalization. For Croatia is used the official Zagreb Stock Exchange share index CROBEX. It is weighted by a free float adjusted market capitalization, where the weight of any individual issuer is limited to 20 percent of the index capitalization. For developed stock markets are used indices CAC 40 for France, DAX for Germany and FTSE 100 for the United Kingdom.

The period from December 1996 to February 2007 is examined, which means that slightly adjusted period January 1997 to February 2007 is used for the monthly returns. For more detailed analysis, this period is also divided into two sub periods – the first one from December 1996/January 1997 to December 2001, and the second one from December 2001/January 2002 to February 2007.

We use stock markets indices in the local currencies since the primary objective was to depict the development of the national stock markets and not the aspects of the international portfolio diversification. Monthly stock market indices are the end-of-period indices for all countries, stock markets returns and risks are own calculations based on these indices in the domestic currency. (Data source: http://ftp.pse.cz, http://www.zse.hr, http://finance. yahoo.com)

Development of Stock Markets in 1997-2007

The developments of particular stock markets in the examined countries from December 1996 to February 2007 are showed in Figure 7-1. As it is apparent, the increasing trend of developed stock markets (with a decrease in the year 1998) was replaced from the beginning of the year 2000 by a plunge continuing up to the first quarter of the year 2003. Decreasing trend of Croatian stock market was replaced from the third quarter of the year 1999 and in the Czech Republic from the third quarter of the year 2001. Yet, in the Czech Republic and Croatia we can notice the stoppage of the decrease or a mild recovery of the stock market as early as in the last quarter of the year 2001.

Figure 7-1 Development of stock market indices in the whole period (January 1997 – February 2007, December 1996 = 100)

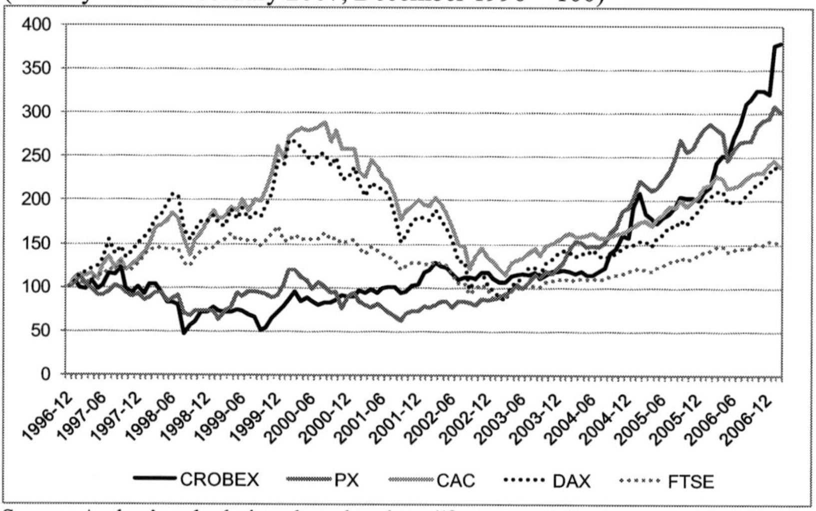

Source: Author's calculations based on http://ftp.pse.cz, http://www.zse.hr, http://finance.yahoo.com

The detailed examination of the development of stock indices in the sub-period from January 1997 to December 2001 is represented in Figure 7-2, from which a relative synchronous development of the stock markets in the Czech Republic, France, Germany and the United Kingdom is evident.

The highest increase in the monthly index in that sub period January 1997 – December 2001 was registered in the Czech Republic (May 1999:

+20.5 percent) and in Croatia (September 1998: +19.2 percent), the highest decrease in Croatia too (August 1998: -54 percent). France recorded in this sub period the highest monthly increase of +13.2 percent (in June 1997), Germany +16.7 percent (in December 1999) and United Kingdom 8.5 percent (in January 1998). The highest decrease France recorded in September 2001 (-14 percent), Germany in August 1998 (-20.6 percent) and United Kingdom in August 1998 (-12.6 percent).

As it is apparent from the Figure 7-2, starting in October 1998 the stock markets in all analysed countries began to turn up; starting in March 2000 the stock markets in the Czech Republic, Germany and the United Kingdom began to turn down.

Figure 7-2 Development of stock market indices in the sub-period from January 1997 to December 2001 (December 1996 = 100)

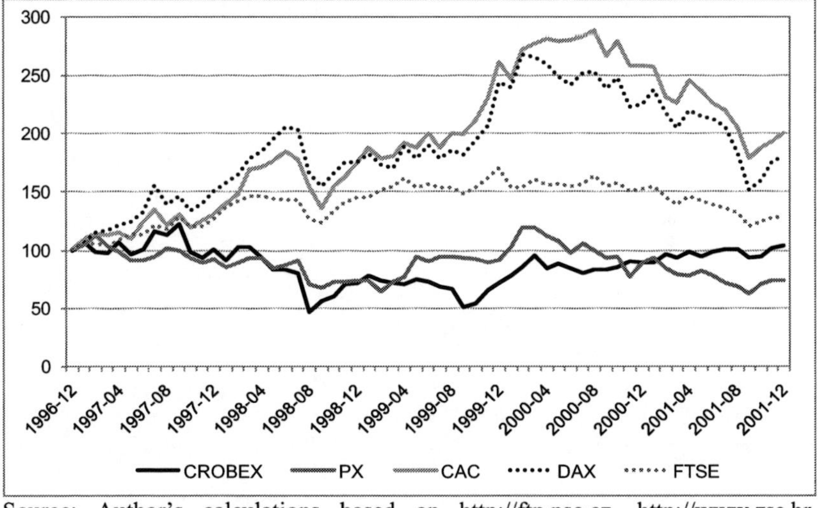

Source: Author's calculations based on http://ftp.pse.cz, http://www.zse.hr, http://finance.yahoo.com

Figure 7-3 represents the development of stock markets in the second sub-period from January 2002 to February 2007. A characteristic feature for this sub period is first stagnation and subsequently the slump of national stock indices practically in all examined countries except the Czech Republic (starting in September 2001 the Czech stock market began to turn up). The decreasing trend of developed stock markets and Croatian stock market was replaced from the first quarter of the year 2003.

For the Czech stock market in this sub period can be noticed with Broz and Ridzak (2006), that accession countries that joined the EU in 2004 had a big increase in values of their stock indices. Dvorak and Podpiera (2005) claim that price increase of equities in the EU accession countries, that happened after accession was certain, has been caused by increased market integration.

The highest monthly increase of the stock market index in that sub period January 2002 – February 2007 was registered in Croatia in January 2005 (+20.6 percent) and in Germany in April 2003 (+19.2 percent), the highest monthly decrease in Germany (in September 2002: -28.8 percent) and in France (September 2002: -18.1 percent). The highest decrease in the United Kingdom (-12.7 percent) was registered in September 2002 too.

Figure 7-3 Development of stock market indices in the sub-period from January 2002 to February 2007 (December 1996 = 100)

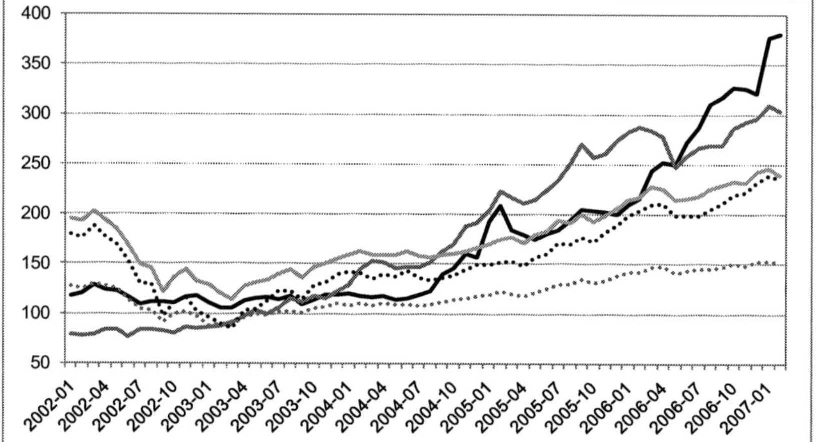

Source: Author's calculations based on http://ftp.pse.cz, http://www.zse.hr, http://finance.yahoo.com

Monthly Returns and Risk

Comparison of Stock Markets Returns and Risk in 1997-2007

Main characteristics of the monthly returns of the national stock markets in Croatia, Czech Republic, France, Germany and United Kingdom (mean of returns and standard deviation of returns) and also other characteristics for the entire period from January 1997 to February 2007 are depicted in Table 7-1. The data confirm general assertions that emerging markets (or stock markets in transition countries) not only may offer higher returns, but also the risks associated with returns are frequently higher than in the established markets as well.[1]

Table 7-1 Selected characteristics of monthly returns (January 1997 – February 2007)

	CROBEX	PX	CAC	DAX	FTSE
Mean	1.09	0.91	0.71	0.70	0.34
Median	1.13	1.24	1.59	2.25	0.77
Maximum	20.57	20.50	13.16	19.16	8.47
Minimum	-53.97	-26.37	-18.17	-28.81	-12.74
Std. Deviation	8.84	6.91	5.99	7.13	4.16
Skewness	-2.111	-0.610	-0.506	-0.904	-0.770
Kurtosis	14.740	4.926	3.397	5.452	4.010
Jarque-Bera	791.30	26.41	6.00	47.21	17.25
Probability	0.0000	0.0000	0.0497	0.0000	0.0002
Sum	133.4	110.4	87.0	85.5	41.4
Sum sq. dev.	9451.1	5785.5	4339.3	6151.8	2093.5
Observations	122	122	122	122	122

Source: Author's calculations

Note: CRO – Croatia, CZE – Czech Republic, FRA – France, GER – Germany, UKI – United Kingdom.

The highest average monthly return in the whole period from January 1997:01 to February 2007:02 was registered in Croatia (it amounted to 1.09%), the Czech stock market recorded in this period average monthly return 0.91%. Developed stock markets indices in France, Germany and the United Kingdom recorded in this period lower average monthly returns (from 0.34% to 0.71%).

The volatility of the monthly returns is in emerging markets generally high (standard deviations of monthly returns are 8.84 for Croatian stock market and 6.91 for Czech stock market in comparison with standard deviations of 4.16 for the United Kingdom or 5.99 for France). In cases of some countries it can be noticed with Kulhánek and Uherek (2003) that a higher risk does not have to be accompanied by higher returns (returns and risk at German stock market in comparison with stock markets in Czech Republic or France, see Figure 7-4).

Figure 7-4 Stock markets monthly returns and risk (January 1997 – February 2007)

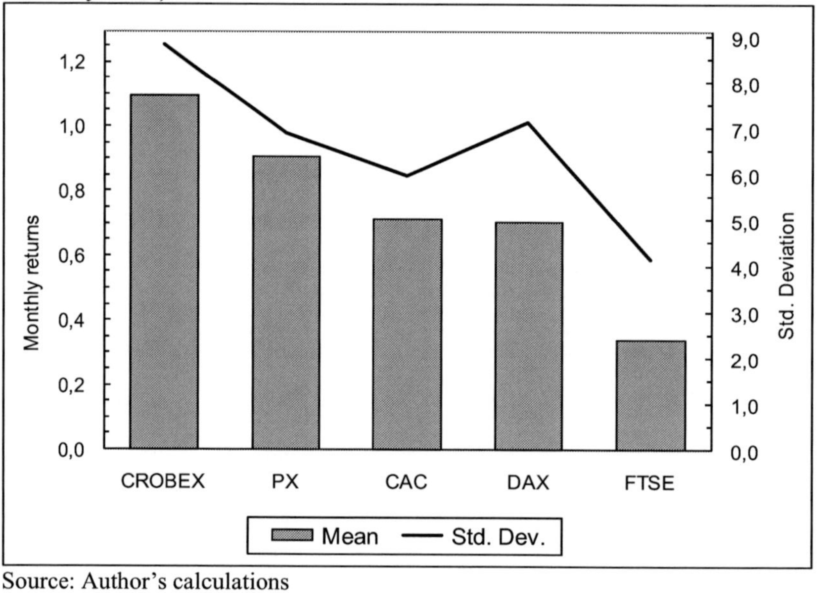

Source: Author's calculations

Changes of Returns and Risk

The comparison of the development of risk and monthly returns of particular countries brings remarkable results too. For the purposes of this comparison, the five-years moving averages of risk and monthly returns for Croatian, Czech, German and British stock markets were obtained, which are showed in Figure 7-5 and Figure 7-6.

Figure 7-5 Development of five-years moving averages of risk and returns for Czech and Croatian stock markets (December 2001 – February 2007)

Czech Republic Croatia

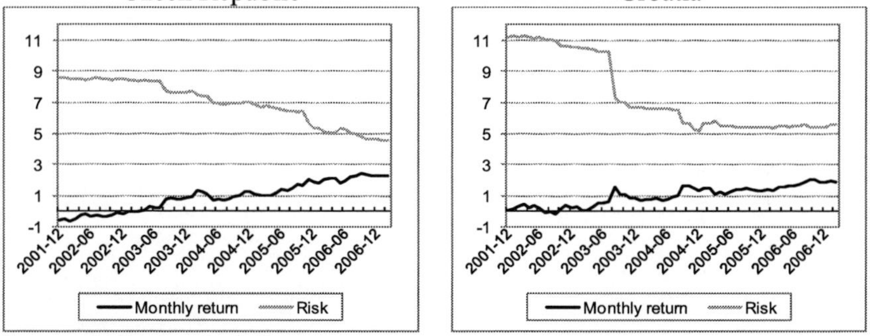

Sourcc: Author's calculations

The monitoring of monthly returns and risk development (measured by five-years moving averages of monthly returns and standard deviation) and their international comparison prove in principle the fundamental relation between returns and risk. As it is obvious from Figures 7-5 and 7-6, the increase of monthly returns was connected with the decrease of standard deviation. Correlation coefficients between five-years moving averages of monthly returns and standard deviations are -0.898 for Croatia, -0.957 for Czech Republic, -0.773 for Germany and -0.622 for the United Kingdom respectively.

Similar relatively high average monthly returns of the Croatian or Czech stock markets were related to the high risk (or standard deviation) in comparison with the United Kingdom. Then again, the British stock market showed the lowest average monthly return and the lowest standard deviation.

Figure 7-6 Development of five-years moving averages of risk and returns for German and British stock markets (December 2001 – February 2007)

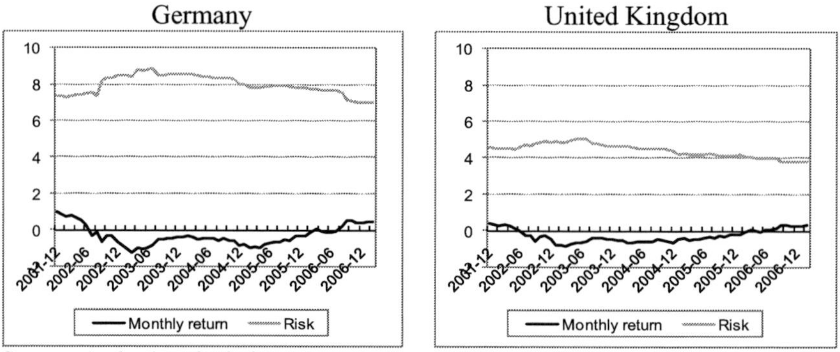

Source: Author's calculations

Stock Markets Linkages

Since the sixties the advantages of the international diversification have been analysed in detail. The results of a number of empirical studies in this area indicate that the benefits from the international diversified portfolios arise from a relatively low interconnection of the individual national stock markets, which is assessed according to the correlation coefficients of proceeds rate among those national stock markets. A question arises legally in connection to the aim of the chapter too; what degree of interdependence stock markets in the old and new EU Member States show.

Due to the changeable character of the development of stock markets, the valuation of mutual relations between the developments of the particular national stock markets was conducted in two steps. First, the correlation[2] coefficients of monthly returns for the entire observed period from January 1997 to February 2007 were identified (see Table 7-2). Subsequently, the correlation coefficients were identified as five-years moving averages beginning from December 2001 to February 2007 (see Figures 7-7 and 7-8).

Table 7-2 Correlation coefficients of returns for the sample period 1997–2007

	CRO	CZE	FRA	GER	UKI
CRO	1	0.381	0.344	0.375	0.421
CZE	0.381	1	0.346	0.352	0.268
FRA	0.344	0.346	1	0.905	0.776
GER	0.375	0.352	0.905	1	0.798
UKI	0.421	0.268	0.776	0.798	1

Source: Author's calculations

Note: CRO – Croatia, CZE – Czech Republic, FRA – France, GER – Germany, UKI – United Kingdom.

As it is noticeable from Table 7-2, high correlation coefficients are (traditionally)[3] showed by the returns of developed stock markets (Germany and France: 0.905, Germany and the United Kingdom: 0.798). Correlation coefficients of these stock markets with Croatia and Czech Republic are considerably lower (between 0.268 and 0.421). Monthly returns of the Croatian stock market in examined period are mostly correlated with British stock market (0.421) and Czech stock market (0.381) respectively. Correlation coefficients of Czech stock market returns with developed stock markets in EU Member States are lower too.

As it is evident from the Figure 7-7, changes of five-years moving averages of correlation coefficients for Czech and Croatian stock markets returns against average are obvious in the course of time. The correlation coefficient between Czech and Croatian markets showed first an increase of correlation coefficients till the April 2002, then it was followed by the decrease up to August 2003, and subsequently the correlation coefficient began to oscillate. Increase of correlation coefficient began from June 2004 and the most correlated returns of these stock markets come around starting November 2005. The development of five-years moving correlation coefficients for France, Germany and United Kingdom is depicted in the right part of Figure 7-7.

The development of five-years moving correlation coefficients for the Croatian both Czech stock markets against the British stock market is depicted in the left part of Figure 7-8. Development trends of correlation coefficients against German stock market are obvious from the right part of this figure.

Figure 7-7 Correlation of returns for selected countries (five-years moving averages, December 2001 – February 2007)

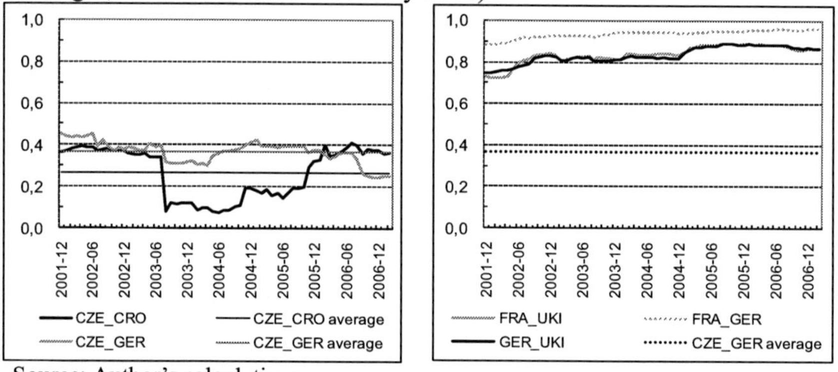

Source: Author's calculations

Figure 7-8 Correlation of returns against British and German stock markets (five-years moving averages, December 2001 – February 2007)

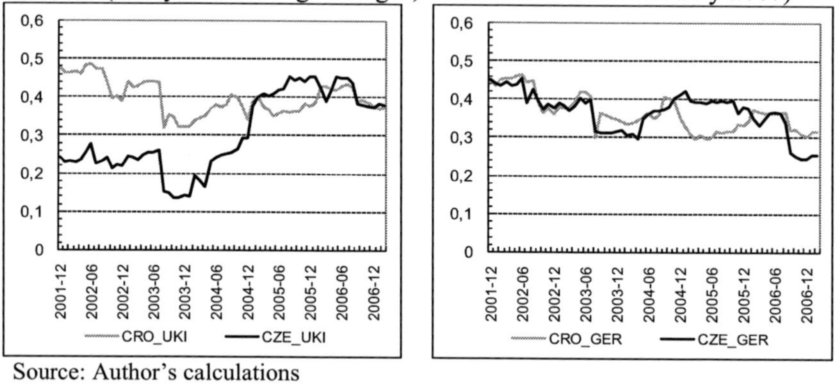

Source: Author's calculations

As Figure 7-8 shows, started in 2003 for both the Czech and Croatian stock markets, the increase from the lowest levels of correlation coefficients against British stock market and the decrease levels of correlation coefficients against German stock market were observed.

Conclusion

In this chapter we have focused on the development of the stock markets in Croatia and in the Czech Republic in comparison with the development of stock markets in selected developed EU Member States.

The comparison of monthly returns and risks on stock markets in the Czech Republic and Croatia in examined period from 1997:01 to 2007:02 has confirmed characteristics which are typical for the emerging markets. Returns and risk are higher than in returns and risk in developed stock markets. The increase of returns in all examined stock markets was connected in examined period with the decrease of risk.

The monthly returns correlation coefficients for Croatia and Czech Republic against developed stock markets are generally positive but low. This fact can contribute to the decrease in portfolio risk by way of international diversification. However our results confirms, that correlation is a time-varying short-term measure and portfolios built accordingly may underestimate long term gains and require frequent rebalancing. Stock markets returns in Croatia and Czech Republic have become increasingly interconnected from end of the year 2005.

References

Adam, K., T. Jappelli, A. Menichini, M. Padula and M. Pagano. 2002. *Analyse, Compare, and Apply Alternative Indicators and Monitoring Methodologies to Measure the Evolution of Capital Market Integration in the European Union.* Centre for Studies in Economics and Finance. University of Salerno, Salerno.

Broz, T. and T. Ridzak. 2006. *Croatian Equity Market in Perspective of European Integration.* Dubrovnik: 12th Dubrovnik Economic Conference 2006. Access from: < www.hnb.hr/dub-konf/12-konferencija/mladi/broz-ridzak.pdf >.

Dvorak, T. and R. Podpiera. 2005. *European Union Enlargement and Equity Markets in Accession Countries.* ECB Working Paper Series No. 552. European Central Bank, Frankfurt am Main.

Kulhánek, L. 2002. Comparison of Capital Markets Returns in the Czech Republic and in the EMU. In *Finance. 50th Anniversary Financial Conference*, 381-95. Svishtov-Veliko Tarnovo: Abagar.

—. 2005. Stock Markets in Poland and Czech Republic. In *Kapitał i źródła jego pozyskiwania dla przedsiębiorstw i regionów*, ed. J. Czekaj, 239-48. Bielsko-Biała: Wyższa Szkoła Bankowości i Finansów.

Kulhánek, L. and D. Uherek. 2003. Globalization, Financial System and Equity Market Linkages in Transition Countries. *Economic Research (Ekonomska Istraživanja)* 16(2): 55-67.

Acknowledgement

The research is due to the support provided by GAČR (Czech Science Foundation – Grantová agentura České republiky) under the project No. 402/08/1237. The support is greatly acknowledged.

Notes

[1] For the Czech Republic, Poland and the Euro Area countries see Kulhánek (2005), among others.
[2] Adam et al. (2002) use price-based and quantity based indicators in order to assess evolution of capital market integration within European Union. As price-based indicator for stock markets they use correlation of stock market returns.
[3] For more detailed analysis see Kulhánek (2002), among others.

CHAPTER EIGHT

FINANCIAL DEVELOPMENT AND REAL INCOME GROWTH IN THE EURO AREA

SALIH TURAN KATIRCIOGLU
AND ELIF KATIRCIOGLU

One of the main issues of development economics is to search the major determinants of economic growth. The relationship and the direction of causality between financial development and economic growth have been empirically tested in the literature. After the extensive studies in this field, it is now well recognized that financial development is crucial for economic growth (Calderon and Liu, 2003). Likewise, it is a necessary condition for achieving a high rate of economic growth (Chang, 2002) and has a strong positive relationship with economic growth (Mazur and Alexander, 2001). But according to De Gregorior and Guidotti (1995) financial development significantly reduces economic growth in countries (especially in Latin America) experiencing relatively high inflation rates. Furthermore, the direction of causality between the financial development and economic growth has been in attention of the researchers in the literature for over three decades. This causal relationship, however, generally remains inconclusive (Calderon and Liu, 2003).

Patrick (1966) developed two hypotheses testing the possible directions of causality between financial development and economic growth: (i) *supply-leading hypothesis* that posits a causal relationship from financial development to economic growth; and (ii) *demand-following hypothesis* where it postulates a causal relationship leading from economic growth to financial development. In the empirical literature, McKinnon (1973), King and Levine (1993), Neusser and Kugler (1998) and Levine et al. (2000) support the supply-leading hypothesis while Gurley and Shaw (1967), Goldsmith (1969), and Jung (1986) support the demand-following hypothesis.

This chapter first examines the stationary nature of financial development measurement and real income by applying panel unit root tests. Second, we test the supply-leading or the demand-following hypothesis through Granger causality tests for the European Union (EU) countries who currently participate in the euro area.

The remainder of this chapter is organized as follows. Next section presents the data and describes the methodology used in the study. The subsequent section discusses the findings and the final section gives the concluding remarks.

Data and Methodology

Data

A panel dataset of 12 EU countries that currently use the euro in their circulation is employed in this chapter. The variables used are on annual basis and cover the period 1960 – 2005. The selected euro countries are Belgium, Germany, Greece, Spain, France, Ireland, Italy, Luxembourg, the Netherlands, Austria, Portugal and Finland. The variables are constructed and measured as follows. The real income growth is the logarithm of the real gross domestic product per capita at 2000 constant USD prices, hereafter L(CAP). The financial development measure was taken as the ratio of the logarithm of domestic credit provided by banking sector to nominal GDP, hereafter L(DC/GDP). The definition of financial development, which is the improvement in quantity, quality, and efficiency of financial intermediary services, cannot be captured by a single measure. Thus, two common measures (M2/GDP and DC/GDP) are advised in the literature (see also Calderon and Liu, 2003). Data was obtained from World Bank Development Indicators (World Bank, 2005).

Methodology

Prior to Granger causality tests, panel unit root tests have been applied to the variables to test the existence of a unit root. The methods developed by Levin et al. (2002), hereafter LLC; Im et al. (2003), hereafter IPS; and Maddala and Wu (1999), henceforth M-W, are implemented in this chapter for the unit root process. LLC unit root test assumes a common unit root process for panel data where the IPS and M-W tests assume individual unit root process for the panel data. Furthermore, all of these unit root tests suggest the null hypothesis of a unit root. M-W test has the advantage over the IPS test that its value does not depend on different lag lengths in the individual Augmented Dickey Fuller regressions (see also Christopoulos and Tsionas, 2004; and Baltagi and Kao, 2000). Furthermore, Baltagi and Kao (2000) also report that Fisher type tests such as M-W are superior to IPS in terms of size-adjusted power.

The causal relationship between stationary variables X and Y can be examined within the following bivariate representation:

$$Y_t = a + \sum_{i=1}^{p} \alpha_i Y_{t-i} + \sum_{j=1}^{q} \beta_j X_{t-j} + \mu_t \tag{8.1}$$

$$X_t = b + \sum_{i=1}^{r} \gamma_i X_{t-i} + \sum_{j=1}^{s} \delta_j Y_{t-j} + v_t \tag{8.2}$$

where μ_t and v_t are serially uncorrelated white-noise residuals; and p, q, r, and s are lag lengths for each variable in each equation. Equations (8.1) and (8.2) are also known as a simple bivariate autoregressive (AR) model testing for Granger causality.

Using the same lag length for the variables in each equation, the model is estimated by least squares. To estimate causal direction, the Granger test employs F-statistics within a framework of restricted and unrestricted models. For causality from X to Y or from Y to X as can be seen in equations (8.1) and (8.2) respectively, lagged values of X in equation (8.1) and Y in equation (8.2) are used as a zero restriction. According to the Granger causality test, having statistically significant F values in (8.1) and (8.2) would be a sufficient precondition to have causation from X to Y and from Y to X respectively.

Another method for testing Granger causality is the one within the framework of block exogeneity test where it carries out pairwise Granger causality tests and shows whether an endogenous variable can be treated as exogenous. For each equation in the VAR, chi-square (χ^2) or Wald statistic tests for joint significance of each of the other lagged endogenous variables in that equation. Furthermore, results obtained from Wald tests will be a justification of results reached by bivariate simple Granger causality tests as modelled in equations (8.1) and (8.2).

Empirical Results

Before testing the direction of causality, panel data properties should be considered. Table 8-1 reports results of the LLC, IPS and M-W unit root tests. The results in Table 8-1 suggest that both L(DC/GDP) and

L(CAP) variables are stationary at their levels. It is important to note that LLC test assumes a common unit root process so that the autoregressive coefficients are identical across the cross-sections. On the other hand, IPS and M-W tests allow for individual unit root processes so that the autoregressive coefficients may vary across the cross-sections. LLC and M-W tests are also characterized by the combining of individual unit root tests to derive a panel-specific result. Lastly, IPS test does not estimate the most restricted model without trend and a drift.

Table 8-1 Panel unit root tests

	LLC	IPS	M-W
L(CAP)			
τ_T	-2.44*	0.78	15.89
τ_μ	-9.94*	-4.23*	90.94*
τ	16.44	---	0.19
L(DC/GDP)			
τ_T	2.16	-0.13	32.75
τ_μ	-0.06	2.51	12.02
τ	-4.99*	---	61.00*

Source: Authors' calculations

Note: τ_T represents the most general model with a drift and trend; τ_μ is the model with a drift and without trend; τ is the most restricted model without a drift and trend. Optimum lag lengths are selected based on Schwartz Criterion. * denotes rejection of the null hypothesis at the 1% level.

Since L(DC/GDP) and L(CAP) are integrated of order zero, I(0), as also summarized in Table 8-2, simple Granger causality tests are now suitable to test the direction of causality between L(DC/GDP) and L(CAP). There are methods for lag the length selection in the recent literature such as Akaike Information Criterion (AIC), Schwartz Information Criterion (SIC) and Hsiao (1979) sequential procedure. The latter one combines Granger's definition of causality and Akaike's minimum final prediction error criterion. However, Pindyck and Rubinfeld (1991) point out that it would be best to run the tests for a few different lag structures and make sure that the results were not sensitive to the choice of lag length. Therefore, Equations (8.1) and (8.2) are estimated for the lags 1 to 3.

Table 8-2 Summary of panel unit root tests

	LLC	IPS	M-W	Individ. result	Final result
L(CAP)					
τ_T	I (0)	I (1)	I (1)	I (0)	
τ_μ	I (0)	I (0)	I (0)	I (0)	I (0)
τ	I (1)		I (1)	I (1)	
L(DC/GDP)					
τ_T	I (1)	I (1)	I (1)	I (1)	
τ_μ	I (1)	I (1)	I (1)	I (1)	I (0)
τ	I (0)		I (0)	I (0)	

Source: Authors' calculations
Note: All variables denoted as in Table 8-1.

Bivariate causality test results in Table 8-3 suggest bidirectional causation between L(DC/GDP) and L(CAP). This causation has been obtained for the lag lengths of 1 to 3, but higher lag lengths did not provide significant results.

Table 8-3 Granger causality tests

	F – Statistic			Conclusion
	Lag 1	Lag 2	Lag 3	
L(DC/GDP) does not Granger cause L (CAP)	26.21^{*}	4.42^{**}	3.22^{**}	L(CAP) ⇔ L(DC/GDP)
L(CAP) does not Granger cause L (DC/GDP)	6.73^{*}	2.60^{***}	2.88^{**}	

Source: Authors' estimation
Note: *, **, and *** significance at 1%, 5% and 10% levels respectively.

Table 8-4 provides estimation results of the Granger causality tests within block exogeneity Wald tests. One can reveal that they are consistent with the results in Table 8-3. In both equations χ^2 statistics are statistically significant for the lags between 1 and 3. Therefore, the endogenous variable of L(DC/GDP) in the first equation and L(CAP) in the second equation in Table 8-4 can also be treated as exogenous. Thus, the bidirectional causation between per capita income and domestic credit in the euro area reported in Table 8-3 is also justified by Wald tests.

Table 8-4 Granger causality tests within block exogeneity Wald tests

Dependent variable	Exclude	χ^2		
		Lag 1	Lag 2	Lag 3
L(CAP)	*L(DC/GBP)*	26.21*	8.84**	9.65**
L(DC/GBP)	*L(CAP)*	6.73*	5.21***	8.64**

Source: Authors' estimations
Note: *, **, and *** significance at 1%, 5% and 10% levels respectively.

Conclusion

The objective of this chapter was to empirically investigate the direction of causality between per capita income and domestic credit provided by banking sector in the EU countries that adopted the euro as of the end of 2005. Panel unit root test results suggest that per capita income and domestic credit by banking sector are stationary at their levels which are both integrated of order zero. Bivariate simple Granger causality tests suggest bidirectional causation between per capita income and domestic credit in the euro area. Thus, we may conclude that there is a feedback relationship between real income and financial development in the euro area countries.

References

Baltagi, B.H. and C. Kao. 2000. Nonstationary Panels, Cointegration in Panels and Dynamic Panels: A Survey. In *Advances in Econometrics 15*, ed. B.H. Baltagi. Oxford: Elsevier Science.

Calderon, C. and L. Liu. 2003. The Direction of Causality between Financial Development and Economic Growth. *Journal of Development Economics* 72(1): 321-34.

Chang, T. 2002. Financial Development and Economic Growth in Mainland China: A Note on Testing Demand-following or Supply-leading Hypothesis. *Applied Economic Letters* 9(13): 869-73.

Christopoulos, D.K. and E.G. Tsionas. 2004. Financial Development and Economic Growth: Evidence from Panel Unit Root and Cointegration Tests. *Journal of Development Economics* 73(1): 55-74.

De Gregorio, J. and P. Guidotti. 1995. Financial Development and Economic Growth. *World Development* 23(3): 433-48.

Goldsmith, R.W. 1969. *Financial Structure and Development.* Yale University Press, New Haven, CT.

Gurley, J. and E. Shaw. 1967. Financial Structure and Economic Development. *Economic Development and Cultural Change* 15(3): 333-46.

Hsiao, C. 1979. Causality in econometrics. *Journal of Economic Dynamics and Control* 1(4): 321-46.

Im, K.S., H. Pesaran and Y. Shin. 2003. Testing for Unit Roots in Heterogeneous Panels. *Journal of Econometrics* 115(1): 53-74.

Jung, W.S. 1986. Financial Development and Economic Growth: International Evidence. *Economic Development and Cultural Change* 34(2): 336-46.

King, R. G. and R. Levine. 1993. Finance and Growth: Schumpeter might be Right. *Quarterly Journal of Economics* 108(3): 717-38.

Levin, A., C.F. Lin and C.S.J. Chu. 2002. Unit Root Tests in Panel Data: Asymptotic and Finite-Sample Properties. *Journal of Econometrics* 108(1): 1-24.

Levine, R., N. Loayza and T. Beck. 2000. Financial Intermediation and Growth: Causality Analysis and Causes. *Journal of Monetary Economics* 46(1): 31-77.

Maddala, G.S. and S. Wu. 1999. Comparative Study of Unit Root Tests with Panel Data and a New Simple Test. *Oxford Bulletin of Economics and Statistics* 61(special issue, November): 631-52.

Mazur, E.A. and W.R.J. Alexander. 2001. Financial Sector Development and Economic Growth in New Zealand. *Applied Economic Letters* 8(8): 545-49.

McKinnon, R.I. 1973. *Money and Capital in Economic Development.* Brookings Institution, Washington, DC.

Neusser, K. and M. Kugler. 1998. Manufacturing Growth and Financial Development: Evidence from OECD Countries. *Review of Economics and Statistics* 80(4): 638-46.

Patrick, H.T. 1966. Financial Development and Economic Growth in Underdeveloped Economies. *Economic Development and Cultural Change* 14(2): 174-89.

Pindyck, R.S. and D.L. Rubinfeld. 1991. *Models and Economic Forecasts.* McGraw-Hill Inc.

World Bank. 2005. *World Development Indicators.* CD-ROM database.

CHAPTER NINE

INFLATION TARGETING AND MONETARY INTEGRATION UNDER ERM 2: MODELLING THIRD-COUNTRY EFFECTS FROM PRODUCTION SHARING*

FELIX HAMMERMANN

In this chapter, we analyse the potential cost of regional monetary integration, i.e., targeting the exchange rate to an anchor currency, while being at the same time integrated with third countries. Recent empirical papers point to the relevance of outsourcing and offshoring for the transmission of business cycle shocks and thereby for the conduct of monetary policy (see, among others, Fontagné and Freudenberg, 1999; Imbs, 2004; Kalemli-Ozcan et al., 2003; Kose et al., 2003a; Kose et al., 2003b; IMF, 2007). This is especially true for the countries that are about to join the euro area, which have to stay for two years in the European Exchange Rate Mechanism (ERM 2) and therefore target inflation and the exchange rate simultaneously. These countries are significantly integrated with third countries through the production chain. How do external shocks originating from a third country affect monetary policy under ERM 2?

Up to now, the empirical analysis had to focus on the early years characterized by inflation stabilization. The central and eastern European countries (CEEC) had to deal with the structural change from centrally planned to market economies. In the beginning of the 1990s, price liberalization and the abolition of price controls led to hyperinflation. The situation got stabilized by pegging the exchange rate. When the economies were ready for a more independent monetary policy, the central banks of the Czech Republic (1998), Poland (1998), Hungary (2001) and Slovakia (2005)[1] introduced inflation targeting. Mohanty and Klau (2005) and Frömmel and Schobert (2006) estimate Taylor rules in these inflation targeting countries. Krusec (2005) investigates the transmission mechanism under inflation targeting in a Vector Error Correction Model, whereas Hammermann (2005) shows the reaction of the interest rate to shocks in inflation, output and the exchange rate in a Vector Autoregressive model.

Empirical studies could not yet analyse how central banks actually solve the trade-off between inflation and exchange rate stabilization under ERM 2 (see Orlowski and Rybinski, 2006).[2] In November 2005, Slovakia was the first inflation targeting country to move into ERM 2. In the next years, other countries of the CEEC that currently target the inflation rate may join ERM 2 and thus target the exchange rate at the same time. ERM 2 allows only for exchange rate movements within a ±15 percent band. After two successful years in ERM 2 and fulfilment of the other convergence criteria specified in the treaty of Maastricht, countries would adopt the euro. In any case, the results from the empirical literature support the assumption that even the inflation targeters among the CEEC did not completely give up exchange rate targeting, which was, of course, more dominant during the initial phase of disinflation and structural change. Incorporating the exchange rate in the conduct of monetary policy may be interpreted as simulating ERM 2, while still avoiding its strictly binding rules.

The theoretical literature looks either at the strategic role of targeting the exchange rate in competitive devaluations and its role as a shock absorber or rejects the role for targeting the exchange rate as the central bank should target domestic inflation and allow the exchange rate to float (Clarida et al., 2001). Svensson (2000) shows in his simulations that a Taylor rule without an exchange rate term is a robust monetary policy strategy despite ignoring part of the available information. De Paoli (2006) finds only for implausibly high elasticities of substitution that exchange rate targeting enters the optimal monetary policy (see also Galí, 2008).

Nonetheless, the existing models are incomplete as they do not address any potential trade-off between the strategic role of the exchange rate and achieving an announced inflation target given third-country effects. As shown in Table 9-1, CEEC with inflation targeting are well integrated into production sharing with the euro area, documented by high trade shares, but a substantial share of their trade is still with the rest of the world (see also Crespo and Fontoura, 2007).

Because a two-country model cannot adequately cope with potential third-country effects, we develop a New Keynesian three-country model. As a starting point, we take a three-country model in which Teo (2005) analyses the choice of invoice currency in Asia but that does not address the role of monetary policy. We, therefore, integrate Teo's three-country framework into a model that analyses monetary policy in a New Keynesian two-country model developed by Monacelli (2001). As a result, we are able to analyse regional monetary integration based on a dynamic, microfounded model allowing for third-country effects. Additionally, following Corsetti et al. (2000), we incorporate a nested consumption basket to distinguish between goods produced in two periphery countries and a core country.

Table 9-1 Trade shares and openness of central European inflation targeting countries and the euro area in 2006

	Imports		**Exports**		**Openness**
	Euro area	**Rest of the world**	**Euro area**	**Rest of the world**	
Czech Republic	0.59	0.41	0.58	0.42	1.31
Hungary	0.52	0.48	0.55	0.45	1.35
Poland	0.56	0.44	0.53	0.47	0.69
Slovakia	0.42	0.58	0.52	0.49	1.56
Average of CEEC	0.52	0.48	0.54	0.46	1.23
Euro Area	0.49	0.51	0.50	0.50	0.65

Source: Eurostat and IFS

Note: Openness is measured as imports and exports over GDP.

The model develops a set of equations for each of the three countries *A*, *B* and *C*. Country *A* is the country under consideration and may represent a CEEC country integrating into the euro area by targeting the euro as its anchor currency. Country *B* constitutes the third country, which is not directly affected by the European integration process and, therefore, stays outside ERM 2. Country *B* may represent either another transition country like Russia or the rest of the world. Both countries *A* and *B* together form the periphery, while country *C* represents the core country, which also provides the anchor currency for country *A*. Hence, country *C* features the euro area.

We analyse monetary policy in this setting given alternative degrees of integration between the euro area (core country *C*), an inflation targeting accession country like the Czech Republic, Hungary, Poland and Slovakia (country *A*) and a non-EU country or the rest of the world as the third country (country *B*). As a short cut for modelling production linkages we use alternative elasticities in consumption baskets. This framework allows us to trace the transmission mechanism of a third-country technology shock. Evaluating the central bank loss function for different simple rules and determining the corresponding optimal simple rules allows us to assess the costs of ERM 2 and derive the implications of production sharing for monetary policy. As a robustness check, we introduce home bias in consumption.

Our results show that a Taylor rule extended for an exchange rate term is a good simple rule for different kinds of integration with a third country. Nevertheless, the costs of ERM 2 in terms of a traditional central bank loss function are considerable. We proceed as follows. First, we derive the New Keynesian three-country model. Next, we present the simulation results and finally the conclusions.

A New Keynesian Three-Country Model for Analyzing Optimal Monetary Rules under ERM 2

The New Keynesian three-country model incorporates explicit microfoundations with dynamic and intertemporal effects as well as Keynesian building blocks such as nominal rigidities and monopolistic competition. Following the microfoundation of the model, all individuals are at the same time consumers and producers. In their role as consumers, we look at the demand side of the economy. The representative household maximizes its utility by deciding about its optimal consumption. In the individuals' role as producers, we look at the supply side of the economy. The representative firm maximizes its profits by deciding about the product's optimal price. Putting the resulting optimality conditions together, the New Keynesian model is made of three core equations for each country. First, the dynamic IS curve stems form the household's choice on the optimal consumption path. Second, the New Keynesian Phillips curve stems from the firm's choice on the optimal price. Third, the model is closed with a monetary policy rule. These three equations form together with market clearing and international risk sharing the three-country model. The derivation follows along the lines of Galí and Monacelli (2005).

Households

The representative household in country i, $i = A, B, C$, maximizes the expected lifetime utility

$$E_0 \sum_{t=0}^{\infty} \beta^t U_t^i \left(C_t^i , L_t^i \right), \tag{9.1}$$

where β is the subjective discount factor, C is consumption and L are hours worked, with the respective period utility

$$U_t^i = \frac{1}{1-\mu} C_t^{i\,1-\mu} - \frac{1}{1+\gamma} L_t^{i\,1+\gamma}, \tag{9.2}$$

where μ is the risk aversion and γ the inverse of the elasticity of labour supply. Households consume from a nested consumption basket as in Corsetti et al. (2000). The utility-based consumption basket distinguishes between goods from the periphery P and the centre C, where n_P is the size of the periphery relative to the centre

$$C_t^i = \left[(n_P)^{1/\theta} \left(C_{P,t}^i \right)^{(\theta-1)/\theta} + (1-n_P)^{1/\theta} \left(C_{C,t}^i \right)^{(\theta-1)/\theta} \right]^{\theta/(\theta-1)}. \tag{9.3}$$

The periphery itself is made up of the two countries A and B, where n_A is the size of country A relative to country B. The consumption basket for the periphery is given by

$$C_{P,t}^i = \left[(n_A)^{1/\psi} \left(C_{A,t}^i \right)^{(\psi-1)/\psi} + (1-n_A)^{1/\psi} \left(C_{B,t}^i \right)^{(\psi-1)/\psi} \right]^{\psi/(\psi-1)}. \tag{9.4}$$

Taken together, the size of country A is $n_P\, n_A$, of country B is $n_P\,(1-n_A)$ and of the centre C is $(1-n_P)$. The nested consumption basket for country i, $i = A, B, C$, is

$$\begin{aligned} C_t^i = \Big[(n_P)^{1/\theta} \Big(\left[(n_A)^{1/\psi} \left(C_{A,t}^i \right)^{(\psi-1)/\psi} + (1-n_A)^{1/\psi} \left(C_{B,t}^i \right)^{(\psi-1)/\psi} \right]^{\psi/(\psi-1)} \Big)^{(\theta-1)/\theta} \\ + (1-n_P)^{1/\theta} \left(C_{C,t}^i \right)^{(\theta-1)/\theta} \Big]^{\theta/(\theta-1)}. \end{aligned} \tag{9.5}$$

Introducing home bias in consumption changes the trade shares. If consumers in each country prefer home goods over foreign goods, the degree of openness, η, is smaller than one. The nested consumption baskets for each country depend on the intratemporal elasticity of substitution between goods from the centre versus the periphery, θ, as well as on the intratemporal elasticity of substitution between goods from country A versus country B, i.e., between the two goods from the periphery, ψ. Thus, the nested consumption baskets with home bias are given by

$$
\begin{aligned}
C_t^A = \Big[& [1-\eta(1-n_P)]^{1/\theta} \Big(\Big[[1-\eta(1-n_A)]^{1/\psi} \left(C_{A,t}^A\right)^{(\psi-1)/\psi} \\
& + [\eta(1-n_A)]^{1/\psi} \left(C_{B,t}^A\right)^{(\psi-1)/\psi} \Big]^{\psi/(\psi-1)} \Big)^{(\theta-1)/\theta} \\
& + [\eta(1-n_P)]^{1/\theta} \left(C_{C,t}^A\right)^{(\theta-1)/\theta} \Big]^{\theta/(\theta-1)}
\end{aligned} \tag{9.6}
$$

$$
\begin{aligned}
C_t^B = \Big[& [1-\eta(1-n_P)]^{1/\theta} \Big(\Big[(\eta n_A)^{1/\psi} \left(C_{A,t}^B\right)^{(\psi-1)/\psi} \\
& + (1-\eta n_A)^{1/\psi} \left(C_{B,t}^B\right)^{(\psi-1)/\psi} \Big]^{\psi/(\psi-1)} \Big)^{(\theta-1)/\theta} \\
& + [\eta(1-n_P)]^{1/\theta} \left(C_{C,t}^B\right)^{(\theta-1)/\theta} \Big]^{\theta/(\theta-1)}
\end{aligned} \tag{9.7}
$$

$$
\begin{aligned}
C_t^C = \Big[& (\eta n_P)^{1/\theta} \Big(\Big[(n_A)^{1/\psi} \left(C_{A,t}^C\right)^{(\psi-1)/\psi} \\
& + (1-n_A)^{1/\psi} \left(C_{B,t}^C\right)^{(\psi-1)/\psi} \Big]^{\psi/(\psi-1)} \Big)^{(\theta-1)/\theta} \\
& + [\eta(1-n_P)]^{1/\theta} \left(C_{C,t}^C\right)^{(\theta-1)/\theta} \Big]^{\theta/(\theta-1)}.
\end{aligned} \tag{9.8}
$$

The consumption indexes for the three countries i, $i = A, B, C$, are given by

$$
C_{A,t}^i = \left[\left(\frac{1}{n_P n_A} \right)^{1/\phi} \int_0^{n_P n_A} \left(C_{A,t}^i(z) \right)^{\phi-1/\phi} dz \right]^{\phi/(\phi-1)} \tag{9.9}
$$

$$
C_{B,t}^i = \left[\left(\frac{1}{n_P(1-n_A)} \right)^{1/\phi} \int_{n_P n_A}^{n_P} \left(C_{B,t}^i(z) \right)^{\phi-1/\phi} dz \right]^{\phi/(\phi-1)} \tag{9.10}
$$

$$C_{C,t}^{i}=\left[\left(\frac{1}{1-n_{P}}\right)^{1/\phi}\int_{n_{P}}^{1}\left(C_{C,t}^{i}(z)\right)^{\phi-1/\phi}dz\right]^{\phi/(\phi-1)} \tag{9.11}$$

where the subscript refers to the country of production and the superscript refers to the country of consumption. The elasticity of substitution for goods of different brands *z*, i.e., "varieties" is given by ϕ.

Prices

The utility-based price indexes are defined analogously to the consumption basket and are therefore broken down into the overall index

$$P_{t}^{i}=\left[n_{P}\left(P_{P,t}^{i}\right)^{1-\theta}+\left(1-n_{P}\right)\left(P_{C,t}^{i}\right)^{1-\theta}\right]^{1/(1-\theta)} \tag{9.12}$$

and the sub-index for prices of goods from the two periphery countries

$$P_{P,t}^{i}=\left[n_{A}\left(P_{A,t}^{i}\right)^{1-\psi}+\left(1-n_{A}\right)\left(P_{B,t}^{i}\right)^{1-\psi}\right]^{1/(1-\psi)}. \tag{9.13}$$

As with the consumption basket, introducing home bias renders the consumer price index for each country

$$P_{t}^{A}=[[1-\eta(1-n_{P})]\left([[1-\eta(1-n_{A})]\left(P_{A,t}^{A}\right)^{1-\psi}+\eta(1-n_{A})\left(P_{B,t}^{A}\right)^{1-\psi}]^{1/(1-\psi)}\right)^{1-\theta}$$
$$+\eta(1-n_{P})\left(P_{C,t}^{A}\right)^{1-\theta}]^{1/(1-\theta)} \tag{9.14}$$

$$P_{t}^{B}=[[1-\eta(1-n_{P})]\left(\left[\eta n_{A}\left(P_{A,t}^{B}\right)^{1-\psi}+\left(1-\eta n_{A}\right)\left(P_{B,t}^{B}\right)^{1-\psi}\right]^{1/(1-\psi)}\right)^{1-\theta} \tag{9.15}$$
$$+\eta(1-n_{P})\left(P_{C,t}^{B}\right)^{1-\theta}]^{1/(1-\theta)}$$

$$P_{t}^{C}=\left[\eta n_{P}\left(\left[n_{A}\left(P_{A,t}^{C}\right)^{1-\psi}+\left(1-n_{A}\right)\left(P_{B,t}^{C}\right)^{1-\psi}\right]^{1/(1-\psi)}\right)^{1-\theta}+\left(1-\eta n_{P}\right)\left(P_{C,t}^{C}\right)^{1-\theta}\right]^{1/(1-\theta)} \tag{9.16}$$

with

$$P_{A,t}^{i}=\left[\frac{1}{n_P n_A}\int_0^{n_P n_A}\left(P_{A,t}^{i}(z)\right)^{1-\phi}dz\right]^{1/(1-\phi)} \tag{9.17}$$

$$P_{B,t}^{i}=\left[\frac{1}{n_P(1-n_A)}\int_{n_P n_A}^{n_P}\left(P_{B,t}^{i}(z)\right)^{1-\phi}dz\right]^{1/(1-\phi)} \tag{9.18}$$

$$P_{C,t}^{i}=\left[\frac{1}{1-n_P}\int_{n_P}^{1}\left(P_{C,t}^{i}(z)\right)^{1-\phi}dz\right]^{1/(1-\phi)} \tag{9.19}$$

where $P_{i,t}^{i}$ is the price index of domestic goods or producer price index (PPI) in country *i*.

Exchange Rates

The terms of trade between country *i* and country *i'* are defined as the relative price of imports

$$ToT_{i',t}^{i}=\frac{P_{i',t}^{i}}{P_{i,t}^{i}} \tag{9.20}$$

that means, the price of imported goods (produced in country *i'*) in home (country *i*) currency relative to the price of home goods.

For convenience, we define the following CPI-PPI ratios, $g_{i,t}(ToT)$, for each country *i*. The expression links CPI prices and domestic prices to the terms of trade (Faia and Monacelli, 2004, 2008)

$$\frac{P_t^A}{P_{A,t}^A}=\left[[1-\eta(1-n_P)]\left[\left([1-\eta(1-n_A)]+\eta(1-n_A)\left(ToT_{B,t}^A\right)^{1-\psi}\right)^{1/(1-\psi)}\right]^{1-\theta}\right.$$
$$\left.+\eta(1-n_P)\left(ToT_{C,t}^A\right)^{1-\theta}\right]^{1/(1-\theta)}\equiv g_{A,t}(ToT) \tag{9.21}$$

$$\frac{P_t^B}{P_{B,t}^B} = \left[\left[1 - \eta \left(1 - n_P \right) \right] \left[\left(\eta \, n_A \left(ToT_{A,t}^B \right)^{1-\psi} + \left(1 - \eta \, n_A \right) \right)^{1/(1-\psi)} \right]^{1-\theta} \right. \tag{9.22}$$
$$\left. + \eta \left(1 - n_P \right) \left(ToT_{C,t}^B \right)^{1-\theta} \right]^{1/(1-\theta)} \equiv g_{B,t}\left(ToT \right)$$

$$\frac{P_t^C}{P_{C,t}^C} = \left[\eta \, n_P \left[\left(n_A \left(ToT_{A,t}^C \right)^{1-\psi} + \left(1 - n_A \right) \left(ToT_{A,t}^C \right)^{1-\psi} \right)^{1/(1-\psi)} \right]^{1-\theta} \right. \tag{9.23}$$
$$\left. + \left(1 - \eta \, n_P \right) \right]^{1/(1-\theta)} \equiv g_{C,t}\left(ToT \right).$$

Households maximize their lifetime utility subject to the period budget constraint,

$$\sum_{h^{t+1}} Q_{t,t+1} \frac{1}{S_{i,t}^C} B_{t+1}^i + P_t^i C_t^i = \frac{1}{S_{i,t}^C} B_t^i + W_t^i L_t^i + \Psi_t^i \tag{9.24}$$

where nominal bonds, B_t^i, are state-contingent claims denominated only in country C's currency, $S_{i,t}^{i'}$, is the nominal exchange rate defined as the price of currency i' in currency i, $Q_{t,t+1} \equiv Q\left(h^{t+1} \middle| h^t \right)$ is the period-t price of one unit of country C's currency in state h^{t+1} divided by the probability of occurrence of that state,[3] W_t^i is the nominal wage; L_t^i are hours worked and Ψ_t^i are nominal profits of the domestic monopolistic firms, which shares are owned by domestic residents. Complete markets ensure stationarity of bonds and consumption (Schmitt-Grohé and Uribe, 2003).

Deriving Demand Functions

First, we derive the individual demand functions for good z as well as the aggregate demand functions from the intratemporal cost minimization of the household's consumption across different countries i and brands z.[4]

Individual demand functions for country i, $i = A, B, C$:

$$C_{A,t}^i\left(z \right) = \left(\frac{P_{A,t}^i\left(z \right)}{P_{A,t}^i} \right)^{-\phi} \left(n_P n_A \right)^{-1} C_{A,t}^i, \tag{9.25}$$

$$C^i_{B,t}(z) = \left(\frac{P^i_{B,t}(z)}{P^i_{B,t}} \right)^{-\phi} \left(n_P(1-n_A)\right)^{-1} C^i_{B,t}, \tag{9.26}$$

$$C^i_{C,t}(z) = \left(\frac{P^i_{C,t}(z)}{P^i_{C,t}} \right)^{-\phi} \left(1-n_P\right)^{-1} C^i_{C,t}. \tag{9.27}$$

Aggregate demand functions for country *i*, *i* = *A*, *B*, *C*:

$$C^i_{A,t} = v^i_A \left(\frac{P^i_{A,t}}{P^i_{P,t}} \right)^{-\psi} \left(\frac{P^i_{P,t}}{P^i_t} \right)^{-\theta} C^i_t \tag{9.28}$$

$$C^i_{B,t} = v^i_B \left(\frac{P^i_{B,t}}{P^i_{P,t}} \right)^{-\psi} \left(\frac{P^i_{P,t}}{P^i_t} \right)^{-\theta} C^i_t \tag{9.29}$$

$$C^i_{C,t} = v^i_C \left(\frac{P^i_{C,t}}{P^i_t} \right)^{-\theta} C^i_t, \tag{9.30}$$

where the trade shares are given by Table 9-2.

Table 9-2 Trade shares for countries *A*, *B* and *C*

Country A	Country B	Country C
$v^A_A = [1-\eta(1-n_P)][1-\eta(1-n_A)]$	$v^B_A = [1-\eta(1-n_P)]\eta n_A$	$v^C_A = \eta n_P n_A$
$v^A_B = [1-\eta(1-n_P)]\eta(1-n_A)$	$v^B_B = [1-\eta(1-n_P)](1-\eta n_A)$	$v^C_B = \eta n_P(1-n_A)$
$v^A_C = \eta(1-n_P)$	$v^B_C = \eta(1-n_P)$	$v^C_C = 1-\eta n_P$

Second, we solve the intertemporal optimization by maximizing the lifetime utility function (9.1) subject to the budget constraint (9.24). Combining the first order conditions for consumption and labour determines the consumption labour trade-off and, thereby, the nominal wage

$$W_t^i = \frac{-\partial U_t^i / \partial C_t^i}{\partial U_t^i / \partial L_t^i} = \frac{\left(L_t^i\right)^{\gamma}}{\left(C_t^i\right)^{-\mu}} P_t^i. \tag{9.31}$$

Combining the first order conditions for consumption and bonds leads to the familiar Euler equation

$$\beta \left(\frac{C_{t+1}^i}{C_t^i} \right)^{-\mu} \frac{P_t^i}{P_{t+1}^i} = \frac{S_{i,t+1}^C}{S_{i,t}^C} Q_{t,t+1}. \tag{9.32}$$

Taking expectations conditional on the information available in period t and defining the gross nominal interest rate, R_t^i, on a riskless one-period bond in country i as

$$R_t^i \equiv \frac{1}{E_t \left\{ \left(S_{i,t+1}^C / S_{i,t}^C \right) Q_{t,t+1} \right\}}, \tag{9.33}$$

we rewrite the Euler equation as

$$\beta\, R_t^i\, E_t \left\{ \left(\frac{C_{t+1}^i}{C_t^i} \right)^{-\mu} \frac{P_t^i}{P_{t+1}^i} \right\} = 1. \tag{9.34}$$

The Euler equation (9.34) leads to the dynamic IS curve, where today's consumption depends on tomorrow's consumption and the interest rate.

International Risk Sharing

The three countries are linked by international risk sharing. Combining the Euler equation (9.32) for two countries *i* and *i'*

$$\beta \left(\frac{C_{t+1}^i}{C_t^i} \right)^{-\mu} \frac{P_t^i}{P_{t+1}^i} = \beta \left(\frac{C_{t+1}^{i'}}{C_t^{i'}} \right)^{-\mu} \frac{S_{i',t}^i \, P_t^{i'}}{S_{i',t+1}^i \, P_{t+1}^{i'}} \tag{9.35}$$

and defining the real exchange rate as

$$RER_{i',t}^{i} \equiv \frac{S_{i',t}^{i} \cdot P_{t}^{i'}}{P_{t}^{i}} \tag{9.36}$$

the following risk sharing condition holds in every period

$$C_{t}^{i} = C_{t}^{i'} \cdot \left(RER_{i',t}^{i}\right)^{1/\mu}. \tag{9.37}$$

The real exchange rate may be written in terms of trade

$$RER_{i',t}^{i} = ToT_{i',t}^{i} \cdot g_{i',t}(ToT) \cdot g_{i,t}(ToT)^{-1}. \tag{9.38}$$

In a three-country model we have two risk sharing conditions expressed in terms of trade

$$C_{t}^{A} = C_{t}^{B}\left(ToT_{B,t}^{A}\right)^{1/\mu} g_{B,t}(ToT)^{1/\mu} g_{A,t}(ToT)^{-1/\mu} \tag{9.39}$$

and

$$C_{t}^{A} = C_{t}^{C}\left(ToT_{C,t}^{A}\right)^{1/\mu} g_{C,t}(ToT)^{1/\mu} g_{A,t}(ToT)^{-1/\mu} \tag{9.40}$$

If purchasing power parity holds, which is the case if there is no home bias in consumption, the real exchange rate in (9.37) is one and international risk sharing implies perfect consumption smoothing across countries, i.e.,

$$C_{t}^{i} = C_{t}^{i'}. \tag{9.41}$$

Firms

Differences in production and thereby in economic integration along the production chain are modelled via the consumption basket to keep the supply side of the model simple. We also abstract from capital as labour is the only input factor. Each monopolistically competitive firm z in country i produces

$$Y_{t}^{i}(z) = F_{t}^{i} L_{t}^{i}(z). \tag{9.42}$$

where $Y_t^i(z)$ is the output of firm z in period t and F_t^i is country specific productivity that follows a first order autoregressive process

$$F_t^i = \rho^i F_{t-1}^i + \varepsilon_t^i . \tag{9.43}$$

Firms maximize profits subject to the production function, demand and staggered producer currency pricing à la Calvo (1983), where α is the degree of price stickiness. The optimal price of variety z is

$$\tilde{P}_{i,t}^i(z) = \frac{\phi}{\phi-1} \cdot \frac{E_t \sum_{\tau=0}^{\infty} \alpha^\tau \rho_{t,t+\tau} Y_{t+\tau}^i(z) MC_{t+\tau}^i(z)}{E_t \sum_{\tau=0}^{\infty} \alpha^\tau \rho_{t,t+\tau} Y_{t+\tau}^i(z)}, \tag{9.44}$$

where $MC_t^i(z) = W_t^i / L_t^i$ are nominal marginal costs given by the Lagrange multiplier associated with the demand constraint, $Y_t^i(z)$ is total "world" output of country i's firm z and $\phi/(\phi-1)$ is the markup of prices over marginal costs.

Market Clearing

Market clearing requires the demand and supply of goods to be equalized in each of the three countries

$$\begin{aligned} Y_t^A = {} & v_A^A \left(ToT_{P,t}^A\right)^{\psi-\theta} \left(g_A(ToT)\right)^\theta C_t^A \\ & + v_B^A \left(ToT_{P,t}^B\right)^{\psi-\theta} \left(ToT_{B,t}^A\right)^\psi \left(g_B(ToT)\right)^\theta C_t^B \\ & + v_C^A \left(ToT_{P,t}^C\right)^{\psi-\theta} \left(ToT_{C,t}^A\right)^\psi \left(g_C(ToT)\right)^\theta C_t^C \end{aligned} \tag{9.45}$$

$$\begin{aligned} Y_t^B = {} & v_A^B \left(ToT_{P,t}^A\right)^{\psi-\theta} \left(ToT_{A,t}^B\right)^\psi \left(g_A(ToT)\right)^\theta C_t^A \\ & + v_B^B \left(ToT_{P,t}^B\right)^{\psi-\theta} \left(g_B(ToT)\right)^\theta C_t^B \\ & + v_C^B \left(ToT_{P,t}^C\right)^{\psi-\theta} \left(ToT_{C,t}^B\right)^\psi \left(g_C(ToT)\right)^\theta C_t^C \end{aligned} \tag{9.46}$$

$$Y_t^C = v_A^C \left(ToT_{C,t}^A\right)^{-\theta} \left(g_A(ToT)\right)^\theta C_t^A + v_B^C \left(ToT_{C,t}^B\right)^{-\theta} \left(g_B(ToT)\right)^\theta C_t^B + v_C^C \left(g_C(ToT)\right)^\theta C_t^C. \tag{9.47}$$

Solving the Model

The model cannot be solved analytically. We follow the strategy of linear approximation of the model's non-linear equations established in the real business cycle literature (e.g., Campbell, 1994; Uhlig, 1999). Kydland and Prescott (1982) proposed taking a linear-quadratic approximation to the true model around its steady state. This method is valid in the special case of Kydland and Prescott (1982) but may not be generalized. Kim and Kim (2007) demonstrate in a small model that log-linearizing the model before deriving the optimality conditions (first order conditions) leads to inaccurate results. Such a "naive" (Benigno and Woodford, 2007) linear-quadratic problem is not correct up to first order. King et al. (1988, 2002) use instead a log-linear-quadratic approximation of the model's (non-linear) optimality conditions.

However, the limitations of this method need to be kept in mind. Ascari and Merkl (2008) show the shortcomings of log-linearizations in a model with a disinflation experiment. The economy moves from one steady state with high inflation to a new steady state with low inflation. Especially with respect to inflation at the starting point (the first steady state) of the disinflation experiment, the economic results may differ dramatically.

Summing up, log-linear approximations are suitable if (i) the non-linearities are not essential (in contrast to models in finance where risk matters) and (ii) the model analyses only small deviations from the steady state. In our model, we already derived the optimality conditions for the household and for the firm. Next, we log-linearize the model around a steady state with no inflation.

Like a closed economy, the model's core equations are an IS curve, a Phillips curve and a monetary policy rule for each country. In an open economy, we need additionally goods market clearing for each country as consumption may deviate from output and, to link the three economies, two international risk sharing conditions. For convenience, we use two shorthand notations. First, the real marginal costs, $\hat{mc}_t^i$ and, second, the frequently used CPI-PPI ratio, $\hat{g}_{i,t}(ToT)$. To analyse monetary policy under ERM 2, we also back out CPI inflation, $\hat{\pi}_t^i$ and the change in the nominal exchange rate, $\Delta\hat{S}_{i',t}^i$, where an increase corresponds to a change in the rate of depreciation of the currency in country *i*. Country *A* is the accession country. Equations of the log-linearized model for country *A*:

$$\hat{C}_t^A = \hat{C}_{t+1}^A - \frac{1}{\mu}\hat{R}_t^A + \frac{1}{\mu}\hat{\pi}_{A,t+1}^A + \frac{v_B^A}{\mu}\hat{T}oT_{B,t+1}^A - \frac{v_B^A}{\mu}\hat{T}oT_{B,t}^A + \frac{v_C^A}{\mu}\hat{T}oT_{C,t+1}^A - \frac{v_C^A}{\mu}\hat{T}oT_{C,t}^A \tag{9.48}$$

$$\hat{\pi}_{A,t}^A = \beta\hat{\pi}_{A,t+1}^A + \frac{(1-\alpha)(1-\alpha\beta)}{\alpha}\hat{mc}_t^A \tag{9.49}$$

$$\hat{mc}_t^A = \mu\hat{C}_t^A + \gamma\hat{Y}_t^A - (1+\gamma)\hat{F}_t^A + \hat{g}_{A,t}(ToT) \tag{9.50}$$

$$\hat{g}_{A,t}(ToT) = v_B^A\hat{T}oT_{B,t}^A + v_C^A\hat{T}oT_{C,t}^A \tag{9.51}$$

$$\hat{R}_t^A = \varphi_\pi\hat{\pi}_t^A + \varphi_Y\hat{Y}_t^A + \varphi_S\Delta\hat{S}_{C,t}^A \tag{9.52}$$

$$\begin{aligned}\hat{Y}_t^A = {} & v_A^A\hat{C}_t^A + \theta v_A^A\hat{g}_{A,t}(ToT) - (\psi-\theta)v_B^A[1-\eta(1-n_A)]\hat{T}oT_{B,t}^A \\ & + v_B^A\hat{C}_t^B + \theta v_B^A\hat{g}_{B,t}(ToT) + (\psi-\theta)v_B^A\eta n_A\hat{T}oT_{A,t}^B + \psi v_B^A\hat{T}oT_{B,t}^A \\ & + v_C^A\hat{C}_t^C + \theta v_C^A\hat{g}_{C,t}(ToT) + (\psi-\theta)v_C^A n_A\hat{T}oT_{A,t}^C \\ & + (\psi-\theta)v_C^A(1-n_A)\hat{T}oT_{B,t}^C + \psi v_C^A\hat{T}oT_{C,t}^A\end{aligned} \tag{9.53}$$

$$\hat{\pi}_t^A = \hat{\pi}_{A,t}^A + v_B^A\hat{T}oT_{B,t}^A - v_B^A\hat{T}oT_{B,t-1}^A + v_C^A\hat{T}oT_{C,t}^A - v_C^A\hat{T}oT_{C,t-1}^A \tag{9.54}$$

$$\Delta\hat{S}_{C,t}^A = \hat{T}oT_{C,t}^A - \hat{T}oT_{C,t-1}^A + \hat{\pi}_{A,t}^A - \hat{\pi}_{C,t}^C \tag{9.55}$$

Consumption in this economy is determined by expected consumption, the interest rate, expected domestic inflation as well as expected changes in the terms of trade between country *A* and countries *B* and *C*, the dynamic IS curve (9.48). Inflation, in turn, is determined by the forward-looking Phillips curve (9.49), which reflects the impact of marginal costs on inflation. To guarantee determinacy the monetary policy rule (9.52) needs to respond to inflation by more than one to one and thereby fulfil the Taylor principle (Woodford, 2003). A productivity shock for country *A* would reduce marginal costs (9.50) and thereby reduce inflation. The central bank would react to lower inflation with an interest rate cut. Consumers would respond to a lower interest rate with increases in today's consumption. In a closed economy, the changes in consumption would lead to equal changes in output. In an open economy, the lower interest rate improves also the terms of trade and thereby the increase in domestic output is shared with the rest of the world (goods market clearing, equation 9.53).

The equations for countries *B* and *C* mirror those for country *A* except for the international risk sharing condition (equations 9.56 and 9.57). In a three-country model, we need two risk sharing conditions to link financial markets

$$\hat{C}_t^A = \hat{C}_t^B + \frac{1}{\mu}\hat{T}oT_{B,t}^A + \frac{1}{\mu} g_{B,t}(ToT) - \frac{1}{\mu} g_{A,t}(ToT) \tag{9.56}$$

$$\hat{C}_t^A = \hat{C}_t^C + \frac{1}{\mu}\hat{T}oT_{C,t}^A + \frac{1}{\mu} g_{C,t}(ToT) - \frac{1}{\mu} g_{A,t}(ToT). \tag{9.57}$$

Calibration

The numerical solution requires calibrating the structural parameters of the model (Table 9-3). Most parameters are standard in the real business cycle literature. The discount factor β equals 0.99, so that the steady state annual real interest rate is 4 percent. The period utility function has a risk aversion of 2 to depart from the case of logarithmic utility[5] and an inverse of the labour supply of 3. The Calvo price staggering parameter is set to 0.75, implying an average frequency of price adjustment of four quarters (Galí, 2003).

In the three-country model, we explicitly consider different types of production sharing. The elasticity of substitution between goods from two countries follows Backus et al. (1995). We take this conventional assumption for the elasticity between goods from the core country *C* and the two periphery countries *A* and *B* and set θ equal to 1.5. Within the two periphery countries, we distinguish two scenarios. Countries *A* and *B* producing complements implies vertical integration along the production chain. We follow Burstein et al. (2008) and model complements with a relatively low elasticity of substitution as ψ equals 0.05. Their calibration is based on survey data on outsourcing and offshoring in Eastern Europe reported in Marin (2006). Horizontal production sharing implies countries producing substitutes. To model strong substitutes, we follow De Paoli (2006) and set ψ equal to 3.

As we focus on the qualitative results, we do not calibrate the model for specific countries. In the benchmark calibration, each country's size is 1/3 and there is no home bias in consumption, i.e., η equals 1. We relax this assumption and introduce home bias as a robustness check (η equals 0.5).

Table 9-3 Calibration of the model

Structural Parameters		Calibration
α	Calvo staggering	0.75
β	subjective discount factor	0.99
γ	inverse of the elasticity of labour supply	3
μ	risk aversion	2
θ	elasticity of substitution between country *C* vs. *P*	1.5
ψ	elasticity of substitution between country *A* vs. *B*	0.05 (complements) 3 (substitutes)
ρ	autocorrelation of technology shock process	0.9
η	degree of openness	1 (completely open) 0.5 (with home bias)
n_P	size of country *C* vs. *P*	2/3
n_A	size of country *A* vs. *B*	0.5

Simulation Results

Technology Shock in a Two-County Model

In order to provide a benchmark for the value added of this model, we briefly revisit a technology shock in a two-country model, where the two countries produce complements in one case and strong substitutes in the other case.[6] We analyse the impulse responses with respect to consumption, output and domestic inflation. The technology shock process is modelled by a first order autoregressive process to productivity in country B

$$\hat{F}_t^B = \rho^B \hat{F}_{t-1}^B + \varepsilon_t^B \tag{9.58}$$

where the persistence parameter ρ^B is set to 0.9 (see Faia, 2007).

As already pointed out by Mundell (1961), monetary policy faces difficulties of dealing with asymmetric shocks in a monetary union. If the two countries produce complements to each other, output would increase in both countries (Figure 9-1, Table 9-4). The technology shock, however, reduces inflation only in country B. In country A, higher consumption and a higher production increase marginal costs (9.50) and thereby domestic inflation increases (9.49). Thus, the inflation rates in the two countries would be negatively correlated. If, in contrast, the two countries produce strong substitutes, output would be negatively correlated (Figure 9-2). The technology shock would again reduce the price of products from country B. The consumers in country A would switch from their own products to the cheaper imports from country B. Consequently, output would fall only in country A, but inflation would fall in both countries. For both cases, we may distinguish between a central bank of the monetary union that is dominated by one country and a central bank of the union that targets the average of the two countries. Obviously, given the negative correlations in either inflation or output, a monetary policy in favour of one country would be inadequate for the other country. If the central bank bases its decisions on the union-wide aggregates, the negative correlations would partly offset each other and none of the two countries would benefit from an appropriate monetary policy.

Table 9-4 Correlation coefficients of inflation and output in a two-country model

	Inflation	**Output**
Complements	-0.24	0.69
Substitutes	0.07	-1.10

Source: Author's calculations

Figure 9-1 Technology shock in a two-country model, complements

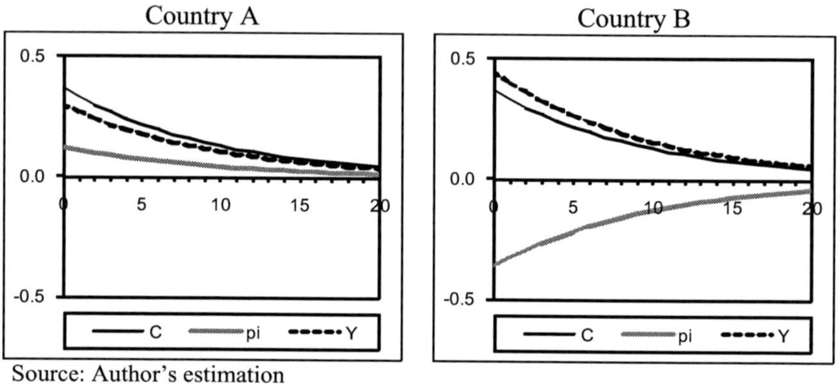

Source: Author's estimation

Figure 9-2 Technology shock in a two-country model, substitutes

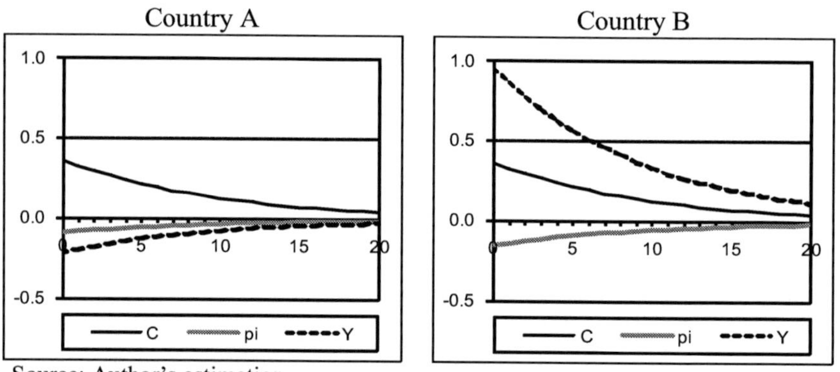

Source: Author's estimation

Technology Shock in a Three-County Model

The three-country model with a nested consumption basket studies the transmission of a technology shock in the third country (country *B*) and its implications for monetary policy in the accession country (country *A*).[7] The model addresses the run-up to a monetary union as the central bank in country *A* may have to target the exchange rate vis-à-vis the anchor country *C*. Further, the model emphasizes the implications of asymmetric production sharing among the three countries. Countries *A* and *C* are not affected by the third-country shock in the same way. Thus, under fully flexible exchange rates, the exchange rate between countries *A* and *C* would also bear part of the adjustment. In particular, this model distinguishes between countries *A* and *B* producing complements and strong substitutes.

We evaluate the effects of eight different simple monetary policy rules (9.52) for country *A*, the euro area accession country. Rules 1 and 2 in Table 9-5 stand for strict inflation targeting, where Rule 1 targets the domestic (i.e., core) inflation rate and Rule 2 targets the inflation of the consumer price index (CPI). Their respective Taylor rule counterparts are Rules 3 and 4, including output targeting. Rules 5 to 8 add an exchange rate term to Rules 1 to 4 in order to investigate the implications of exchange rate targeting under ERM 2. For the impulse responses presented in the graphs, we focus on the traditional CPI inflation Taylor rule (Rule 4) and adding an exchange rate term for ERM 2 (Rule 8).

Countries *B* and *C* conduct strict domestic inflation targeting, $\varphi_{\pi_i^i}$ equals 1.5. The central bank in country *B* neither mitigates the effect of the technology shock on output nor second-round effects from abroad showing up in CPI inflation. Otherwise, positive weights for output targeting in the monetary policy rule would reduce the shock in country *B* and, hence, also its impact on the other countries. Countries *B* and *C* are assumed to produce substitutes throughout the simulations. Hence, their output reactions are negatively correlated. Again, a positive weight for output targeting in the monetary policy rule of country *C* would dampen the (inverse) shock in the anchor currency country. Any weight on output targeting in the monetary policy rules of countries *B* and *C* would lead to biased results with respect to the analysis of monetary policy in country *A*.

Table 9-5 Simple monetary policy rules for country *A*

Monetary policy rule		$\varphi_{\pi_i^i}$	φ_{π^i}	φ_Y	φ_S
Rule 1	domestic inflation targeting	1.5	–	–	–
Rule 2	CPI inflation targeting	–	1.5	–	–
Rule 3	domestic inflation Taylor rule	1.5	–	0.5	–
Rule 4	CPI inflation Taylor rule	–	1.5	0.5	–
Rule 5	domestic inflation targeting under ERM 2	1.5	–	–	0.5
Rule 6	CPI inflation targeting under ERM 2	–	1.5	–	0.5
Rule 7	domestic inflation Taylor rule under ERM 2	1.5	–	0.5	0.5
Rule 8	CPI inflation Taylor rule under ERM 2	–	1.5	0.5	0.5

As standard in the literature, we evaluate the different monetary policy rules based on the loss function of the central bank. The central bank wishes to minimize volatility in output and inflation (Monacelli, 2005).[8] The loss function is defined as

$$L_0^{CB} = E_0 \sum_{t=0}^{\infty} \delta^t \left(\lambda_\pi \hat{\pi}_t^2 + \lambda_Y \hat{Y}_t^2 \right), \tag{9.59}$$

where $0 < \delta < 1$ is a discount factor. Woodford (2003) shows that such a loss function is consistent with maximizing a social utility function in a closed economy setup. Both, society as well as the Maastricht criteria specify inflation measured by the CPI. As weights in the loss function we take $\lambda_\pi = \lambda_Y = 0.5$.

However, although such a loss function is meaningful as a benchmark for the evaluation of monetary policy, it would be incomplete for the case of regional monetary integration. If the central bank in country *A* would not give any positive weight to exchange rate smoothing, it would be difficult to establish the case for integrating into the euro area. Hence, we assume that the central bank minimizes the volatility in the exchange rate as an additional objective. In case the central bank operates under ERM 2, the loss function with a positive weight on exchange rate smoothing could be defined as

$$L_0^{ERM2} = E_0 \sum_{t=0}^{\infty} \delta^t \left(\lambda_\pi \hat{\pi}_t^2 + \lambda_Y \hat{Y}_t^2 + \lambda_S \Delta \hat{S}_t^2 \right), \tag{9.60}$$

where $\lambda_\pi = 1$ and $\lambda_Y = \lambda_S = 0.5$. The value of the intertemporal loss functions approaches the unconditional mean of the period loss functions as $\delta \to 1$, which equals the sum of the unconditional variances of the policy objectives.

Thus, the two loss functions for country *A* are

$$\textit{Loss CB:} \qquad 0.5\left(\pi^A\right)^2 + 0.5\left(\hat{Y}^A\right)^2 \tag{9.61}$$

$$\textit{Loss ERM 2:} \qquad \left(\pi^A\right)^2 + 0.5\left(\hat{Y}^A\right)^2 + 0.5\left(\Delta \hat{S}_C^A\right)^2. \tag{9.62}$$

Technology Shock I: Countries A and B Producing Complements

We start by analyzing the case where countries *A* and *B*, the two periphery countries, produce complements, while the periphery goods and country *C*'s goods are substitutes. A common feature for all countries stems from international risk sharing. Consequently, in the absence of home bias in consumption, the technology shock is evenly distributed and leads to equal increases in consumption in the three countries (see equation 9.41).

First, we consider the impulse responses according to Rule 4, when country *A* conducts a CPI inflation Taylor rule without exchange rate smoothing (Figure 9-3, left column). Following the technology shock in country *B*, output in that country increases. Country *A*, producing complements to country *B*, benefits by a significant increase in its output. Country *C* in contrast looses output as its consumers substitute home goods by the products from the periphery countries *A* and *B*, taking also upward pressure from prices. As a consequence, inflation decreases in all countries. However, the decline in prices is more pronounced in country *A* than in country *C*. The inflation differential leads to an increased appreciation of country *A*'s currency vis-à-vis country *C*'s currency (Figure 9-3, bottom row, dashed line).

Second, we turn to the case when country *A*'s central bank operates under ERM 2 (Figure 9-3, right column). The exchange rate between country *A* and *C* is not allowed to adjust to the full extent as the central bank in country *A* conducts a CPI inflation Taylor rule augmented for exchange rate smoothing (Rule 8). As implicitly uncovered interest rate parity holds in the model, the central bank of country *A* has to reduce its interest rate in order to counter the appreciation vis-à-vis the anchor currency, thereby driving up inflation at home. Table 9-6 shows how volatility in domestic as well as CPI inflation increases when comparing the rules without an exchange rate term (Rules 1 to 4) with their ERM 2 counterparts (Rules 5 to 8). Hence, with relatively stable exchange rates, domestic inflation in country *A* increases sharply, displaying the costs of an asymmetric shock under exchange rate targeting.

Figure 9-3 Technology shock in a three-country model, complements

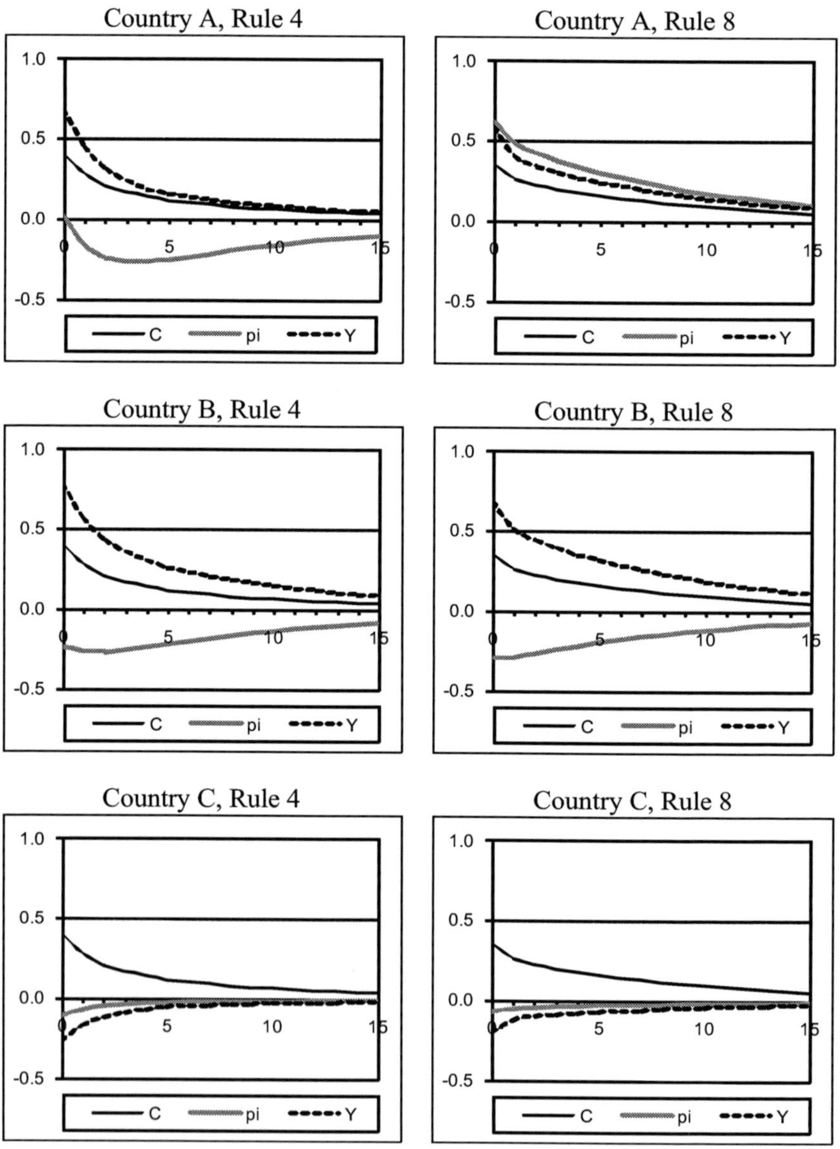

Figure 9-3 (cont.)

ΔS^A

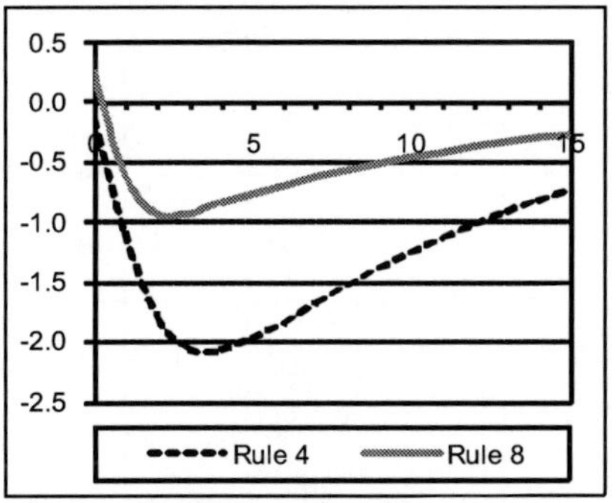

Source: Author's estimation

To analyse the relative change in the central bank loss of joining ERM 2, we construct the ratio of the loss for each monetary policy rule with an exchange rate term over its counterpart without that term (Table 9-7). Moving to ERM 2 more than doubles the loss for the traditional central bank loss function (Loss CB) as it increases up to 2.39-times. For the two Taylor Rules 3 and 4 moving to their ERM 2 counterparts still increases the loss but by less than 30 percent. If the central bank adapts ERM 2 as its policy targets (Loss ERM 2), the loss drops when adding the exchange rate to the policy rule to half or almost a quarter of the loss without exchange rate term (Table 9-7, last column).

Table 9-6 Performance of simple monetary policy rules, complements

Rule		Standard deviation					Loss	
		π_A^A	π^A	Y^A	ΔS_C^A	C^A	**CB**	**ERM2**
Rule 1	*domestic inflation targeting*	0.33	1.35	0.8	4.59	0.56	1.23	12.67
Rule 2	*CPI inflation targeting*	0.46	0.37	1.11	4.71	0.70	0.68	11.85
Rule 3	*domestic inflation Taylor rule*	0.19	1.57	0.70	5.76	0.52	1.49	19.34
Rule 4	*CPI inflation Taylor rule*	0.77	1.03	0.99	5.96	0.64	1.02	19.33
Rule 5	*domestic inflation ERM 2*	1.65	1.86	1.01	1.69	0.67	2.24	5.40
Rule 6	*CPI inflation ERM 2*	1.51	1.43	1.10	1.91	0.71	1.63	4.48
Rule 7	*domestic Taylor ERM 2*	1.39	1.71	0.96	2.28	0.65	1.92	5.98
Rule 8	*CPI Taylor ERM 2*	1.24	1.22	1.05	2.44	0.68	1.30	5.02

Source: Author's estimation

Table 9-7 Ratio of loss for joining ERM 2, complements

Ratio	Rule	Loss CB	Loss ERM 2
Rule 5 / Rule 1	domestic inflation targeting	1.82	0.43
Rule 6 / Rule 2	CPI inflation targeting	2.39	0.38
Rule 7 / Rule 3	domestic inflation Taylor rule	1.29	0.31
Rule 8 / Rule 4	CPI inflation Taylor rule	1.28	0.26

Source: Author's calculations

Technology Shock II: Countries A and B Producing Substitutes

As it was in the case with countries *A* and *B* producing complements, the technology shock in country *B* increases consumption in all three countries by the same amount due to perfect international risk sharing when the two periphery countries produce strong substitutes (Figure 9-4). This time, however, the technology shock goes one to one into country *B*'s output. As not only country *A* but also country *C* produces substitutes to country *B*, output declines in both countries. Without a reaction of monetary policy to the shock, CPI inflation would decline in all three countries. However, country *A* conducting monetary policy with a CPI inflation Taylor rule (Rule 4), the central bank reacts evenly to inflation and output (Figure 9-4, left column). Table 9-8 shows how the volatility in domestic and CPI inflation as well as output falls when moving from strict inflation targeting (Rules 1 and 2) to a Taylor rule (Rules 3 and 4). As a result of the central bank lowering the interest rate to accommodate the decline in output, inflation in country *A* increases slightly.

Figure 9-4 Technology shock in a three-country model, substitutes

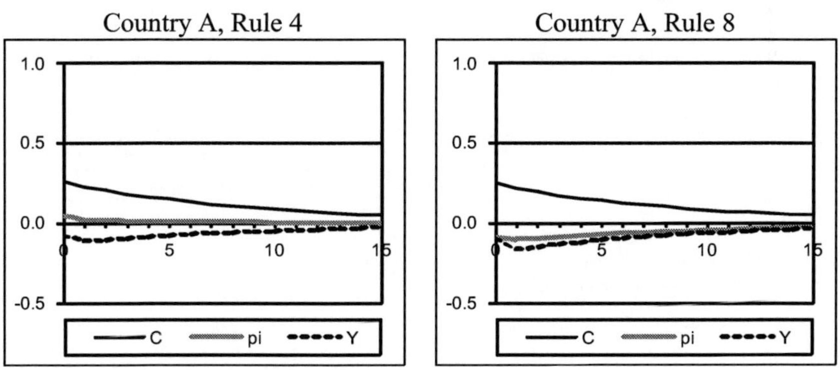

Figure 9-4 (cont.)

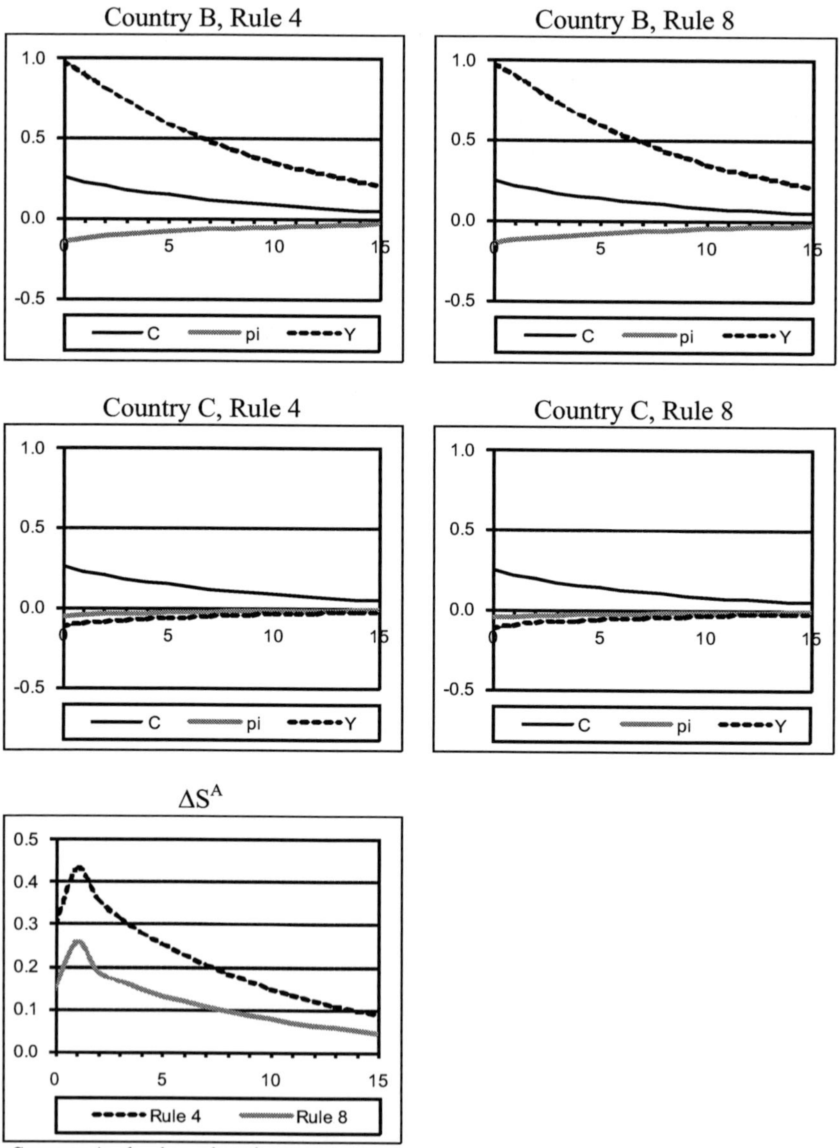

Source: Author's estimation

In the case of substitutes, the technology shock in country *B* affects only a little the exchange rate between countries *A* and *C*. The magnitude of the exchange rate reaction to the external shock is small with the peak of the devaluation at only 0.43 standard deviations compared to the peak of the appreciation at 2.07 standard deviations in the case of complements. Thus, moving to a monetary policy rule consistent with ERM 2, where the interest rate reacts also to movements in the exchange rate (Rule 8), exhibits less changes in the impulse responses as seen before in the case of complements in Figure 9-3. Table 9-8 shows that volatility in the domestic and CPI inflation as well as output has to increase in order to reduce volatility in the exchange rate (Rules 1 to 4 versus Rules 5 to 8).

Concerning the consequences for the loss function (Loss CB), adding the exchange rate more than doubles the loss for all four rules (Table 9-9). However, the loss for the classical CPI inflation Taylor rule increases 2.79-times when the exchange rate term is incorporated. For the strict inflation targeting rules (Rules 1 and 2), the loss for an ERM 2 central bank (Loss ERM 2) is virtually alike with or without the exchange rate term as the ratio is close to 1. For the two Taylor rules (Rules 3 and 4), the loss halves.

Table 9-8 Performance of simple monetary policy rules, substitutes

Rule		Standard deviation					Loss	
		π_A^A	π^A	Y^A	ΔS_C^A	C^A	CB	ERM2
Rule 1	*domestic inflation targeting*	0.16	0.19	0.38	0.63	0.56	0.09	0.310
Rule 2	*CPI inflation targeting*	0.18	0.20	0.35	0.65	0.57	0.08	0.309
Rule 3	*domestic inflation Taylor rule*	0.08	0.10	0.30	0.96	0.58	0.05	0.512
Rule 4	*CPI inflation Taylor rule*	0.07	0.06	0.28	0.95	0.59	0.04	0.499
Rule 5	*domestic inflation ERM 2*	0.41	0.44	0.45	0.30	0.55	0.20	0.340
Rule 6	*CPI inflation ERM 2*	0.43	0.45	0.43	0.31	0.55	0.19	0.342
Rule 7	*domestic Taylor ERM 2*	0.26	0.28	0.40	0.51	0.56	0.12	0.290
Rule 8	*CPI Taylor ERM 2*	0.27	0.29	0.39	0.51	0.56	0.12	0.290

Source: Author's estimation

Table 9-9 Ratio of loss for joining ERM 2, substitutes

Ratio	Rule	Loss CB	Loss ERM 2
Rule 5 / Rule 1	domestic inflation targeting	2.17	1.10
Rule 6 / Rule 2	CPI inflation targeting	2.40	1.11
Rule 7 / Rule 3	domestic inflation Taylor rule	2.41	0.57
Rule 8 / Rule 4	CPI inflation Taylor rule	2.79	0.58

Source: Author's calculations

Table 9-10 Ranking of simple monetary policy rules

Rule		Complements		Substitutes		Sum	
		Loss CB	Loss ERM 2	Loss CB	Loss ERM 2	Loss CB	Loss ERM 2
Rule 1	*domestic inflation targeting*	3	6	4	4	7	10
Rule 2	*CPI inflation targeting*	1	5	3	3	4	8
Rule 3	*domestic inflation Taylor rule*	5	8	2	8	7	16
Rule 4	*CPI inflation Taylor rule*	2	7	1	7	3	14
Rule 5	*domestic inflation ERM 2*	8	3	8	5	16	8
Rule 6	*CPI inflation ERM 2*	6	1	7	6	13	7
Rule 7	*domestic Taylor ERM 2*	7	4	6	1	13	5
Rule 8	*CPI Taylor ERM 2*	4	2	5	2	9	4

Source: Author's calculations

The evaluation of simple monetary policy rules leads us to the following conclusions (Table 9-10). For countries *A* and *B* producing complements the CPI inflation Taylor rule with exchange rate smoothing (Rule 8), shows in the ranking a remarkably good performance for Loss ERM 2. Under Loss CB, this rule even outperforms the domestic inflation Taylor rule (Rule 3). For countries *A* and *B* producing substitutes, each of the monetary policy rules without an exchange rate term performs better than the rules that are in line with ERM 2 under the traditional central bank loss function. This result does not hold when adjusting the central bank loss function to take into account exchange rate smoothing (Loss ERM 2). The last two columns of Table 9-10 serve as a robustness check in case the kind of production sharing is not known. Under a traditional central bank loss function (Loss CB) the best performance is given by Rule 4, the traditional CPI inflation Taylor rule. In case the central bank operates under ERM 2 (Loss ERM 2), the best results are achieved by the CPI inflation Taylor rule with exchange rate smoothing (Rule 8).

Robustness Checks

As a robustness check, we introduce home bias in consumption in all three countries by setting the parameter for openness, η, equal to 0.5. The home bias affects also the nested consumption basket as we could think of a bias not only towards home goods but also towards goods from the periphery countries generally. The altered trade shares are shown in Table 9-11. Country *A* trades not anymore as much as before with countries *B* and *C*. The technology shock in country *B* affects country *A* less, leading to strictly lower losses for the central bank. The ranking of the eight monetary policy rules alters only little in the case of complements and not at all for substitutes (Table 9-12 and Appendix 9-A).

Table 9-11 Trade shares under home bias in consumption

Country *A*	**Country *B***	**Country *C***
$v_A^A = 0.6250$	$v_A^B = 0.2083$	$v_A^C = 0.1667$
$v_B^A = 0.2083$	$v_B^B = 0.6250$	$v_B^C = 0.1667$
$v_C^A = 0.1667$	$v_C^B = 0.1667$	$v_C^C = 0.6667$

Source: Author's calculations

Note: Trade shares are based on relative country size n_A = 0.5 and n_P = 2/3 and degree of openness η = 0.5.

Table 9-12 Ranking of simple monetary policy rules

Rule		Complements		Substitutes		Sum	
		Loss CB	Loss ERM 2	Loss CB	Loss ERM 2	Loss CB	Loss ERM 2
Rule 1	*domestic inflation targeting*	2	5	4	4	6	9
Rule 2	*CPI inflation targeting*	1	6	3	3	4	9
Rule 3	*domestic inflation Taylor rule*	4	7	2	8	6	15
Rule 4	*CPI inflation Taylor rule*	3	8	1	7	4	15
Rule 5	*domestic inflation ERM 2*	8	3	8	5	16	8
Rule 6	*CPI inflation ERM 2*	7	1	7	6	14	7
Rule 7	*domestic Taylor ERM 2*	6	4	6	1	12	5
Rule 8	*CPI Taylor ERM 2*	5	2	5	2	10	4

Source: Author's calculations

Optimal Simple Rules in a Three-Country Model

In this section, we identify optimal monetary policy rules by minimizing the central bank loss function. The Matlab routine "fminsearch" is an unconstrained non-linear optimization using the Simplex search method of Lagarias et al. (1998). The method does not rely on numerical or analytical gradients and may therefore handle discontinuity. The search starts from initial values and may only give a local solution. We take the parameters of the respective simple monetary policy rules specified in Table 9-5 as starting values. As the method is unconstrained, it searches the entire parameter space and may find optimal coefficients minimizing the loss for implausible policy parameters.

To circumvent this problem, we follow Schmitt-Grohé and Uribe (2007) and conduct additionally a grid search.[9] Rules 3 to 6 are evaluated on a grid in 0.05 steps for $\varphi_{\pi_i^i}$ or φ_{π^i} from 1 to 3 and for φ_Y or φ_S from 0 to 1.51. The grid for Rules 7 and 8 is in 0.1 steps for $\varphi_{\pi_i^i}$ or φ_{π^i} from 1 to 3 and for φ_Y or φ_S from 0 to 1.51. Our interpretation focuses on the optimal simple rules based on that grid search. We limit our attention on the traditional Taylor rule (Rule 4) and its ERM 2 counterpart with an exchange rate term (Rule 8).[10]

The traditional central bank loss function (Loss CB) minimizes the volatility in CPI inflation and output. All results in Tables 9-13 and 9-15, including those based on "fminsearch", in general adhere to the Taylor principle (Woodford, 2003). Most of the time, there is no role for targeting the exchange rate as the respective coefficient is zero. Only in the case of complements, Rules 6 and 8 find a positive but small coefficient for the exchange rate term (Table 9-13). In the analysis of simple monetary policy rules, we already saw that the exchange rate between countries *A* and *C* is hardly affected in the case of substitutes. However, in the case of complements, the exchange rate bears part of the macroeconomic adjustment. The exchange rate plays a more important role in the model with complements than in the model with substitutes. The analysis of optimal simple rules confirms the findings of Svensson (2003, 442), who states: "A first obvious problem for a Taylor-type rule, with or without interest-rate smoothing, is that, if there are other important state variables than inflation and the output gap, it will not be optimal." The numerical analysis reveals that the exchange rate approximates other important state variables of the model in the case of complements but not in the case of substitutes. Having an additional policy parameter available pays off as even a small exchange rate coefficient of 0.1 reduces the central bank loss to 0.64 down from 0.67 (Table 9-13, Rules 4 and 8).

If the loss function captures the requirements of ERM 2 (Loss ERM 2) and therefore the central bank aims to additionally reduce volatility in the exchange rate, the monetary policy rules with the lowest loss include the exchange rate as a target. If the central bank includes an exchange rate in the monetary policy rule, the Taylor principle is occasionally violated (Tables 9-14 and 9-16). For a technology shock being the only disturbance, the optimal coefficients are in general lower for production sharing via complements than via substitutes. In the latter case, the exchange rate has the same weight as inflation (Table 9-16, Rule 8). This result applies also with home bias in consumption (see more in Table 9-B4 in Appendix 9-B).

Table 9-13 Optimal simple rules, complements, Loss CB

Rule	**Method**	$\varphi_{\pi_i^i}$	φ_{π^i}	φ_Y	φ_S	**Loss CB**
Rule 1	F	1.2957	---	---	---	1.2196
Rule 2	F	---	2.0104	---	---	0.6696
Rule 3	F	1.2956	---	0.0001	---	1.2196
	G	1.3	---	0	---	1.2196
Rule 4	F	---	1.0025	-0.1625	---	0.6462
	G	---	2	0	---	0.6696
Rule 5	F	1.0315	---	---	-0.0280	1.1897
	G	1.3	---	---	0	1.2196
Rule 6	F	---	1.1501	---	0.0268	0.6365
	G	---	1.6	---	0.05	0.6453
Rule 7	F	1.0271	---	0.0223	-0.0244	1.1937
	G	1.3	---	0	0	1.2196
Rule 8	F	---	0.9866	-0.0646	0.0129	0.6363
	G	---	2	0.3	0.1	0.6377

Source: Author's estimation. Note: F is "fminsearch" and G is "grid search"

Table 9-14 Optimal simple rules, complements, Loss ERM 2

Rule	**Method**	$\varphi_{\pi_i^i}$	φ_{π^i}	φ_Y	φ_S	**Loss ERM 2**
Rule 1	F	1.2957	---	---	---	1.2196
Rule 2	F	---	2.0104	---	---	0.6696
Rule 3	F	1.2956	---	0.0001	---	1.2196
	G	1.3	---	0	---	1.2196
Rule 4	F	---	1.0025	-0.1625	---	0.6462
	G	---	2	0	---	0.6696
Rule 5	F	1.0315	---	---	-0.0280	1.1897
	G	1.3	---	---	0	1.2196
Rule 6	F	---	1.1501	---	0.0268	0.6365
	G	---	1.6	---	0.05	0.6453
Rule 7	F	1.0271	---	0.0223	-0.0244	1.1937
	G	1.3	---	0	0	1.2196
Rule 8	F	---	0.9866	-0.0646	0.0129	0.6363
	G	---	2	0.3	0.1	0.6377

Source: Author's estimation. Note: F is "fminsearch" and G is "grid search".

Table 9-15 Optimal simple rules, substitutes, Loss CB

Rule	Method	$\varphi_{\pi_i^i}$	φ_{π^i}	φ_Y	φ_S	Loss CB
Rule 1	F	6.3215 e+006	---	---	---	0.0570
Rule 2	F	---	2.4712 e+012	---	---	0.0401
Rule 3	F	30.104	---	11.853	---	0.0496
	G	2.55	---	1	---	0.0496
Rule 4	F	---	1.1871 e+009	736,56 7	---	0.0401
	G	---	3	0.95	---	0.0406
Rule 5	F	3.1654 e+008	---	---	-1.2515 e+006	0.0570
	G	3	---	---	0	0.0643
Rule 6	F	---	6.4676 e+007	---	-4.5584 e+006	0.0372
	G	---	3	---	0	0.0480
Rule 7	F	1.0406	---	0.2350	-0.0462	0.0509
	G	1.1	---	1.5	0.3	0.0467
Rule 8	F	---	1.3221	-0.2446	-0.2122	0.0310
	G	---	3	0.9	0	0.0406

Table 9-16 Optimal simple rules, substitutes, Loss ERM 2

Rule	Method	$\varphi_{\pi_i^i}$	φ_{π^i}	φ_Y	φ_S	Loss ERM 2
Rule 1	F	1.2746	---	---	---	0.2947
Rule 2	F	---	1.3027	---	---	0.2935
Rule 3	F	1.2744	---	0.0001	---	0.2947
	G	1.2	---	0.05	---	0.2948
Rule 4	F	---	0.9937	0.2053	---	0.2905
	G	---	1	0.2	---	0.2906
Rule 5	F	2.9138	---	---	0.7985	0.2895
	G	2.9	---	---	0.8	0.2895
Rule 6	F	---	1.3613	---	0.0320	0.2935
	G	---	1.4	---	0.05	0.2935
Rule 7	F	2.9551	---	-0.0589	0.7731	0.2895
	G	2.2	---	1.1	1.3	0.2895
Rule 8	F	---	0.6994	1.6413	0.9747	0.2894
	G	---	1	1.5	1	0.2895

Source: Author's estimation. Note: F is "fminsearch" and G is "grid search"

Conclusion

We analyse monetary policy given alternative degrees of integration between the euro area, an inflation targeting accession country like the Czech Republic, Hungary, Poland and Slovakia and a non-EU country as the third country.

The model developed here is based on Teo (2005) and Monacelli (2001) and allows us to simulate the impact of a technology shock originating in a third country on an accession country considering feedback from the euro area as well. The New Keynesian three-country model incorporates explicit microfoundations with dynamic and intertemporal effects as well as Keynesian building blocks such as nominal rigidities and monopolistic competition. The core equations, i.e., the IS curve, the Phillips curve and the monetary policy rule, are derived following Galí and Monacelli (2005). As a short cut for modelling production linkages, we use alternative elasticities in consumption baskets. This allows us to trace the transmission mechanism of a third-country technology shock in the alternative cases that a third country produces complements or substitutes, i.e., that a third country is vertically or horizontally integrated with the accession country.

Evaluating the central bank loss function without ERM 2 (Loss CB) and with ERM 2 (Loss ERM 2) under strict inflation targeting and Taylor rules as well as both types of rules extended by exchange rate smoothing allows us to assess the costs of ERM 2 and derive the implications of production sharing for monetary policy. Optimal rules are derived by minimizing the central bank loss function. The Matlab routine "fminsearch" uses the entire parameter space and therefore tends to find optimal coefficients minimizing the loss for implausible policy parameters. To circumvent this problem, we follow Schmitt-Grohé and Uribe (2007) and conduct additionally a grid search.

The simulations reveal the following results. First, we revisit an asymmetric shock in a two-country model. A common monetary policy cannot address the implications of a technology shock on inflation and output adequately. Under production sharing via complements, inflation in one country is negatively correlated with inflation in the other country. If the two countries produce strong substitutes, output is negatively correlated.

Second, our simulations of a third-country technology shock show that the exchange rate between the accession country and the anchor currency country bears part of the adjustment if production sharing is via complements, but only little if the accession country and the third-country produce strong substitutes.

Third, our evaluation of simple monetary policy rules reveals that targeting the exchange rate, if the central bank has no exchange rate objective (Loss CB), increases the loss. The loss more than doubles in case the accession country and the third country produce substitutes. If the loss of the central bank takes into account the volatility of the exchange rate (Loss ERM 2), the CPI inflation Taylor rule augmented for exchange rate smoothing performs well under any type of production sharing.

Fourth, our results for optimal monetary policy rules depend on the assumed loss function of the central bank. For a traditional central bank loss function (Loss CB), minimizing volatility in CPI inflation and output, the exchange rate generally does not matter. However, having an additional policy parameter still pays off in the case of complements as even a small exchange rate coefficient of 0.1 reduces the central bank loss. If the loss function captures the requirements of ERM 2 (Loss ERM 2), i.e., exchange rate smoothing is an objective of the central bank, allowing for a reaction of the interest rate to the exchange rate lowers the loss. Further, the optimal coefficients are lower for production sharing via complements than via substitutes. In the latter case, the exchange rate has in fact the same coefficient in the optimal monetary policy rule as inflation.

All in all, the results show that a Taylor rule extended for an exchange rate term is a good simple rule for different kinds of integration with a third country and even in case the loss function does not account for a preference for exchange rate smoothing.

References

Ascari, G. and C. Merkl. 2008. Real Wage Rigidities and the Cost of Disinflations. *Journal of Money, Credit and Banking,* forthcoming.

Backus, D.K., P.J. Kehoe and F.E. Kydland. 1995. International Business Cycles: Theory vs. Evidence. In *Frontiers of Business Cycle Research,* ed. Thomas F. Cooley, 331-56. Princeton, NJ: Princeton University Press.

Benigno, P. 2004. Optimal Monetary Policy in a Currency Area. *Journal of International Economics* 63(2): 293-320.

Benigno, P. and M. Woodford. 2007. *Linear-Quadratic Approximation of Optimal Policy Problems.* Mimeo. Columbia University, New York.

Burstein, A., C. Kurz and L. Tesar. 2008. Trade, Production Sharing, and the International Transmission of Business Cycles. *Journal of Monetary Economics*, forthcoming.

Calvo, G. 1983. Staggered Prices in a Utility-Maximizing Framework. *Journal of Monetary Economics* 12(3): 383-98.

Campbell, J.Y. 1994. Inspecting the Mechanism: An Analytical Approach to the Stochastic Growth Model. *Journal of Monetary Economics* 33(3): 463-506.

Clarida, R., J. Galí and M. Gertler. 2001. Optimal Monetary Policy in Open versus Closed Economies: An Integrated Approach. *American Economic Review* 91(2): 248-52

Corsetti, G., P. Pesenti, N. Roubini and C. Tille. 2000. Competitive Devaluations: Toward a Welfare-Based Approach. *Journal of International Economics* 51(1): 217-41.

Crespo, N. and M.P. Fontoura. 2007. Integration of CEECs into EU Market: Structural Change and Convergence. *Journal of Common Market Studies* 45(3): 611-32.

De Paoli, B. 2006. *Monetary Policy and Welfare in a Small Open Economy.* CEP Discussion Paper 639. Centre for Economic Performance, London.

Faia, E. 2007. Financial Differences and Business Cycle Co-Movements in a Currency Area. *Journal of Money, Credit and Banking* 39(1): 151-85.

Faia, E. and T. Monacelli. 2004. *Ramsey Monetary Policy and International Relative Prices.* European Central Bank Working Paper 344. European Central Bank, Frankfurt am Main.

—. 2008. Optimal Monetary Policy in a Small Open Economy with Home Bias. *Journal of Money, Credit and Banking* 40(4): 721-50.

Fontagné, L. and M. Freudenberg. 1999. Endogenous Symmetry of Shocks in a Monetary Union. *Open Economies Review* 10(3): 263-87.

Frömmel, M. and F. Schobert. 2006. *Monetary Policy Rules in Central and Eastern Europe.* Discussion Paper 341. University of Hanover, Hanover.

Galí, J. 2003. New Perspectives on Monetary Policy, Inflation, and the Business Cycle. In *Advances in Economics and Econometrics: Theory and Applications*, ed. M. Dewatriport, L.P. Hansen and S. J. Turnovsky, 151-97. Cambridge: Cambridge University Press.

—. 2008. Monetary Policy and the Open Economy. In *Monetary Policy, Inflation, and the Business Cycle*, ed. J. Galí, 149-84. Princeton, NJ: Princeton University Press.

Galí, J. and T. Monacelli. 2005. Monetary Policy and Exchange Rate Volatility in a Small Open Economy. *Review of Economic Studies* 72(3): 707-34.

Ghironi, F. 2006. Macroeconomic Interdependence under Incomplete Markets. *Journal of International Economics* 70(2): 428-50.

Hammermann, F. 2005. Do Exchange Rates Matter in Inflation Targeting Regimes? Evidence from a VAR Analysis for Poland and Chile. In *Monetary Policy and Macroeconomic Stabilization in Latin America*, ed. R.J. Langhammer and L. Vinhas de Souza, 115-48. Berlin: Springer.

Imbs, J. 2004. Trade, Finance, Specialization, and Synchronization. *Review of Economics and Statistics* 86(3): 723-34.

IMF. 2007. Decoupling the Train? Spillovers and Cycles in the Global Economy. In *World Economic Outlook: April 2007*, ed. International Monetary Fund, 121-161.Washington, DC.

Kalemli-Ozcan, S., B.E. Sørensen and O. Yosha. 2003. Risk Sharing and Industrial Specialization: Regional and International Evidence. *American Economic Review* 93(3): 903-18.

Kim, J. and S.H. Kim. 2007. Two Pitfalls of Linearization Methods. *Journal of Money, Credit and Banking* 39(4): 995-1001.

King, R.G., C.I. Plosser and S.T. Rebelo. 1988. Production, Growth and Business Cycles I: The Basic Neoclassical Model. *Journal of Monetary Economics* 21(2-3): 195-232.

—. 2002. Production, Growth and Business Cycles: Technical Appendix. *Computational Economics* 20(1-2): 87-116.

Kose, M.A., C. Otrok and C.H. Whiteman. 2003. International Business Cycles: World, Region, and Country-Specific Factors. *American Economic Review* 93(4): 1216-39.

Kose, M.A., E.S. Prasad and M. Terrones. 2003. How Does Globalization Affect the Synchronization of Business Cycles? *American Economic Review* 93(2): 56-62.

Krusec, D. 2005. *Is Inflation Targeting Effective? Monetary Transmission in Poland, the Czech Republic, Slovakia and Hungary.* Mimeo. European University Institute, Firenze.

Kydland, F.E. and E.C. Prescott. 1982. Time to Build and Aggregate Fluctuations. *Econometrica* 50(6): 1345-70.

Lagarias, J.C., J.A. Reeds, M.H. Wright and P.E. Wright. 1998. Convergence Properties of the Nelder-Mead Simplex Method in Low Dimensions. *SIAM Journal of Optimization* 9(1): 112-47.

Lipińska, A. 2006. *The Maastricht Convergence Criteria and Optimal Monetary Policy for the EMU Accession Countries.* Mimeo. London School of Economics, London.

Liu, Z. and E. Pappa. 2007. Gains from International Monetary Policy Coordination: Does It Pay to Be Different? *Journal of Economic Dynamics and Control*, forthcoming.

Marin, D. 2006. A New International Division of Labor in Europe: Outsourcing and Offshoring to Eastern Europe. *Journal of the European Economic Association* 4(2-3): 612-22.

Miranda, M.J. and P.L. Fackler. 2002. *Applied Computational Economic and Finance.* Cambridge, MA: MIT Press.

Mohanty, M.S. and M. Klau. 2005. Monetary Policy Rules in Emerging Market Economies: Issues and Evidence. In *Monetary Policy and Macroeconomic Stabilization in Latin America*, ed. R.J. Langhammer and L. Vinhas de Souza, 205-45. Berlin: Springer.

Monacelli, T. 2001. New International Monetary Arrangements and the Exchange Rate. *International Journal of Finance and Economics* 6(4): 389-400.

Mundell, R.A. 1961. A Theory of Optimal Currency Areas. *American Economic Review* 51(4): 657-65.

Orlowski, L.T. and K. Rybinski. 2006. Implications of ERM2 for Poland's Monetary Policy. *Economic Systems* 30(4): 346-65.

Pappa, E. 2004. Do the ECB and the Fed really Need to Cooperate? Optimal Monetary Policy in a Two-Country World. *Journal of Monetary Economics* 51(4): 753-79.

Schmitt-Grohé, S. and M. Uribe. 2003. Closing Small Open Economy Models. *Journal of International Economics* 61(1): 163-85.

—. 2007. Optimal Simple and Implementable Monetary and Fiscal Rules. *Journal of Monetary Economics* 54(6): 1702-25.

Svensson, L.E.O. 2000. Open-Economy Inflation Targeting. *Journal of International Economics* 50(1): 155-83.

—. 2003. What Is Wrong with Taylor Rules? Using Judgement in Monetary Policy through Targeting Rules. *Journal of Economic Literature* 41(2): 426-77.

Taylor, J.B. 1993. Discretion Versus Policy Rules in Practice. *Carnegie-Rochester Conference Series on Public Policy* 39: 195-214.

Teo, W.L. 2005. *Should East Asia's Currencies Be Pegged to the Yen? The Role of Invoice Currency.* Mimeo. Johns Hopkins University, Baltimore, MD.

Uhlig, H. 1999. A Toolkit for Analysing Nonlinear Dynamic Stochastic Models Easily. In *Computational Methods for the Study of Dynamic*

Economies, ed. R. Marimon and A. Scott, 30-61. Oxford: Oxford University Press.

Woodford, M. 2003. *Interest and Prices: Foundations of a Theory of Monetary Policy.* Princeton, NJ: Princeton University Press.

Notes

* I would like to thank Paul Bergin, Alper Çenesiz, Ester Faia, Jordi Galí, Rafael Gerke, Rolf Langhammer, Thomas Lux, Tommaso Monacelli, Christian Pierdzioch, Rainer Schweickert, Mewael Tesfaselassie, and Roland Winkler as well as seminar and conference participants at the University of Kiel and the Silesian University in Karviná for helpful comments and suggestions. This study was written during my time at the Kiel Institute for the World Economy. I am also grateful for the hospitality of the Universitat Pompeu Fabra and financial support of the German Academic Exchange Service (DAAD) as well as the Monetary Stability Foundation of the Deutsche Bundesbank. The views expressed are my own and do not involve the responsibility of the institutions mentioned above. I am responsible for all remaining shortcomings.

[1] Slovakia had an implicit inflation target since 1999.

[2] The currency board countries Estonia, Latvia and Lithuania are already in ERM 2; Slovenia adopted the euro in January 2007.

[3] Each asset in the portfolio B^{i}_{t+1} pays one unit of country *C*'s currency at time $t+1$ and in state h^{t+1}.

[4] The detailed optimization is available upon request.

[5] External shocks would not affect the home country under complete markets and logarithmic utility (Ghironi, 2006, 429).

[6] In this two-country example both central banks target domestic inflation.

[7] In principle, the model could be extended to the analysis of monetary shocks. Such a shock could be implemented by a reduction in the third country's interest rate, which could be interpreted as a competitive devaluation or contagion following a financial crisis. The evaluation of simple monetary policy rules could give insights on the strategic costs of ERM 2 and giving up a floating exchange rate for the accession country. We leave this for future research and focus on a third-country technology shock.

[8] In principle, it would be possible to calculate welfare as a second-order approximation to the representative agent's utility function, see Benigno (2004), Pappa (2004), De Paoli (2006), Lipińska (2006) and Liu and Pappa (2007). We take the perspective of the policy maker and focus on the central bank's loss function.

[9] Rules 1 and 2 are only one-dimensional and are therefore not evaluated on a grid. The density of the grid needs to be adjusted in the case of three parameters to avoid the well-known curse of dimensionality (Miranda and Fackler, 2002).

[10] The results with home bias in consumption are extremely similar (Tables in Appendix 9-B).

Appendix 9-A

Technology Shock with Home Bias in Consumption

Figure 9-A1 Technology shock in a three-country model, complements, home bias ($\eta = 0.5$)

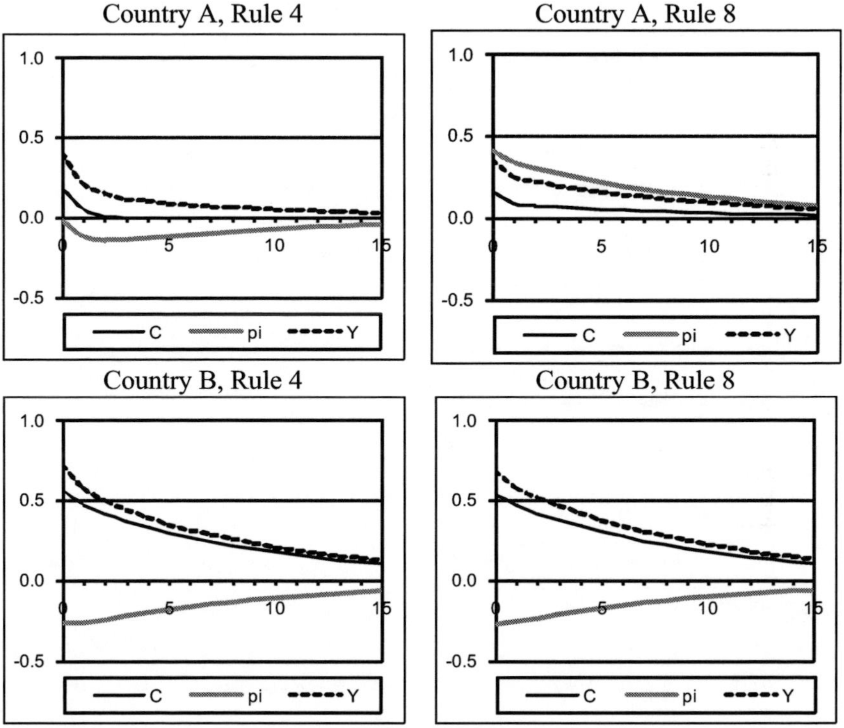

Figure 9-A1 (cont.)

Country C, Rule 4

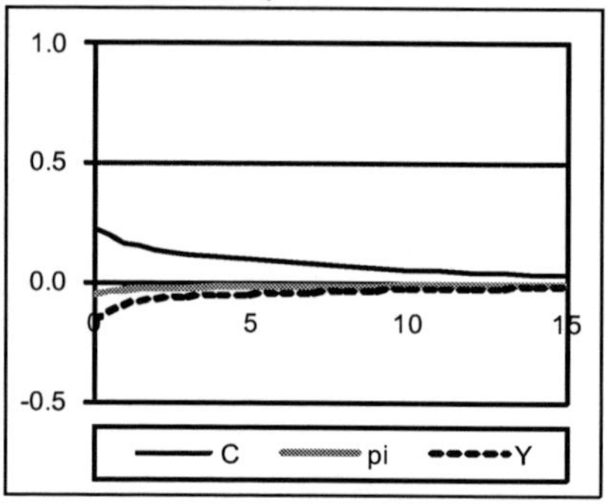

Country C, Rule 8

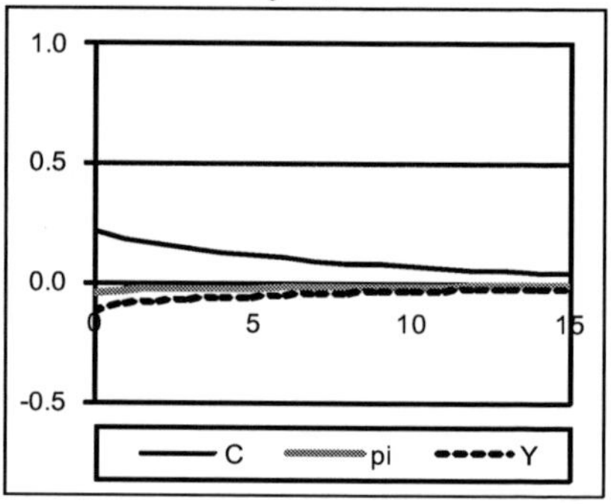

ΔS^A

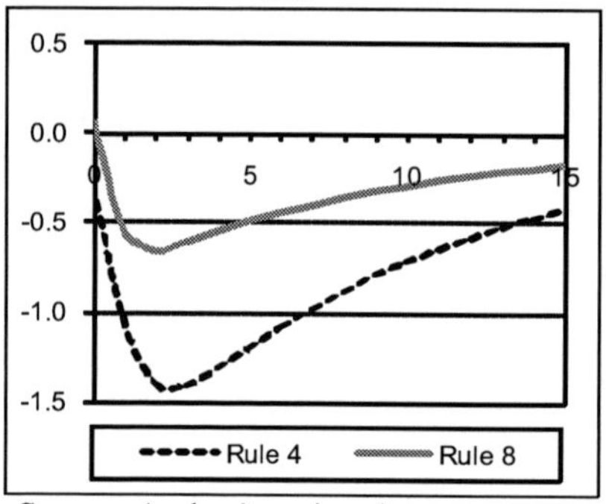

Source: Author's estimation

Table 9-A1 Performance of simple monetary policy rules, complements, home bias

Rule		**Standard deviation**					**Loss**	
		π_A^A	π^A	Y^A	ΔS_C^A	C^A	**CB**	**ERM 2**
Rule 1	*domestic inflation targeting*	0.20	0.60	0.48	3.06	0.09	0.298	5.1600
Rule 2	*CPI inflation targeting*	0.18	0.26	0.63	3.20	0.25	0.234	5.3750
Rule 3	*domestic inflation Taylor rule*	0.11	0.69	0.41	3.70	0.04	0.321	7.3843
Rule 4	*CPI inflation Taylor rule*	0.37	0.56	0.54	3.82	0.19	0.304	7.7696
Rule 5	*domestic inflation ERM 2*	1.15	1.18	0.67	1.19	0.26	0.921	2.3208
Rule 6	*CPI inflation ERM 2*	1.07	1.02	0.71	1.29	0.29	0.778	2.1325
Rule 7	*domestic Taylor ERM 2*	0.96	1.03	0.63	1.56	0.22	0.728	2.4756
Rule 8	*CPI Taylor ERM 2*	0.88	0.86	0.67	1.63	0.25	0.596	2.2995

Source: Author's estimation

Table 9-A2 Ratio of loss for joining ERM 2, complements, home bias

Ratio	**Rule**	**Loss CB**	**Loss ERM 2**
Rule 5 / Rule 1	domestic inflation targeting	3.09	0.45
Rule 6 / Rule 2	CPI inflation targeting	3.32	0.40
Rule 7 / Rule 3	domestic inflation Taylor rule	2.27	0.34
Rule 8 / Rule 4	CPI inflation Taylor rule	1.96	0.30

Source: Author's calculations

Figure 9-A2 Technology shock in a three-country model, substitutes, home bias ($\eta = 0.5$)

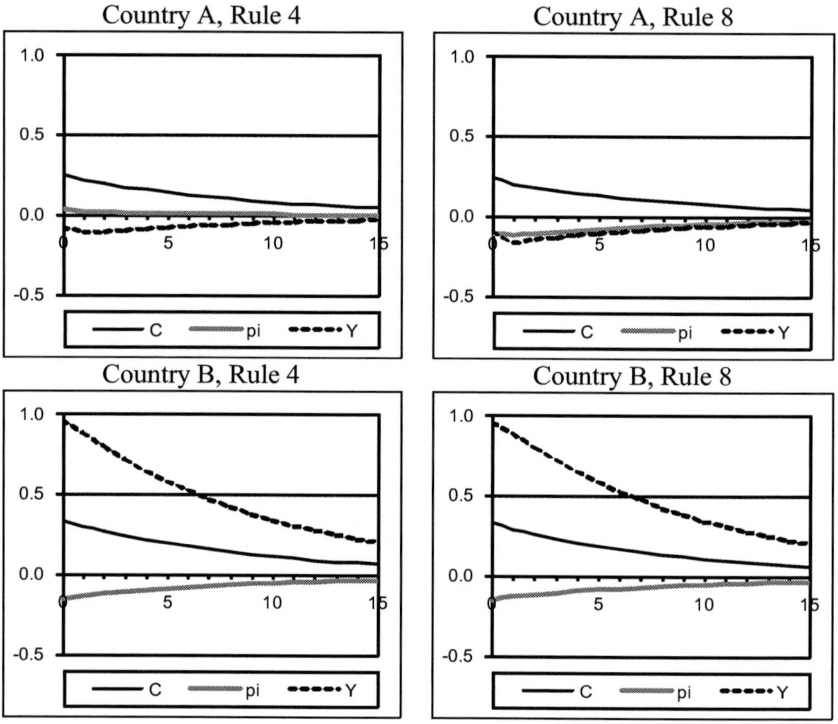

Figure 9-A2 (cont.)

Country C, Rule 4

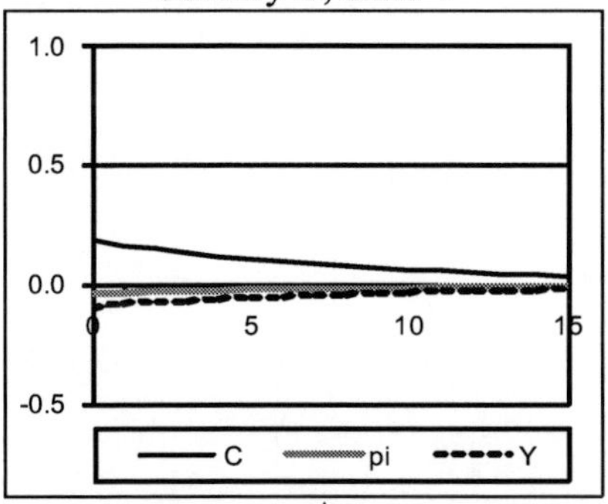

Country C, Rule 8

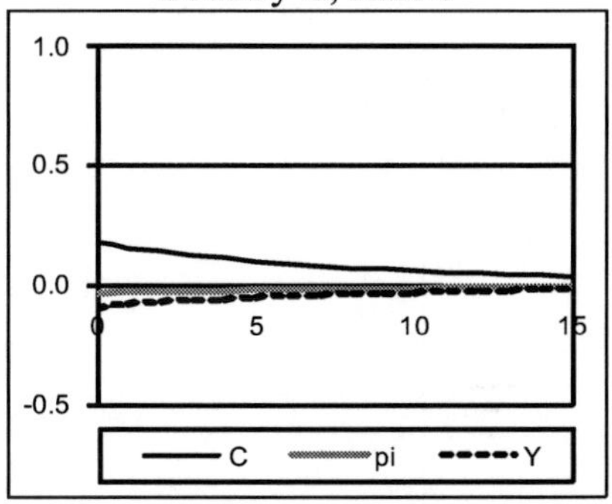

ΔS^A

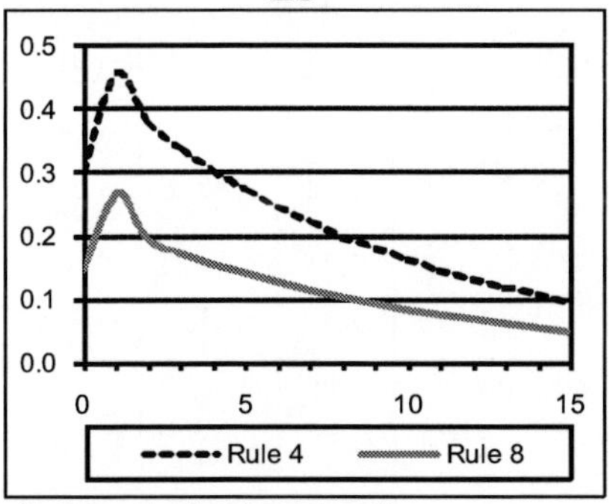

Source: Author's estimation

Table 9-A3 Performance of simple monetary policy rules, substitutes, home bias

Rule		Standard deviation					Loss	
		π_A^A	π^A	Y^A	ΔS_C^A	C^A	**CB**	**ERM 2**
Rule 1	*domestic inflation targeting*	0.15	0.18	0.37	0.70	0.53	0.084	0.3438
Rule 2	*CPI inflation targeting*	0.18	0.19	0.35	0.70	0.54	0.078	0.3423
Rule 3	*domestic inflation Taylor rule*	0.08	0.09	0.29	1.02	0.56	0.047	0.5732
Rule 4	*CPI inflation Taylor rule*	0.06	0.06	0.28	1.02	0.56	0.041	0.5603
Rule 5	*domestic inflation ERM 2*	0.43	0.45	0.45	0.33	0.51	0.199	0.3531
Rule 6	*CPI inflation ERM 2*	0.44	0.46	0.43	0.33	0.51	0.198	0.3573
Rule 7	*domestic Taylor ERM 2*	0.28	0.30	0.40	0.53	0.52	0.123	0.3097
Rule 8	*CPI Taylor ERM 2*	0.29	0.30	0.39	0.54	0.53	0.121	0.3115

Source: Author's estimation

Table 9-A4 Ratio of loss for joining ERM 2, substitutes, home bias

Ratio	Rule	Loss CB	Loss ERM 2
Rule 5 / Rule 1	domestic inflation targeting	2.37	1.03
Rule 6 / Rule 2	CPI inflation targeting	2.54	1.04
Rule 7 / Rule 3	domestic inflation Taylor rule	2.63	0.54
Rule 8 / Rule 4	CPI inflation Taylor rule	3.00	0.56

Source: Author's calculations

Appendix 9-B

Optimal Simple Rules with Home Bias in Consumption

Table 9-B1 Optimal simple rules, complements, home bias, Loss CB

Rule	Method	$\varphi_{\pi_i^i}$	φ_{π^i}	φ_Y	φ_S	Loss CB
Rule 1	F	2.0349	---	---	---	0.2933
Rule 2	F	---	1.2338	---	---	0.2321
Rule 3	F	2.0321	---	0.0007	---	0.2933
	G	1.4	---	0.15	---	0.2933
Rule 4	F	---	1.0010	-0.0493	---	0.2233
	G	---	1.25	0	---	0.2321
Rule 5	F	1.0348	---	---	-0.0316	0.2869
	G	2.05	---	---	0	0.2933
Rule 6	F	---	0.9937	---	0.0057	0.2228
	G	---	1.25	---	0	0.2321
Rule 7	F	7.5924	---	-3.6602	-0.4588	0.2255
	G	1.2	---	0.2	0	0.2933
Rule 8	F	---	0.9899	0.0433	0.0107	0.2227
	G	---	1.7	0.6	0.1	0.2223

Source: Author's estimation. Note: F is "fminsearch" and G is "grid search"

Table 9-B2 Optimal simple rules, complements, home bias, Loss ERM 2

Rule	**Method**	$\varphi_{\pi_i^i}$	φ_{π^i}	φ_Y	φ_S	**Loss ERM 2**
Rule 1	F	1	---	---	---	2.6023
Rule 2	F	---	4.2849 e+012	---	---	4.2976
Rule 3	F	1.0054	---	-0.0910	---	2.2144
	G	1	---	0.05	---	3.0974
Rule 4	F	---	1.0048	-0.2447	---	2.1445
	G	---	3	0	---	4.7546
Rule 5	F	0.9755	---	---	0.0223	2.2214
	G	1	---	---	0.05	2.2303
Rule 6	F	---	0.9363	---	0.0581	2.1060
	G	---	1.05	---	0.15	2.1095
Rule 7	F	0.8876	---	0.2888	0.0970	2.2415
	G	1	---	0.1	0.1	2.2423
Rule 8	F	---	0.9356	0.0023	0.0585	2.1059
	G	---	1	0	0.1	2.1107

Source: Author's estimation. Note: F is "fminsearch" and G is "grid search"

Table 9-B3 Optimal simple rules, substitutes, home bias, Loss CB

Rule	**Method**	$\varphi_{\pi_i^i}$	φ_{π^i}	φ_Y	φ_S	**Loss CB**
Rule 1	F	5.0332 e+006	---	---	---	0.0528
Rule 2	F	---	7.9162 e+012	---	---	0.0382
Rule 3	F	31.182	---	11.854	---	0.0463
	G	1.3	---	0.5	---	0.0463
Rule 4	F	---	3.4862 e+009	2.1631 e+006	---	0.0382
	G	---	3	0.95	---	0.0389
Rule 5	F	2.7036 e+008	---	---	-1.0689 e+006	0.0528
	G	3	---	---	0	0.0594
Rule 6	F	---	2.0715 e+008	---	-1.3076 e+007	0.0353
	G	---	3	---	0	0.0466
Rule 7	F	1.0375	---	0.2283	-0.0427	0.0475
	G	1	---	1.5	0.3	0.0438
Rule 8	F	---	2.6733 e+007	1.1226 e+006	-1.3612 e+006	0.0358
	G	---	3	1	0	0.0390

Source: Author's estimation

Note: F is "fminsearch" and G is "grid search".

Table 9-B4 Optimal simple rules, substitutes, home bias, Loss ERM 2

Rule	**Method**	$\varphi_{\pi_i^i}$	φ_{π^i}	φ_Y	φ_S	**Loss ERM 2**
Rule 1	F	1.2197	---	---	---	0.3128
Rule 2	F	---	1.2526	---	---	0.3130
Rule 3	F	1.2192	---	0.0003	---	0.3128
	G	1.15	---	0.05	---	0.3128
Rule 4	F	---	0.9945	0.1842	---	0.3109
	G	---	1.05	0.15	---	0.3113
Rule 5	F	2.4044	---	---	0.6175	0.3095
	G	2.45	---	---	0.65	0.3095
Rule 6	F	---	1.1226	---	-0.0720	0.3128
	G	---	1.25	---	0	0.3130
Rule 7	F	2.5251	---	-0.1494	0.5695	0.3095
	G	1.9	---	0.6	0.8	0.3095
Rule 8	F	---	-5.3088	16.545	8.9680	0.3094
	G	---	1	1.5	1	0.3100

Source: Author's estimation

Note: F is "fminsearch" and G is "grid search".

CHAPTER TEN

THE EFFECTIVENESS OF THE INTEREST RATE CHANNEL IN THE EU NEW MEMBER STATES

BOGDAN MURARAŞU AND NICOLETA CIURILA

This chapter presents an empirical analysis of the monetary policy interest rate pass-through phenomenon in four EU New Member States: Czech Republic, Hungary, Poland and Romania (NMS hereafter). For this purpose, we estimate four Error Correction Models using the Engle-Granger cointegration approach for each of the countries analysed. The study distinguishes between the response of interest rates charged on loans and interest rates paid for deposits by commercial banks. For each country and for each type of interest rate, we analyse the degree of interest rate pass-through, speed of the pass-through and the size of the contemporary adjustment to the long-term equilibrium. Likewise, for the Czech Republic and Hungary, we determine the responsiveness to monetary policy measures of lending and deposit interest rates used by commercial banks distinctively in their relationship with households and corporate clients. Finally, we conclude about the similarities and differences existing between the four NMS in terms of the monetary policy effectiveness.

Interest Rate Pass-through as a Measure of Monetary Policy Effectiveness

A key issue regarding the transmission mechanism of monetary policy is the extent to which the monetary policy interest rate affects market interest rates, in particular money market rates and, eventually, government bond yields and retail banking lending and deposit rates. The interest rate pass-through from the monetary policy interest rate to the retail interest rates is essential from the monetary policy decision making point of view because changes in the lending and deposit rates affect financial conditions of households and non-financial corporations. The pass-through of monetary policy interest rate changes into other types of interest rates and, hence, monetary policy effectiveness has been a widely analysed topic, especially in the EU countries. This is mainly due to the fact that the speed and degree of the interest rate pass-through of the monetary policy interest rate and money market interest rates into retail banking interest rates quantify the strength of the monetary policy transmission. In the view of joining the euro area where the monetary policy decisions of the European Central Bank must be passed into commercial banks' lending and deposit taking activities in a manner similar to other euro area countries, the interest rate pass-through becomes a topic of outmost importance for the NMS too.

The current framework of the EU enlargement in 2004 and 2007 will be completed by an Eastern enlargement of the euro area. In this context, the nominal convergence – specified through the Maastricht criteria in terms of inflation rates, market interest rates, exchange rates and government budget deficit and debt – plays a central role. The nominal convergence criteria are fulfilled with the need of achieving sufficient integration with the financial system of the euro area. The importance of this topic is twofold: (i) retail banking sector is the least integrated market of the financial sector (Baele et al., 2004), and (ii) differences in the financial structure are the most important cause of national asymmetries in the monetary transmission mechanism generating a less homogenous monetary transmission in the euro area (Cecchetti, 1999). Campa and Gonzalez Minguez (2006) find that in Europe, pass-through is relatively slow and heterogeneous across both financial products and countries. For example, the pass-through is slower for retail banking products such as deposits, consumer loans and mortgages than for corporate products such as corporate loans. Moreover, short-term products are more responsive than long-term products.

The explanation for this weak responsiveness is related to various factors among which we may principally point out the market structure and competition along with the lack of integration in retail banking. Such factors were suggested in Mojon (2000), Sander and Kleimeier (2004), de Bondt (2005) or Sander and Kleimeier (2006). Furthermore, Cottarelli and Kourelis (1994), Borio and Fritz (1995), Mojon et al. (2002) and de Bondt (2002) study the financial structure heterogeneity within the current euro area and other European countries using the interest rate pass-through analysis. These studies find considerable differences in the pass-through across the countries of the euro area. Moreover, the evidence of substantial short-run bank interest rate stickiness and limited evidence for a full pass-through in the long run are also documented. Moreover, it is argued that retail interest rates present an asymmetric adjustment. Finally, the current research shows that the euro adoption could make the pass-through faster, more homogeneous and more complete.

Horváth et al. (2004) find the complete pass-through of market interest rates into corporate loans interest rates in Hungary, while rates on household loans and deposits adjust incompletely or sluggishly. Also, a significant asymmetry is found with respect to the size of the money market interest rate change, the sign of the yield shocks and the volatility of the market rate. Égert et al. (2007) study the interest rate pass-through for five Central and Eastern European countries and find no cointegration between policy rates and short-term or long-term market rates. Moreover, the pass-through has apparently declined in time although being higher than in some of the euro area countries. On the other hand, Sander and Kleimeier (2006) investigate the interest rate pass-through convergence for eight Central and Eastern European Countries and find that the pass-through has become faster over time and is more complete than in the euro area. Crespo-Cuaresma et al. (2004) analyse three NMS using an ARDL model and find complete pass-through in the case of Poland and incomplete pass-through in the case of Hungary and the Czech Republic. No presence of asymmetry is found, except for the short-term lending rate in Hungary.

Linear Econometric Modelling of the Pass-through Phenomenon

The focus of this chapter is the pass-through from the monetary policy rates into money market interest rates and finally into retail banking rates in four NMS with inflation targeting strategy: Czech Republic, Hungary, Poland and Romania. Taking into account the non-stationarity of all types of interest rates, we employ an Error Correction Model (ECM) estimated using the Engle-Granger technique. The purpose of the analysis is threefold: (i) to estimate the size of the spread between money market interest rates and retail banking rates, (ii) to estimate the speed and degree of adjustment of market and retail interest rates to a change in the monetary policy interest rate and to check for any asymmetry of the pass-through, and (iii) to establish the similarities and differences of the interest rate pass-through phenomenon in the four NMS countries. The study distinctively takes into consideration the response of interest rates charged on loans and that of interest rates paid for deposits by commercial banks.

In order to estimate ECM, we use monthly data for the monetary policy interest rate, the one-month interbank offered and bid rates and the retail banking lending and deposit rates. The models are fitted to monthly data for the period from January 2003 to December 2007. For Hungary and the Czech Republic, the analysis is separately performed for corporate loans and deposits and household loans and deposits. The data for the monetary policy interest rate and the retail banking rates are provided by the central banks while the interbank interest rates (PRIBID/PRIBOR in the Czech Republic, BUBID/BUBOR in Hungary, WIBID/WIBOR in Poland and ROBID/ROBOR in Romania) are taken from Reuters.

In the case of Romania, the monetary policy interest rate has been only used since April 2005. In order to ensure the comparability with the data available for the other three NMS, we use the effective interest rate as a proxy for the monetary policy interest rate. The effective rate is computed as a weighted average of the interest rates used by the National Bank of Romania in different open market operations: deposits, certificates of deposit and reverse repo operations. Figure 10-1 shows the monetary policy interest rate and the effective interest rate in Romania for the period of April 2005 – December 2007. The similar development of the two types of interest rates leads us to the conclusion that the NBR effective interest rate is a good proxy for the monetary policy interest rate.

Figure 10-1 NBR effective interest rate and monetary policy interest rate (April 2005 – December 2007)

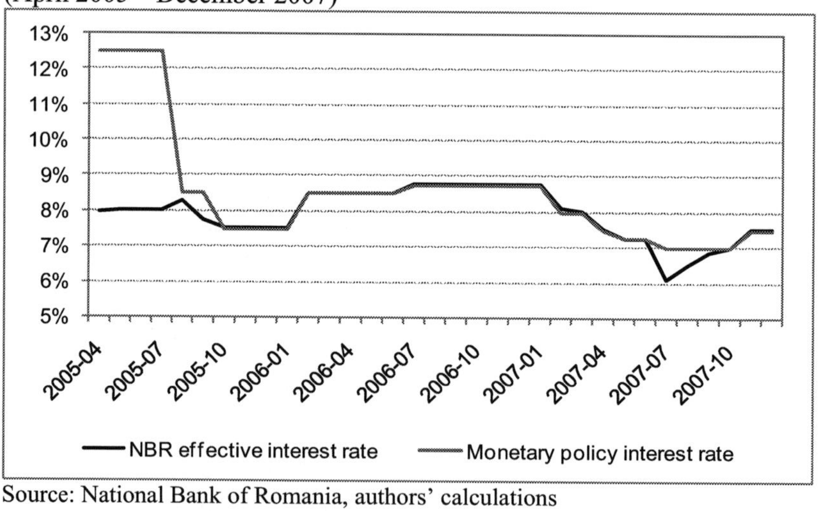

Source: National Bank of Romania, authors' calculations

Figure 10-2 shows the developments of the monetary policy interest rates in the NMS countries analysed. Romania exhibits significantly higher interest rates due to its persistently higher inflation rate compared to the other NMS. Moreover, Romania switched to the inflation targeting not sooner than in August 2005, while the Czech Republic adopted this monetary policy framework in 1998, Poland in 1999 and Hungary in 2001.

Figure 10-2 Monetary policy interest rate developments in NMS (January 2003 – December 2007)

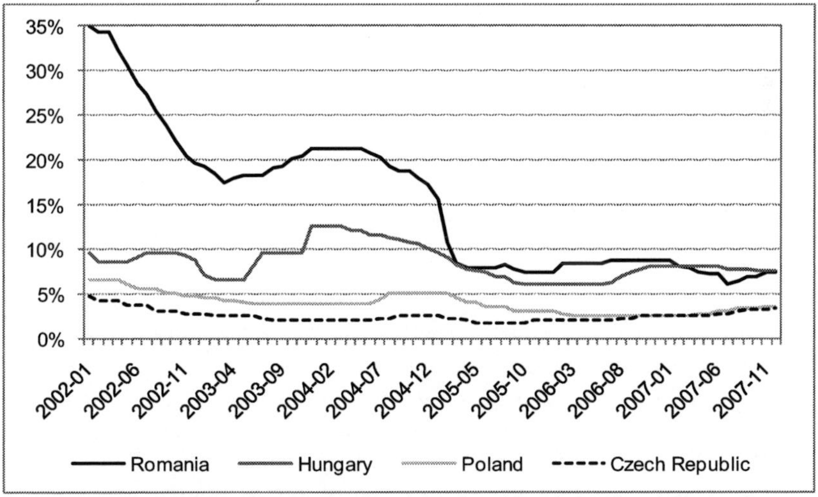

Source: National Bank of Romania, Czech National Bank, National Bank of Hungary and National Bank of Poland

The estimation of the interest rate pass-through is split in two sub-channels: (i) influence of the monetary policy interest rate on bid and offered interbank market rates, and (ii) influence of the interbank market rates on the retail lending and deposit interest rates. Specifically, the transmission of the monetary policy interest rate changes into retail interest rates is summarized in Scheme 10-1.

Scheme 10-1: The monetary policy transmission mechanism

$$\text{Monetary policy interest rate} \rightarrow \begin{cases} \text{Offered interbank interest rate} \rightarrow \text{Average lending rate} \\ \text{Bid interbank interest rate} \rightarrow \text{Average deposit rate} \end{cases}$$

For the each sub-channel presented in Scheme 10-1, a long-run equilibrium relationship and a short-term error correction equation are estimated. The stationarity of the residuals in the long-run relationship indicate whether the interest rates are cointegrated. The models used to assess the speed and size of the interest rate pass-through are described in equations (10.1) and (10.2).

$$\Delta i_t^{MR} = \beta_0 + \alpha \Delta i_{t-1}^{MR} + \beta_1 \Delta i_t^{MP} + \beta_2 \Delta i_{t-1}^{MP} - \\ -\gamma (i_{t-1}^{MR} - m - \lambda i_{t-1}^{MP}) \tag{10.1}$$

$$\Delta i_t^{\text{Retail}} = \beta_0 + \alpha \Delta i_{t-1}^{\text{Retail}} + \beta_1 \Delta i_t^{MR} + \beta_2 \Delta i_{t-1}^{MR} - \\ -\gamma (i_{t-1}^{\text{Retail}} - m - \lambda i_{t-1}^{MR}) \tag{10.2}$$

where i^{MP} represents the monetary policy interest rate, i^{MR} represents the interbank interest rate (bid or offered) and i^{Retail} represents the average interest rates used by commercial banks on deposits and loans respectively.

The terms in brackets describe the long run relationship between the two interest rates analysed in each equation and represent the lagged residuals of the equation estimated in levels.

The coefficients estimated in these equations have certain economical interpretations: m is the interest rate spread, λ is the degree of interest pass-through, namely the extent to which changes in the policy rate are passed through to money market rates and further to retail banking rates in the long run, β_1 represents the contemporary adjustment of the explained variables to a one percent change in the explanatory variable, β_2 represents the lagged adjustment of the explained variable to a one percent change in the explanatory variable and γ is the speed of the interest rate pass-through. According to Égert and Macdonald (2006), the delay with which interest rates adjust to the long run pass-through (λ) is given by the expression: $(1-\beta_1)/\gamma$. We will further refer to this coefficient as the speed of adjustment in number of months and label it with l.

Estimation and Results

The first step in estimating equations (10.1) and (10.2) is to test the order of integration of the variables. The Augmented Dickey Fuller (ADF) test indicates that all the variables are integrated of order one I(1) and, hence, we can test for cointegration. As we have previously mentioned, this is done by testing the stationarity of the residuals from the equations estimated in levels. In all cases, we found that the residuals are stationary at 1 percent significance level which implies cointegration between the nonstationary variables. We summarize the results of the estimations for equations (10.1) and (10.2) in a number of separate tables. Table 10-1 presents the results of the estimations for equation (10.1) performed for all four NMS and for both bid and offered interbank interest rates.

Table 10-1 Estimation of equation (10.1)

	Czech Rep.		**Hungary**		**Poland**		**Romania**	
	bid	**offer**	**bid**	**offer**	**bid**	**offer**	**bid**	**offer**
m	-0.06	0.03	-0.20	-0.15	-1.50	-1.47	-1.99	0.58
λ	1.00	1.00	1.00	1.02	0.85	0.88	0.98	0.99
β_1	1.01	1.02	1.00	1.15	0.40	0.60	0.76	1.03
γ	0.85	0.84	0.80	0.84	0.60	0.61	0.34	0.44
l	0	0	0	0	1	0.6	0.6	0

Source: Authors' estimation

The results show that the long-term pass-through, measured by λ, is complete in the Czech Republic, Hungary and Romania and close to complete in Poland. The speed of adjustment l is instantaneous in the countries that exhibit complete pass-through with the exception of the bid interbank interest rate in Romania which finishes its adjustment in 0.6 months. In Poland, the adjustment after a change in the monetary policy interest rate ends in one month for the bid rate and in 0.6 months for the offered rate.

Table 10-2 presents the results of the estimations for equation (10.2) for both lending and deposit interest rates in Romania and Poland.

Table 10-2 Estimation of equation (10.2) for Poland and Romania

	Poland		Romania	
	Deposit interest rate	Lending interest rate	Deposit interest rate	Lending interest rate
m	0.36	1.73	0.98	8.35
λ	0.76	0.97	0.65	0.92
β_1	0.42	1.06	0.16	0.21
γ	0.62	0.83	0.19	0.25
l	0.94	0	4.42	3.16

Source: Authors' estimation

The results show almost complete pass-through into lending rates, but the adjustment to the long-term pass-through is almost instantaneous in Poland, while in Romania adjustment takes more than three months. Also, the spread between the offered interbank interest rate and the retail lending interest rate is almost five times higher in Romania than in Poland. In the case of deposit interest rates, the pass-through is clearly incomplete and the adjustment to the long-term pass-through takes as much as 4.42 months in Romania. Both lending and deposit interest rates respond sluggishly in the short-term in Romania.

Table 10-3 presents the results of the estimations for the Czech Republic and Hungary performed distinctly for household and corporate deposits and loans.

Table 10-3 Estimation of equation (10.2) for the Czech Republic and Hungary

	Czech Republic				Hungary			
	HD	CD	HL	CL	HD	CD	HL	CL
m	0.38	0.23	9.90	2.37	0.67	-0.27	8.34	2.37
λ	0.23	0.46	0.54	0.80	0.76	0.92	0.87	0.88
β_1	0.14	0.34	---	0.58	0.50	0.76	0.25	0.66
γ	0.26	0.86	0.36	0.57	0.46	0.31	0.13	0.51
l	3.34	0.77	---	0.73	1.07	0.77	5.70	0.65

Source: Authors' estimation

Note: HD stands for household deposits, CD is corporate deposits, HL denotes household loans and CL is corporate loans.

The long-term pass-through of interbank interest rates into deposit interest rates is clearly lower than in the case of lending interest rates. In both countries, household deposits and loans interest rates show a lower long-term adjustment than corporate deposits and loans interest rates. The short-term pass-through is extremely low for household deposits in the Czech Republic and for household loans in Hungary. In both countries, the spread between the interbank interest rates and the retail lending rate is more than four times higher in the case of household loans compared to corporate loans.

We can also observe in Romania that the retail interest rates adjust slower than in other countries, although the long-term pass-through is higher than in the Czech Republic, for example. Also, the country exhibiting the highest long-term interest rate pass-through is Poland for lending interest rates and Hungary for deposit interest rates.

Conclusion

The long-term analysis shows that the interest rate pass-through is complete in the case of the transmission mechanism from the monetary policy interest rate to interbank interest rates. Hence, any change in the policy rate is fully incorporated into money market interest rates.

In the case of the pass-through from interbank interest rates to retail interest rates some conclusions arise. First, the long-term pass-through into deposit interest rates is incomplete in all countries. Second, the long-term pass-through and, in most cases, also the short-term pass-through into household loans and deposits interest rates are lower than in the case of corporate loans and deposits interest rates. Third, Poland exhibits the highest long-term pass-through for lending interest rates while Hungary exhibits the highest long-term pass-through for deposit interest rates. Fourth, although Romania has long-term pass-through coefficients similar to the other three NMS, the adjustment to this long-term pass-through is extremely slow.

References

Baele, L.M., A. Ferrando, P. Hordahl, E. Krylova and C. Monnet. 2004. *Measuring financial integration in the euro area.* ECB Occasional Paper no. 14. European Central Bank, Frankfurt am Main.

Borio, C. and W. Fritz. 1995. *The response of short-term bank lending rates to policy rates: A cross-country perspective.* BIS Working Paper No. 27. Bank for International Settlement, Basel.

Campa, J.M. and J.M. Gozalez Minguez. 2006. Differences in exchange rate pass-through in the euro area. *European Economic Review* 50(1): 121-45.

Cecchetti, S. 1999. *Legal Structure, Financial Structure, and the Monetary Policy Transmission Mechanism.* NBER Working Papers No. 7151. National Bureau of Economic Research, Cambridge, MA.

Cottarelli, C. and A. Kourelis. 1994. Financial structure, bank lending rates and the transmission mechanism of monetary policy. *IMF Staff Papers* 41: 587-623.

Crespo-Cuaresma, J., B. Égert and T. Reininger. 2004. *Interest rate pass-through in the new EU member states: The case of the Czech Republic, Hungary, and Poland.* William Davidson Institute Working Paper no. 2004-671. University of Michigan, Ann Arbor, MI.

de Bondt, G.J. 2002. *Retail bank interest rate pass-through: new evidence at the euro area level.* ECB Working Paper No. 136. European Central Bank, Frankfurt am Main.

—. 2005. Interest rate pass-through: Empirical results for the euro area. *German Economic Review* 6(1): 37-78.

Égert, B., J. Crespo-Cuaresma and T. Reiniger. 2007. Interest rate pass-through in central and Eastern Europe: Reborn from ashes merely to pass away? *Journal of Policy and Modeling* 29 (2): 209-25.

Égert, B. and R. MacDonald. 2006. *Monetary Transmission Mechanisms in Transition Economies:Surveying the Surveyable.* MNB Working Paper no. 5. National Bank of Hungary, Budapest.

Horváth, C., J. Krekó and A. Naszódi. 2004. *Interest rate pass-through: the case of Hungary.* MNB Working Paper no. 8. National Bank of Hungary, Budapest.

Mojon, B. 2000. *Financial structure and the interest rate channel of ECB monetary policy.* ECB Working Paper no. 40. European Central Bank, Frankfurt am Main.

Mojon, B., F. Smets and P. Vermeulen. 2002. Investment and monetary policy in the euro area. *Journal of Banking & Finance* 26(11): 2111-29.

Sander, H. and S. Kleimeier. 2004. Convergence in eurozone retail banking? What interest rate pass-through tells us about monetary policy transmission, competition and integration. *Journal of International Money and Finance* 23(3): 461-92.

—. 2006. Convergence of Interest Rate Pass-Through in a Wider Euro Zone? *Economic Systems* 30(4): 405-23.

CHAPTER ELEVEN

MONETARY INTEGRATION AND COUNTRY RISK OF THE EU NEWCOMERS BULGARIA AND ROMANIA

GERHARD FINK, PETER HAISS, WOLFGANG RAINER AND MADGALENA OEBERSEDER

The recent European Union (EU) accession, which has enlarged the EU to 27 member states, has brought Bulgaria and Romania even more to the focus of European and international investors. While the economic integration and the advancement of the institutional framework that the EU accession has brought the two new members is an important step towards more credibility, there are still inherent macroeconomic risks that should not be disregarded.

In the wake of EU accession, the boom in the Eastern and South-Eastern European Economies has also reached Bulgaria and Romania. In 2001, Romania's GDP) per capita amounted to USD 1,790. Until 2006 this figure more than tripled to USD 5,632. Bulgaria has reached similar growth patterns. Its GDP per capita increased from USD 1,724 in 2001 to USD 4,136 in 2005. Both countries have also managed to foster their exports especially to the EU. During the period 2001 to 2006 exports of Romania grew on average 24 percent per year. Over the same period, Bulgaria's exports grew on average 20.3 percent each year. Given these impressive growth figures it is not surprising that investors from the EU and beyond are eager to get their share of the pie. In 2006, Foreign Direct Investment (FDI) into Romania reached an unprecedented high of EUR 11.5 billion. This is nearly 44 percent of all FDI inflows into the Balkan region this year. Also Bulgaria attracted inflows of FDI amounting to EUR 5.2 billion in 2006 or 19.8 percent of all FDI into the Balkan region. As can be seen, real sector and monetary integration of Bulgaria and Romania with the EU rose considerably over time.

However, a tempting rose may have thorns. One should not be dazzled by the growth patterns both countries have shown in recent years and neglect to analyse also the downside of the catch-up race. A very concerning development is the rapid increase of the current account deficit of Bulgaria and Romania. With only two exceptions in 1996 and 1997, respectively, Bulgaria has always run a current account deficit. In 2006 Bulgaria recorded a current account deficit of USD 5.9 billion, or 15.6 percent of GDP.

The development of Romania is even more dramatic. Its current account deficit soared from USD 2.2 billion in 2001 to USD 12.6 billion or 10.3 percent of GDP in 2006. The forecasts for 2007 show a further increase to a deficit of USD 17.6 billion. As a consequence of the growing current account deficits, Bulgaria and Romania have cumulated large stocks of external debt. Whereas Romania's external debt increased moderately over the last decade, Bulgaria's external indebtedness soared. While its external debt accounted for only USD 11.2 billion in 2001, it reached an unprecedented high in 2006, accounting for USD 26.5 billion. This is equivalent to 49.3 percent of GDP, up from 32.7 percent in 2005. Especially concerning is the recent increase in short-term external debt in both countries.

Regarding the above, one can see the different pictures that different economic indicators paint. On the one hand are GDP growth and inflows of foreign direct investment, which are normally considered of having a positive influence on the economy via fostering real sector integration. On the other hand are the large current account deficits (only partly covered by FDI) and cumulated external debt positions, which raise considerable concerns about the probability of a currency crisis and the sustainability of monetary integration into the euro area (Breuss, 2004; Eller and Haiss, 2002; Rahman, 2008). This raises the request for an objective assessment of the economic country risk of Bulgaria and Romania. We close this gap by applying the Fink (1993) scoring model to Bulgaria and Romania. While the companion papers (Fink, Haiss, Oeberseder and Rainer, 2007; and Fink, Haiss, Paripovic and Aschauer, 2007) apply this model to compare selected new EU Member States to the euro area, we concentrate on Bulgaria and Romania as the latest entrants to the EU.

Methodology

Since country risk varies in definition, there are many different methods for assessing it (see Litchtlen, 1997, 63). Scoring models in general are the epitome of qualitative-quantitative methods, which are characterized by a subdivision into a qualitative pre-analysis and a quantitative main analysis (see Gorbach, 2005, 37). The scoring model that we use to assess the country risk was developed by Fink (1993, 1995). It uses a wide range of macroeconomic indicators, which relate to competitiveness of nations on debt stock, debt service, international liquidity and net capital flows (transfer quota). For an application and discussion of the predictive power of the individual indicators see for example Fink (1993), Fink (1995), Ciarloe and Trebeschi (2005) or Kaminsky et al. (1998).

Assuming constant elasticities, the model projects the indicators with the last observed growth rates. This enables us to draw conclusions about the sustainability of the current economic development path and to indicate whether policy changes would be advised. The logic of the model is as follows: the difference between projected imports and the projected exports results in the projected balance on current account (*CA*). In turn, the current account balance is assumed to be equal to the change in the stock of external liabilities, a deficit increases the external debt stock by the same amount and a surplus decreases it.

$$external\_debt_{t+1} = external\_debt_t + CA_{t+1} \tag{11.1}$$

The main purpose of the model is the development of a risk score that reflects the overall country risk. In the first step the macroeconomic indicators are transformed into key-ratios (*k*), which have been found to have predictive power for currency and economic crises. We alter the model developed by Fink (1993) to include changes in the real exchange rate and short-term external debt to reserves. Kaminsky (2006) found that real exchange rate appreciations are the most important signal of a forthcoming crisis (Kaminsky, 2006, 510). Rodrick and Valasco (1999) find strong support that potential illiquidity and the ratio of short-term foreign debt to reserves, in particular, are important precursors of financial crises triggered by reversal in capital flows (Rodrick and Valasco, 1998, 18).

In the second step, all key-ratios are evaluated according to the specific assessment function for each ratio (Table 11-1). The outcome is a score of 0 to 100 points for each key-ratio, where 100 points is the best possible score. Afterwards the assessed key-ratios are weighted (μ) and clustered into four categories: economic power, economic stability, debt burden, and transfer quota. The key-ratios on debt burden are given a high weight (55 percent) in this model, because it can be assumed that they have the greatest predictive power of economic instability or a crisis (Fink, 1995). Finally, the sum of the scores of the four categories, which is equivalent to the sum of weighted scores of the individual key-ratios, represents the overall country risk score.

$$RiskScore = \sum_{i=1}^{12} \mu_i * f(k_i) \qquad (11.2)$$

Table 11-1 shows the weights and assessment criteria for each key-ratio.

While most of the key ratios are self explanatory, the transfer quota probably needs some explanation. In the long run foreign debt is only sustainable if interest rates do not exceed growth of exports. If interest rates remain higher than growth of exports an increasing share of revenue from exports has to be used for interest payments. A value of zero indicates that a country is at the verge of the debt trap.

All raw data used in the model are taken from the database of the Economist Intelligence Unit (EIU) Country Data. The time series used consist of a 6-year period from 2001 to 2006, for which we use actual observed data. Additionally to ex-post analysis, the model is designed to project the macroeconomic indicators into the future over a 4-year time frame from 2007 to 2010, thereafter named the projection period.

Country Risk Assessment

The aim of this section is to present an independent country risk analysis of Bulgaria and Romania. Our analysis includes two time frames: the first ranges from 2001 to 2006 and deals with the actual development of the fundamentals. The second time frame ranges from 2007 to 2010 and shows the projected development of the indicators.

Country Risk Bulgaria

The country risk assessment of Bulgaria shows a continuous improvement of the risk score from 48 points in 2001 to 66 points in 2005 (see Figure 11-1). This is in line with the positive development of Bulgaria since the second economic crisis in 1998 and the following implementation of long-needed structural reforms. Another positive influence was the perspective of EU accession for Bulgaria and the associated "credibility import". The establishment of EU institutions in a transition country is regarded as major advancement with positive influence on economic development and country risk. De Souza and Selitska (2006), for example, find that appropriate institutions, defined in a very broad sense, can substantially reduce the occurrence of debt distress episodes. However, this positive development stopped and was even reversed in 2006, actually before accession to the EU. The risk score falls by 12 percent to 58 points. The projections for 2007 to 2010 indicate a high chance of a further decline of the risk score. Therefore, in the following we discuss each of the individual clusters of key-ratios.

Figure 11-1 Assessment of the country risk of Bulgaria, 2001 – 2010 (projection 2007 – 2010)

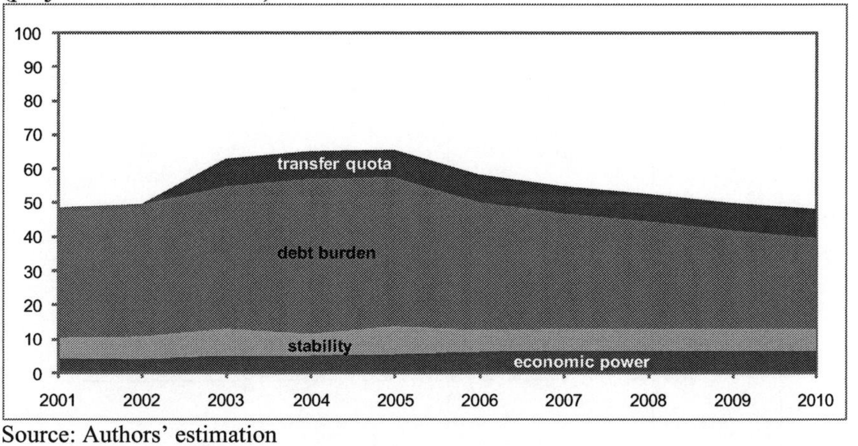

Source: Authors' estimation
Note: best assessment = 100, worst assessment = 0

Table 11-1 Weights and assessment criteria of each key-ratio

Key-ratio k	Weight μ	Assessment			
		0-point border	100-point border	Assessment function f(k)	Graph f(k)
Economic power					
GDP per capita (USD)	0.02	< 0	> 19,951	$f(k)=\frac{21.715}{1.15*LN(\frac{k}{100})}$	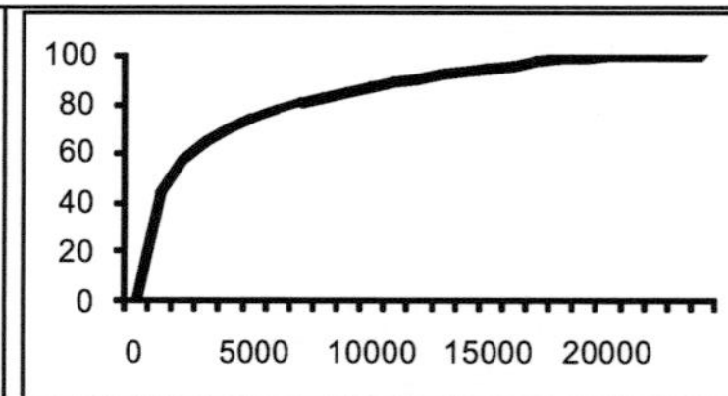
GDP, real change (%)	0.05	< -2 %	> 6.25 %	$f(k)=12.5x+25$	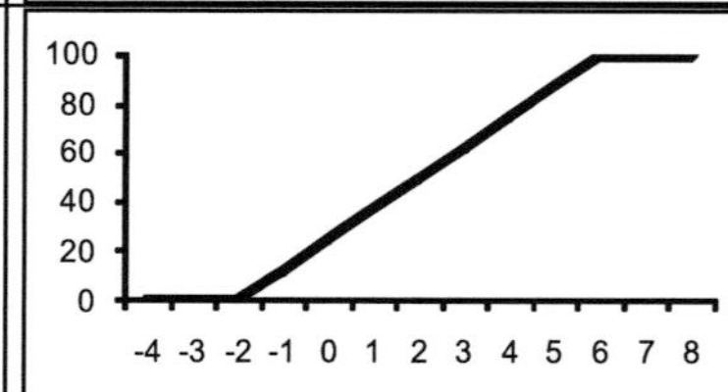
Export / import (%)	0.10	< 90 %	> 110 %	$f(k)=5k-450$	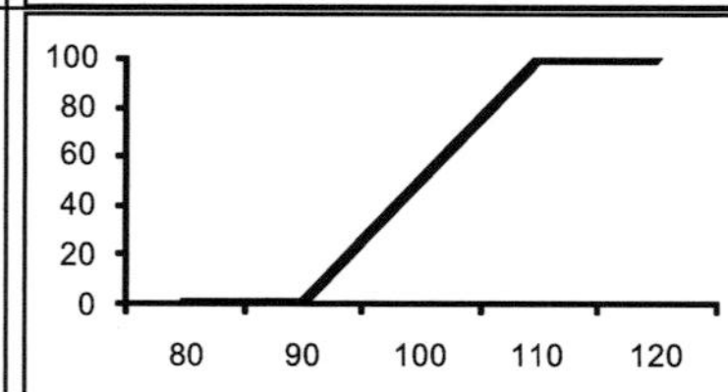

Table 11-1 (cont.)

Stability					
Inflation rate (%)	0.05	> 80 %	< 2 %	$f(k) = 100 - 100 * \sqrt{0.98^2 - (k-1)^2 + 0.05k}$	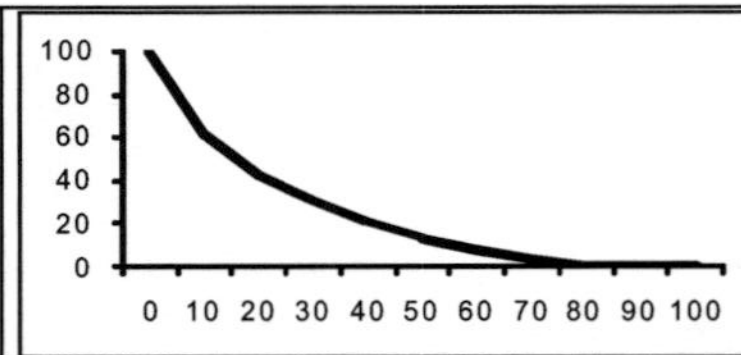
Current account / GDP (%)	0.05	< -5 %	> 1 %	$f(k) = 16.67k + 83.33$	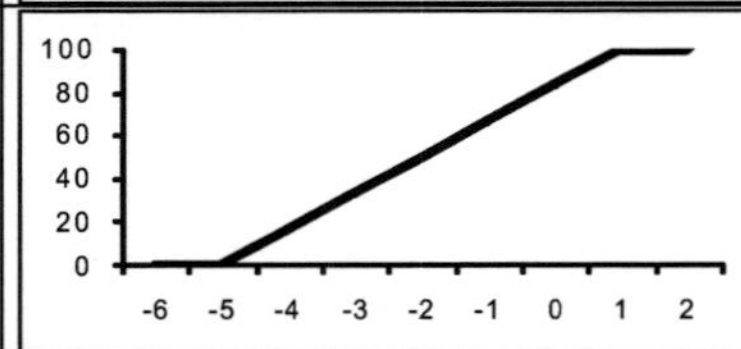
Real exchange rate change (%)	0.10	> 10 %	< -10 %	$f(k) = -5x + 50$	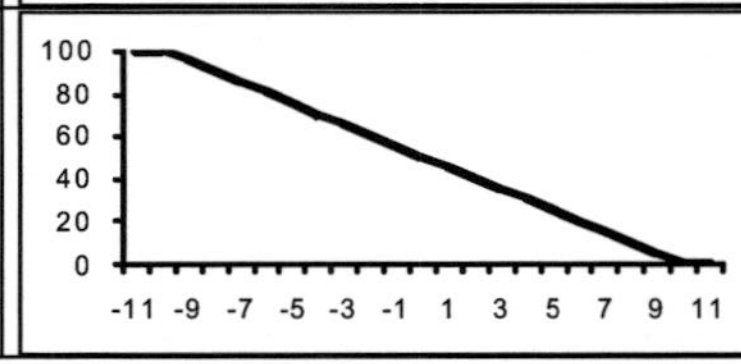
Debt burden					
External debt / GDP (%)	0.05	> 90 %	< 10 %	$f(k) = -1.25k + 112.5$	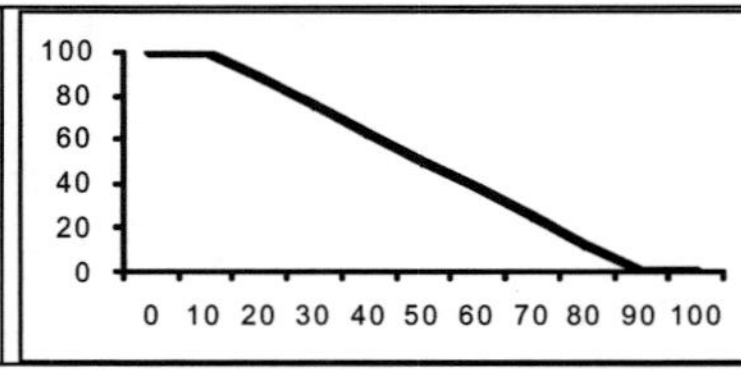

Table 11-1 (cont.)

External debt / exports (%)	0.10	> 250 %	< 50 %	$f(k) = -0.5k + 125$	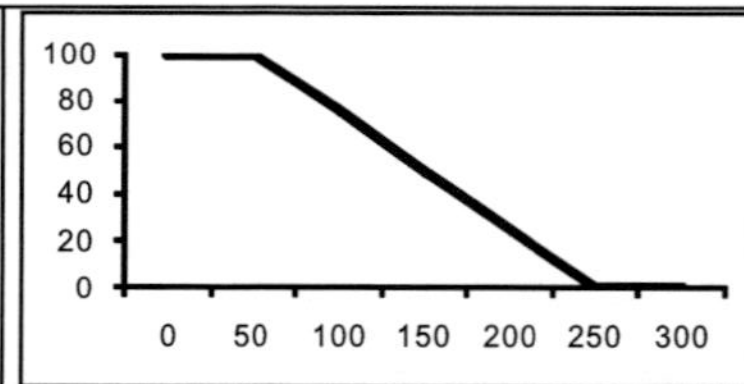
Short-term debt / reserves (%)	0.10	> 100 %	< 5 %	$f(k) = -1.053k + 105.26$	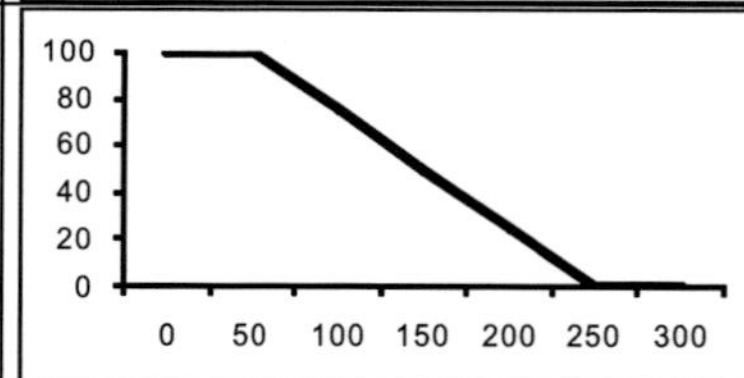
Debt service ratio (%)	0.20	> 90 %	< 10 %	$f(k) = -1.25k + 112.5$	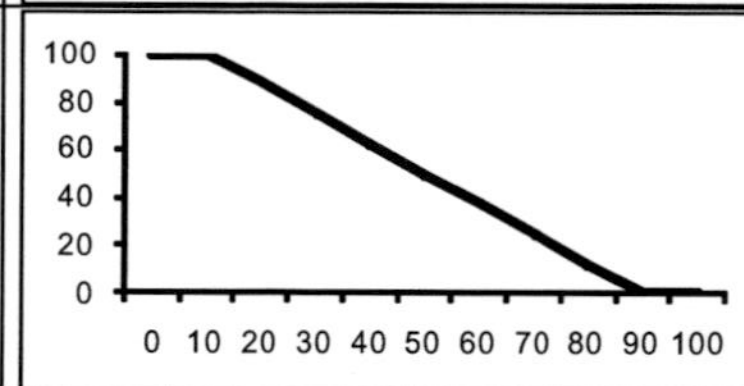
Forex reserves (excl. gold) / imports (%)	0.10	< 5 %	> 25 %	$f(k) = 100 * \sqrt{0.95^2 - (k-1)^2 + 1.67k}$	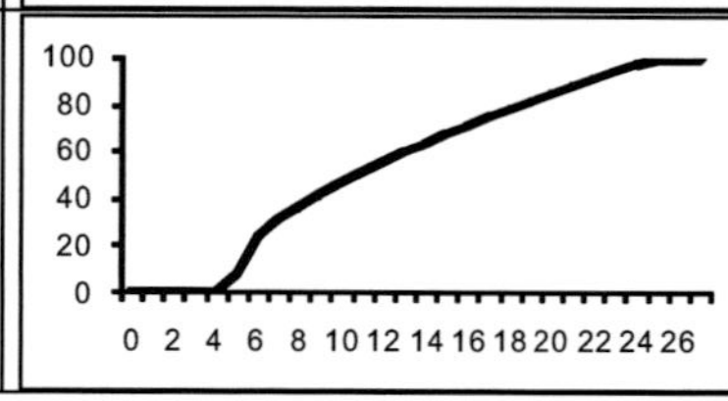

Table 11-1 (cont.)

Transfer quota					
Interest rate / growth rate of exports (%)	0.08	> 100 %	< 50 %	$f(k) = -200k + 200$	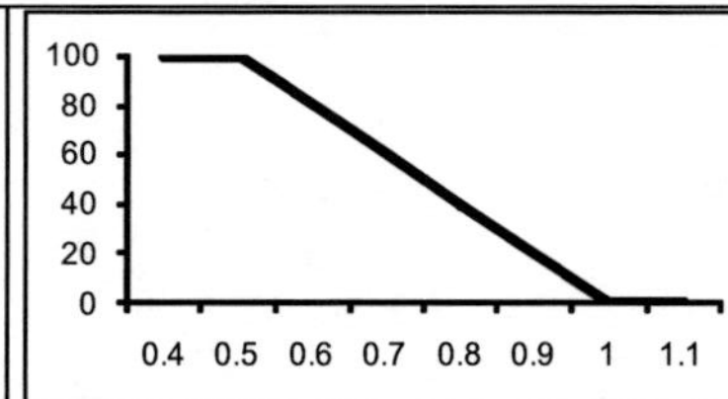
Sum of weights μ	1.00				

Source: Authors' model based on Fink (1993), Fink (1995) and Fink, Haiss, Oeberseder and Rainer (2007).

Economic Power

Bulgaria's economic upswing of the past years is mapped by an increase of the score for economic power from 41 points in 2001 to 57 points in 2006 out of 100 possible points (see Figure 11-3a). This development is underpinned by the strong average real GDP growth of 4.8 percent per year over the observation period 2001 – 2006. The nominal GDP increased from USD 1,724 in 2001 to USD 4,136 in 2006. However, the export/import ratio puts a damper on the economic power score of Bulgaria. Over the whole observation period Bulgaria's imports always exceeded its exports. The export/import ratio declined from 76.4 percent in 2001 to 68.9 percent in 2006.

Stability

The stability score declined since its peak in 2003 (see Figure 11-3b). While the inflation rate declined from 7.36 percent in 2001 to a low of 2.35 percent in 2003, in recent years, Bulgaria's inflation accelerated again, reaching 7.26 percent in 2006. Another concerning development is the worsening current account deficit. Over the whole observation period Bulgaria's current account deficit to GDP ratio permanently stayed below the –5 percent reference mark and increased on average by 36 percent each year (see Figure 11-3b). In 2006 the current account deficit amounted to USD 5.8 billion or 18.5 percent of GDP[1], the highest observed value. So far there is no indication that this trend could be reversed.

The large and increasing deficit on current account is a consequence of the fixed exchange rate of the lev to the appreciating euro. After the economic crisis of 1996 – 1997 the Bulgarian government decided to peg its currency to the euro. The aim of this measure was to import stability. Indeed the introduction of the currency board led to a decline of the inflation rate and boosted economic growth (ECE/UN, 1998, 2). However, in the last years Bulgaria experienced the negative side effects associated with a fixed exchange rate. Since 2001 the euro has appreciated enormously against the dollar. The average USD/EUR exchange rate rose from 0.895 in 2001 to 1.269 in 2006, representing an appreciation of over 50 percent. As a consequence the Bulgarian lev appreciated against the dollar, too, what made exports more expensive and imports cheaper. Since the rate of inflation of Bulgaria is higher than in the euro area, the lev also appreciated in real terms against the euro (see Figure 11-2). From January 2000 to December 2007 the CPI-based real effective exchange rate increased by 133 percent from 105 to 245. This helps to explain the tremendous rise in the current account deficit in the past years. Consequently, Bulgaria's external debt stock has increased (discussed in detail further below). Overall, these developments have negative effects on Bulgaria's international competitiveness. It is disconcerting to imagine what consequences a further appreciation of the euro against the dollar could have on economies like Bulgaria that have pegged their currencies to the euro.

Figure 11-2 Real effective exchange rate, Bulgaria (2000 – 2007, 1997 = 100)

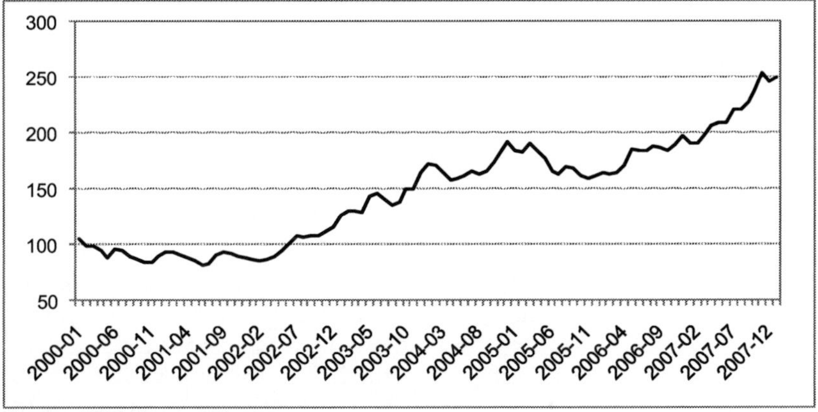

Source: EIU Country Data

Debt Burden

The large and persistent current account deficits have increased Bulgaria's external liabilities. Since 2001 its external debt stock rose from USD 11.2 billion to USD 26.5 billion in 2006. In relation to GDP the development is different. From 2001 to 2004 external debt to GDP declined from 53 percent to 25.4 percent. In the last two years, however, this ratio doubled its 2004 value, reaching 49 percent in 2006. This trend is also reflected in the ratio external debt to exports. Whereas this ratio declined from 140 percent in 2001 to 63 percent in 2004, it increased since then again to 103 percent in 2006 (Table 11-2, Figure 11-3c). Even more concerning is the recent increase in short-term external debt. This figure literally exploded from USD 1.5 billion or 13 percent of total external debt in 2001 to USD 9.7 billion or 37 percent of total external debt in 2006. This recent increase in foreign currency denominated credit has generated concerns about a credit risk that Bulgaria is facing (ECB, 2006, 5).

The ratio of short-term external debt in relation to foreign exchange reserves is another important indicator of liquidity. Over the whole observation period this ratio soared from 37 percent in 2001 to 89 percent in 2006, which is close to the critical limit as defined by the "Guidotti rule". According to this rule a prudently managed economy will have short-term external debt no greater than its stock of foreign exchange reserves (Lubin, 2002, 4). The conclusion is that a further increase of this ratio would imply a significant risk to short-term liquidity.

Transfer Quota

In this category, which measures the ratio of interest rates to the growth rate of exports, Bulgaria has reached the maximum of 100 points since 2003. The driving force is the high growth rate of exports, which averaged 22 percent each year over the observation period 2001 to 2006.

Projection 2007 – 2010

Year 2006 was a turning point. Half of the indicators deteriorated on a year-to-year basis. The risk score declined by 12 percent from 66 points in 2005 to 58 points in 2006. Based on the latest growth figures, the projection for 2007 to 2010 signals the high risk of a further decline of the risk score (Figure 11-1). The model projects a decrease of the risk score from 58 points in 2006 to 48 points in 2010, equal to a decline of 17 percent. This is a strong signal that the current growth path will not be sustainable in the medium term. If imports continue to grow faster than exports, this will result in an enormous increase of the current account deficit in the coming years. Bulgaria would have to raise additional external debt. If the deficit in the current account cannot be financed by FDI or external borrowing, Bulgaria will have to draw on its foreign exchange reserves, which are also projected to decline drastically in relation to imports (Figure 11-3). A high foreign exposure carries an inherent risk of negative shocks to the economy based on a reversal of capital flows, from inflows to capital flight, as was the case in the Russian crisis of 1997 – 1998 (ECE/UN, 1998, 10).

Figure 11-3a Key-ratios of economic power, Bulgaria (2001 – 2007, projection 2007 – 2010)

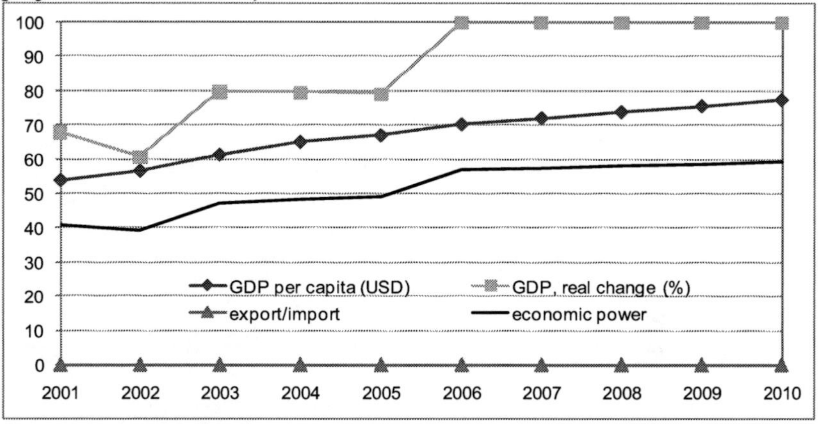

Source: Authors' estimation

Figure 11-3b Key-ratios of stability, Bulgaria (2001 – 2007, projection 2007 – 2010)

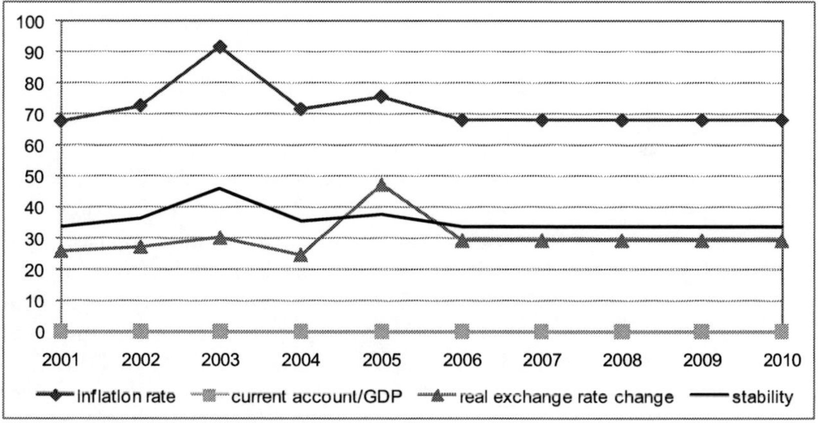

Source: Authors' estimation

Figure 11-3c Key-ratios of debt burden, Bulgaria (2001 – 2007, projection 2007 – 2010)

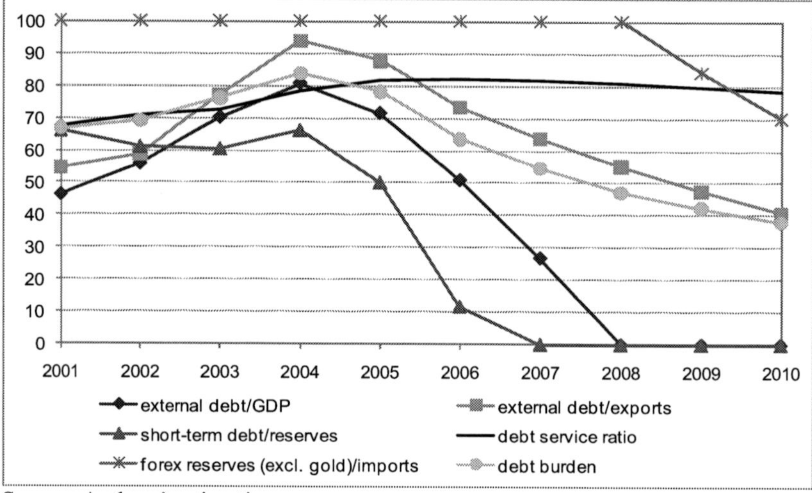

Source: Authors' estimation

Comparison of the Projection Results with the Actual 2007 Data

This section focuses on a comparison of the projections of the scoring model with the newly released actual data for 2007. From 2006 to 2007 inflation increased from 7.26 percent to 9.75 percent. The growth of exports increased only slightly from 22.7 percent to 23.2 percent. However, imports soared, with an increase of 37.9 percent compared to 26.7 percent the year before. The export/import ratio consequently declined to 61.1 percent and the current account balance increased to 21.6 percent of GDP. Real GDP change slowed down from 9.1 percent in 2006 to 4.9 percent in 2007. Although the external debt burden increased sharply in nominal terms, from USD 26.5 billion in 2006 to USD 34.4 billion in 2007, in terms of GDP it actually decreased to 46 percent from 49 percent in 2006. This is due to a still high nominal GDP growth of 14.5 percent in 2007. Taking the actual 2007 data into account the model calculates a risk score of 56 points, down from 58 points in 2006. Compared with our original projection of 55 points for 2007, this reveals that the model was capable of displaying the trend of a worsening economic situation in Bulgaria.

Table 11-2 Key-ratios of Bulgaria (2001 – 2010, projection 2007 – 2010)

	2001	2002	2003	2004	2005	2006	2007	2008	2009	2010
GDP per capita (USD)	1,724	1,994	2,567	3,147	3,479	4,136	4,548	5,001	5,500	6,048
GDP, real change (%)	3.4	2.9	4.4	4.4	4.3	9.1	9.1	9.1	9.1	9.1
Export / import (%)	76.4	76.3	73.3	72.9	68.2	68.9	69.5	70.2	70.9	71.6
Inflation rate (%)	7.4	5.8	2.3	6.1	5.0	7.3	7.3	7.3	7.3	7.3
Current account / GDP (%)	-9.6	-5.5	-8.6	-10.7	-16.2	-18.5	-23.4	-28.9	-35.3	-42.6
Real exchange rate change (%)	4.8	4.6	4.0	5.1	0.6	4.2	4.2	4.2	4.2	4.2
External debt / GDP (%)	53.0	45.3	33.8	25.4	32.7	49.3	68.6	91.8	119.4	152.1
External debt / exports (%)	140.9	132.1	95.4	62.3	74.3	103.2	122.3	139.7	155.0	168.4
Short-term debt / reserves (%)	37.0	41.7	42.3	36.9	52.3	88.8	115.7	152.1	200.6	264.4
Debt service ratio (%)	19.3	36.0	33.4	31.8	27.2	24.7	24.2	24.7	25.4	26.2
Forex reserves (excl. gold) / imports (%)	35.4	47.1	48.2	48.5	36.5	39.7	31.6	25.0	19.8	15.7
Interest rate / growth rate of exports (%)	1.1	1.1	0.2	0.2	0.4	0.2	0.2	0.2	0.2	0.2

Source: Authors' estimation

Country Risk Romania

Romania's development, with regards to the country risk, is even more concerning than the development of Bulgaria. The risk score of Romania declined by 16 percent from 70 points in 2003 to 59 points in 2006. The projection for 2007-2010 yields an inherent risk of a further decline to 35 points in 2010 (see Figure 11-4). This indicates that the current economic development of Romania is not sustainable in the medium term.

Figure 11-4 Assessment of the country risk of Romania, 2001 – 2010 (projection 2007 – 2010)

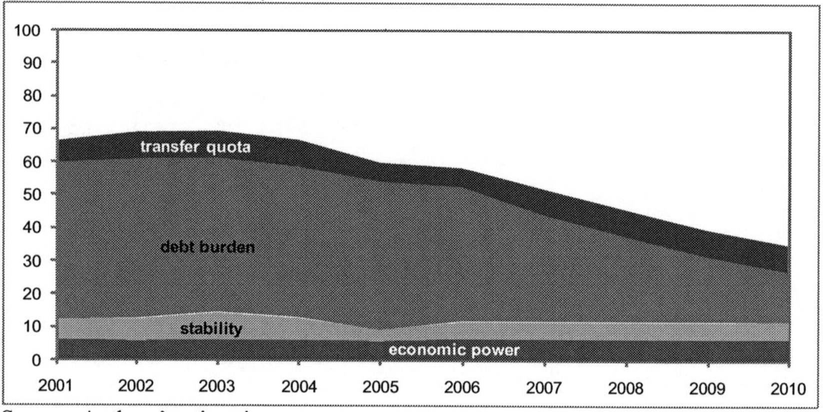

Source: Authors' estimation
Note: best assessment = 100, worst assessment = 0

Economic Power

The key-ratios of economic power show a similar picture to that of Bulgaria. Romania's GDP per capita more than tripled from USD 1,790 in 2001 to USD 5,632 in 2006 (Table 11-3). In real terms it grew on average by a remarkable 9.6 percent each year. However, also Romania suffers from a declining export/import ratio (Figure 11-6a). This figure decreased from 79 percent in 2001 to 69 percent in 2006. The widening gap between exports and imports is due to a higher growth rate of imports than exports, which in turn puts enormous pressure on the current account.

Stability

The mentioned gap between exports and imports manifests itself in a growing current account deficit. While in 2002 Romania ran a current account deficit of 6.7 percent of GDP, this figure has grown to 15.3 percent in 2006. The CPI-based inflation rate, which Romania managed to decrease from 34.5 percent in 2001 to 6.6 percent in 2006 (see Figure 11-6b), has a positive influence on the stability score. However, Romania also experiences the negative effects of an appreciating currency. Its real effective exchange rate appreciated tremendously in the past few years, from a value of 122 in January 2004 to 171 in December 2007 (see Figure 11-5). This is equal to an increase of 40 percent. In turn, this development explains the persistent and growing current account deficits of Romania, as imports are getting cheaper and exports more expensive. Overall, Romania's competitiveness weakened.

Figure 11-5 Real effective exchange rate, Romania (2000 – 2007, 1997 = 100)

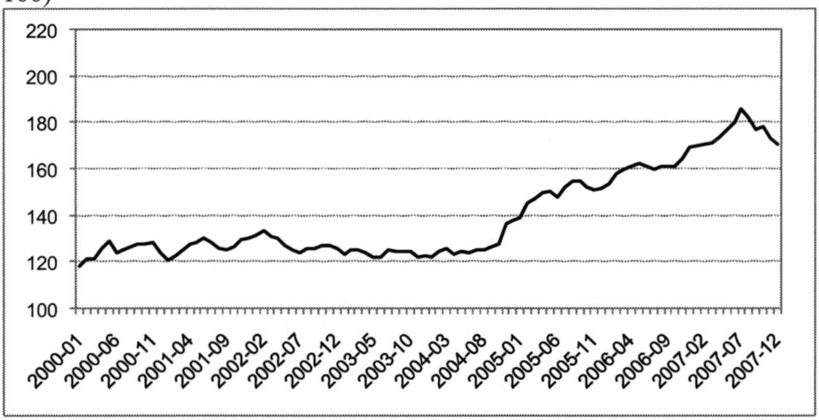

Source: EIU Country Data

Debt Burden

Despite a huge nominal increase from USD 11.2 billion in 2001 to USD 54.4 billion in 2006, external debt in relation to GDP stayed more or less constant, with a rate of 22 percent in 2006 (see Figure 11-6c). By contrast, Romania's external debt stock in percent of exports increased from 76.7 percent in 2001 to 81 percent in 2006. The quick increase of short-term external debt is another worrying signal. Short-term external debt soared from 6.8 percent of total external debt in 2001 to 33 percent in 2006, with a sharp increase of 60 percent since 2005. This development is mapped by the ratio of short-term external debt to foreign exchange reserves, increasing from 25 percent in 2001 to 36 percent in 2005 with a dramatic jump to 63 percent in 2006. The debt service ratio, which measures the effective debt service in relation to a country's exports of goods, also indicates this negative development. It increased steadily from 19 percent in 2001 to 33 percent in 2006, indicating that increasing portions of revenue from exports have to be used for principal and interest payment on external debt.

Transfer Quota

Romania scores relatively high on this measure. The reason is the high growth rate of its exports (in the broader sense), on average 21.2 percent per year over the observation period.

Projection 2007 – 2010

Similar to Bulgaria, the projection for the next three years does not offer a splendid perspective. The projection yields a decline of the country risk rating from 59 points in 2006 to 35 points in 2010. This means that if price and income elasticities remain constant, the country risk of Romania will increase significantly. The projected increase of the current account deficit will give rise to the external debt stock. Other things equal, external debt is projected to increase from 22 percent of GDP in 2006 to 103 percent of GDP by 2010. The model signals that the current growth path is not sustainable. The model gives clear signals that the increase in short-term finance for Romania indeed is a reflection of increased perceived country risk. Since import and export flows react to changes in the real exchange rate only with some time lag, Romanian policy makers need to reassess their current economic policies, possibly within shortly.

The appreciating currency has become the main reason of concern. Although Romania officially remains a freely floating currency, the exchange rate system is characterized by frequent central banks interventions (Cuaresma et al., 2008, 197). From 2000 to 2007 the real effective exchange rate increased by 39 percent, with a very rapid appreciation since 2004. This development of the real effective exchange rate is largely accounted for by the nominal appreciation of the domestic currency against both the euro and dollar in 2005 compared to 2004 (National Bank of Romania, 2006, 24). This in turn has a negative impact on the external competitiveness of Romania, making imports cheaper and exports more expensive. This trend of the foreign exchange rate is likely to continue, as the returns on capital are still relatively high in Romania, entailing large capital inflows, which put higher pressure on domestic currency appreciation (National Bank of Romania, 2006, 21). The resulting increase in the current account deficits will boost foreign borrowing further. The main concern is that for countries that have built-up large stocks of foreign-currency-denominated debt, a currency depreciation raises the real burden of servicing and repaying that debt in terms of domestic consumption that must be forgone, which heightens the prospect of debt payment difficulties (Isard, 2005, 120).

Figure 11-6a Key-ratios of economic power, Romania (2001 – 2007, projection 2007 – 2010)

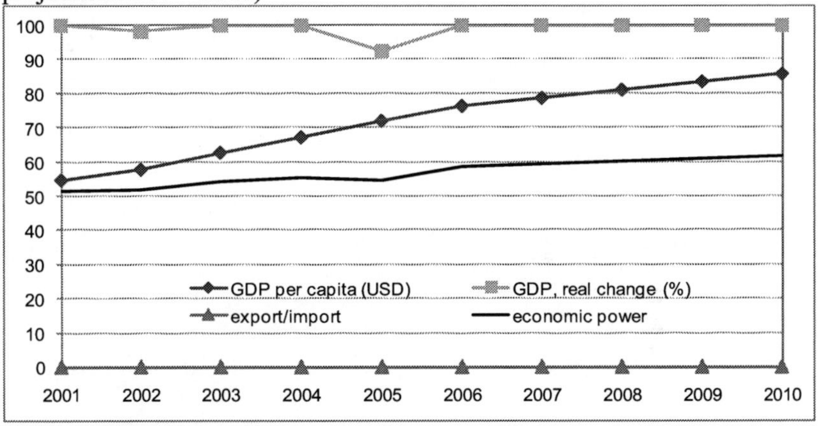

Source: Authors' estimation

Figure 11-6b Key-ratios of stability, Romania (2001 – 2007, projection 2007 – 2010)

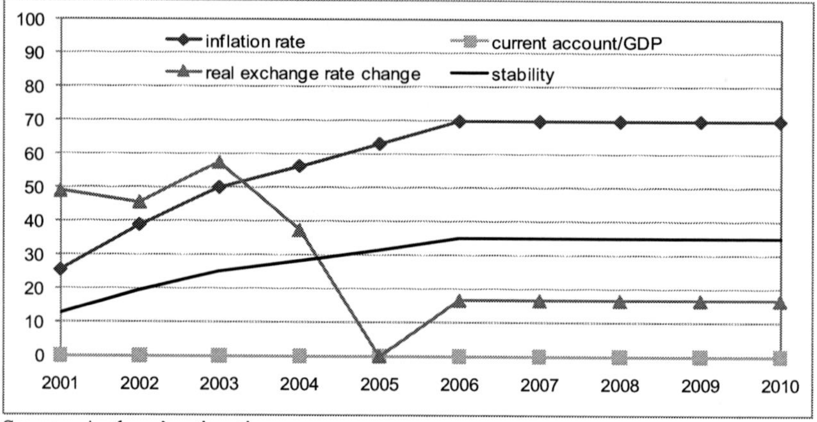

Source: Authors' estimation

Figure 11-6c Key-ratios of debt burden, Romania (2001 – 2007, projection 2007 – 2010)

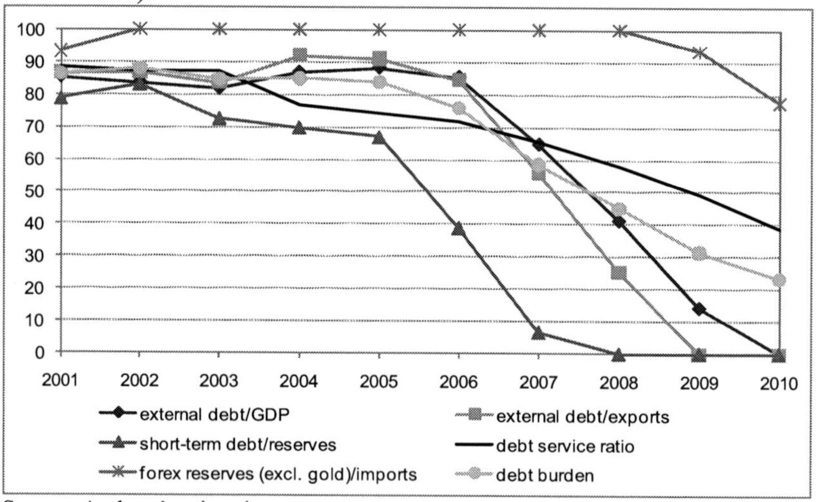

Source: Authors' estimation

Comparison of the Projection Results with the Actual 2007 Data

The newly revealed 2007 data for Romania show an increase in real GDP growth to 14.7 percent, largely due to a decline in inflation from 6.6 percent in 2006 to 4.8 percent in 2007. Exports grew 28.7 percent, compared to 21.5 percent in 2006. Imports, on the other hand, literally exploded, with a y-o-y growth of 47.4 percent in 2007, up from 27.4 percent in 2006. The export/import ratio consequently declined from 68.8 percent in 2006 to 57.7 percent in 2007 and the current account (excluding current transfers) increased to 20.9 percent of GDP. External debt in relation to GDP fell slightly from 21.6 percent in 2006 to 20.8 percent in 2007. In relation to exports, however, it increased from 81.0 percent to 87.4 percent. Using the actual data, the model reveals a country risk score of 58.3 points, more or less constant since 2006 with a score of 58.5 points. Still, the projections based on the new price and income elasticities show a high risk of a decline of the risk score in the future.

Economic Policy Implications

After severe economic crises in the nineties Bulgaria and Romania developed quite well, with real sector and monetary integration with the rest of the EU on the rise. Both countries managed to improve their country risk score. Bulgaria's rating increased from 48 points in 2001 to 66 points in 2005. However, 2006 indicated a turn to the negative, as the risk score fell to 58 points. The score of Romania rose from 67 points in 2001 to 70 points in 2003. Since then the score declined continuously to 59 points in 2006. For the years to come the model projects a continuing negative trend. This gives a clear signal to policy makers in Bulgaria and Romania to reconsider economic policy, and exchange rate policy in particular. To avoid an increase in the country risk, special attention should be given to the real exchange rate development which directly affects the export/import ratio: If imports continue to grow faster than exports, both Bulgaria and Romania will face large current account deficits. Both countries have to find ways and means to foster exports and control imports.

Table 11-3 Key-ratios of Romania (2001 – 2010, projection 2007 – 2010)

	2001	2002	2003	2004	2005	2006	2007	2008	2009	2010
GDP per capita (USD)	1,790	2,103	2,738	3,479	4,492	5,632	6,386	7,241	8,211	9,311
GDP, real change (%)	8.0	5.9	13.1	11.5	5.4	13.5	13.5	13.5	13.5	13.5
Export / import (%)	79.3	84.2	79.5	77.9	74.2	68.7	63.6	58.9	54.5	50.5
Inflation rate (%)	34.5	22.5	15.3	11.9	9.0	6.6	6.6	6.6	6.6	6.6
Current account / GDP (%)	-8.4	-6.7	-8.7	-13.4	-13.4	-15.3	-19.1	-23.4	-28.3	-33.9
Real exchange rate change (%)	0.2	0.9	-1.5	2.5	17.6	6.7	6.7	6.7	6.7	6.7
External debt / GDP (%)	21.7	23.1	24.5	20.5	19.4	21.6	38.1	57.0	78.6	103.1
External debt / exports (%)	76.7	76.2	82.8	66.0	67.9	81.0	138.0	199.4	265.6	336.7
Short-term debt / reserves (%)	25.3	21.2	31.1	33.7	36.4	63.1	93.7	136.3	194.9	274.3
Debt service ratio (%)	19.27	19.3	20.2	20.4	28.7	30.5	32.6	37.5	43.5	50.7
Forex reserves (excl. gold) / imports (%)	22.7	31.1	30.7	38.9	41.9	46.5	36.7	29.0	22.8	17.9
Interest rate / growth rate of exports (%)	0.6	0.2	0.2	0.4	0.6	0.6	0.5	0.5	0.4	0.4

Source: Authors' estimation

External debt/GDP and external debt/exports: The increasing current account deficits need to be financed, what will cause the external debt stock to rise. Soaring short-term external debt clearly signals that foreign lenders share these concerns. Bulgaria's short-term external debt amounted to 37 percent of total external debt in 2006 and Romania's to 33 percent. An increase in short-term debt gives a clear signal of decreasing creditworthiness.

Short-term external debt/foreign exchange reserves: This indicator of short-term liquidity increased rapidly over the observation period to levels of 63 percent in Romania and 89 percent in Bulgaria in 2006, respectively. Policy makers in both countries should definitely keep an eye on this key-ratio, as it is one of the most powerful predictors of a currency crisis, possibly triggered by reversals of capital flows.

Debt service ratio: The debt service ratio measures principal and interest payments as a percentage of exports. A higher external debt stock results in higher principal and interest payments. Although exports of Bulgaria and Romania are growing rapidly, in the years to come the debt service ratio might increase considerably, because external debt might grow even faster.

Foreign exchange reserves: The increasing current account deficits are likely to reduce the foreign exchange reserves. However, both Bulgaria and Romania need to keep their foreign exchange reserves on a level adequate for maintaining short-term liquidity. Apparently, reserves could be borrowed abroad, but increasingly on the very short-term only.

Inflation rate: Although Romania has managed to reduce its inflation rate from of 34 percent in 2001 to about 6.6 percent in 2006 it should try to at least to stabilize this rate at this level. Bulgaria should try to keep down the inflation rate, which has recently begun to rise again. More flexibility in Bulgaria's exchange rate may require more emphasis on incomes policy and monetary policy to keep inflation rates from soaring again.

Conclusion

The presented country risk analyses aim at an assessment of the EU newcomers Bulgaria and Romania. The analyses indicate that both countries managed to improve their ratings during the first years of the observation period 2001 – 2006. However, the past years have seen a declining risk score for Bulgaria and Romania and hence increasing country risk. These findings are similar to those for Croatia and Latvia (Fink, Haiss, Paripovic and Aschauer, 2007). Our projections, assuming constant income and price elasticities, show that Bulgarian and Romanian policy makers would be well advised to revise the current economic and exchange rate policies. If economic challenges like soaring current account deficits and growing foreign debt stocks are not met, there is a considerable risk of an aggravating situation, which in the end might trigger a currency crisis and thus may challenge or delay monetary integration in Europe.

References

Breuss, F., G. Fink and P. Haiss. 2004. How well prepared are the New Member States for the European Monetary Union? *Journal of Policy Modeling* 26(7): 769-91.

Ciarlone, A. and G. Trebeschi. 2005. Designing an early warning system for debt crises. *Emerging Markets Review* 6(4): 376-95.

Cuaresma, J.C., J. Fidrmuc and M. Silgoner. 2008. Fundamentals, the exchange rate and prospects for the current and future EU enlargements: evidence from Bulgaria, Croatia, Romania and Turkey. *Empirica* 35(2): 195-211.

Datamonitor. Country Profile Bulgaria. 2004. United Kingdom.

De Souza, L.V. and N. Selitska. 2006. Debt sustainability in the Wider Eastern European Region: The long shadow of the EU. In *Return to Growth in CIS Countries*, ed. L.V. De Souza and O. Havrylyshyn, 300-16. Heidelberg: Springer, Berlin

Dobrinsky, R. 2000. The transition crisis in Bulgaria. *Cambridge Journal of Economics* 24(5): 581-602.

ECE/UN. 1996/97. *Chapter 3 – The Transition Economies*, 59-179. United Nations, New York and Geneva.

—. 1998. *Chapter 1 – An overview of the Economic Situation and Selected Issues in the ECE Region*, 1-10. United Nations, New York and Geneva.

Eller, M. and P. Haiss. 2002. Integrationsspezifische, aussenhandelsseitige und finanzsektor-spezifische Analyse der Teilnahme der Mittel- und Osteuropaeischen Laender am EURO-Waehrungsraum, *Osteuropa-Wirtschaft* 26(2): 200-15.

European Central Bank. 2006. *Macroeconomic and Financial Stability Challenges for Acceding and Candidate Countries*. ECB Occasional Paper No. 48. European Central Bank, Frankfurt am Main.

Fink, G. 1993a. Über die Mechanik des Schuldenmachens. *Bankarchiv* 1993(4): 261-69.

—. 1993b Unternehmenswert der Banken und Länderrisiko. *Bankarchiv* 1993(8): 599-613.

—. 1995. Kreditrationierung mittels Länderrisikoanalyse. *Bankarchiv* 1995(6): 455-64.

Fink, G., P. Haiss, M. Oeberseder and P. Rainer. 2007. Dollar depreciation – Euro pain. *Journal of Policy Modeling* 29(5): 739-63.

Fink, G., P. Haiss, I. Paripovic and D. Aschauer. 2007. Pressure on the Euro: Country risk of Croatia, Latvia and the Eurozone In *Proceedings of the Conference "Money, Banking and Financial Markets"*, 123-50. Bratislava: University of Economics

Gorbach, O. 2005. *Laenderrisiko, Ratingagenturen und das Country Risk Assessment Model der OECD*. Master Thesis. Vienna University of Economics and Business Administration, Vienna.

Isard, P. 2005. *Globalization and the International Financial System*. Cambridge: Cambridge University Press

Kaminsky, G., S. Lizondo and C.M. Reinhart. Leading indicators of currency crises. *IMF Staff Papers* 45(1): 1-48.

—. 2006. Currency Crises: Are they all the same? *Journal of International Money and Finance* 25(3): 503-27.

Lichtlen, M. 1997. *Management von Laenderrisiken*. Bern: Verlag Paul Haupt.

Lubin, D. 2002. *Bank Lending to Emerging Markets*. UNU/WIDER Discussion Paper No 61. United Nations University, World Institute for Development Economics Research.

National Bank of Romania. 2006. *Financial Stability Report*. National Bank of Romania, Bucharest.

Rahman, J. 2008. *Current Account Developments in New Member States of the European Union: Equilibrium, Excess, and EU-Phoria*. IMF Working Paper No. 08/92. International Monetary Fund, Washington DC.

Rodrick, D. and A.Velasco. 1999. *Short-Term Capital Flows*. NBER Working Paper, No. 7364. National Bureau of Economic Research, Cambridge, MA.

Notes

[*] The opinions expressed are the authors' personal views. For further research on related subjects by the authors, see www.wu-wien.ac.at/europainstitut/forschung/nexus.

[1] According to own calculations using exports in the broader sense (excluding current transfers).

CHAPTER TWELVE

SHOCK SYNCHRONICITY BETWEEN THE EU NEWCOMERS AND THE EURO AREA

GABRIEL BOBEICA, ELENA BOJESTEANU AND IONELA COSTICA

The perspective of adopting the euro by the new EU member states has generated an increased interest in the Optimum Currency Area (OCA) theory. The theoretical background needed in order to document the decision of giving up the monetary policy independence has been laid down by the pioneer work of Mundell (1961), followed by McKinnon (1963), Kenen (1969) and many others. The recent strand in the OCA literature focuses on the more specific case of the euro area, with a special emphasis on the empirical implications of the OCA theory.

This chapter is a contribution to the empirical literature which investigates the extent to which OCA preconditions are satisfied by soon-to-be euro area member states, focusing on the newest EU Member States, namely Bulgaria and Romania. The theory surrounding the OCA properties has evolved since it first came into being (for a comprehensive survey, see Mongelli, 2002). The early 1960s, spanning to early 1970s, experienced a pioneering phase, during which fundamental prerequisites have been laid down and these included price and wage flexibility, mobility of factors, financial market integration, economic openness, diversification in production and consumption, similarities in inflation rates, stable inflation rates, fiscal and political integration. What lacked the first available framework of the OCA conditions was a unifying view, particularly important when a country satisfied a number of criteria, but not the entire set, and there was no generally agreed upon ranking of the prerequisites.

This chapter adds to the existing literature by presenting statistical evidence of shock similarity between the euro area and Romania and Bulgaria together with a thorough economic analysis. The investigation will shed some light on important issues regarding the imminent adoption of the euro in Bulgaria and Romania and it can easily lead the way for similar investigations. The research in this study has two distinct goals: (i) to establish the economic facts that favour or not the similarity of shocks with the euro area; (ii) to determine to what extent the two economies satisfy the OCA prerequisite regarding shock synchronicity.

The rest of the chapter is organized as follows. The next section presents a brief literature review. Next, a series of economic insights that help us understand the macroeconomic similarities with the countries forming the euro area is provided. In the following section, we discuss the dataset and the methodology employed to isolate the supply and demand shocks as well as the monetary shocks originating in each analysed country. The subsequent section interprets the results, and, finally, some conclusions are drawn.

Review of Relevant Literature

The holistic interpretation of the theoretical OCA criteria led to an emphasis on the similarity of shocks that affect the economies of the common currency area. This is seen, including several others, as a comprehensive prerequisite or "meta-property", as it was named by Mongelli (2002), suited for determining the success or failure of a common currency project. It is acknowledged that countries that experience large asymmetric shocks would face severe costs in the case of losing the monetary independence that could have served for reaction to these shocks.

The recognition of the importance of shock similarity between the countries that form a monetary union is given by extensive empirical research that investigates this particular property. Frenkel et al. (1999), Fidrmuc and Korhonen (2001), Frenkel and Nickel (2002), Babetskii et al. (2002), and Eickmeier and Breitung (2006) follow the structural VAR identification methodology pioneered by Blanchard and Quah (1989) and developed by Bayoumi and Eichengreen (1993). They use different measures for the symmetry of the identified shocks as indicators of the synchronicity of business cycles between countries in the euro area and the new EU Member States (NMS). They also investigate the transmission of disturbances from the euro area to other countries assessing the sources (internal vs. external) of business cycle fluctuations.

Another direction in the literature of economic similarities within a common currency area analyses the degree of business cycle synchronization. Such studies employ different filtering techniques to isolate the cyclical component from the trend within a time series that reflects the economic activity (GDP and its components, industrial production index, unemployment level). Numerous studies use different measures of correlation between business cycles, ranging from simple correlations in the early research to dynamic spectral correlations as in Eickmeier and Breitung (2006).

This chapter is a contribution to the first mentioned strand of OCA empirical literature. It refers to the analysis of macroeconomic shock similarity that is considered as a fundamental prerequisite for entering a monetary union. This shock similarity can be regarded as an indicator of business cycle synchronization as we would expect the economies experiencing similar shocks to be in a similar stage of development. Moreover, business cycles can be interpreted as a result of different shocks that affect the economy. It is noteworthy that we deal in this study only with idiosyncratic shocks; and although a small open economy is subject to substantive external influence we leave the analysis of the shock sources to future research.

The empirical investigation conducted in this chapter focuses on Romania and Bulgaria. These countries represent an interesting object of study because the transition process, itself painful and costly, has been prolonged and not accomplished yet in a number of aspects. This is one of the reasons why there are just a few studies that include these two economies. The second reason is the fact that any econometric modelling may be irrelevant in the case of numerous institutional changes or administrative control of the key macroeconomic variables. Another explanation for the scarcity of empirical studies on Romania and Bulgaria is the lack of reliable and long enough data series. Fidrmuc and Korhonen (2006) provide a comprehensive review of studies on business cycle correlation between the euro area and Central and Eastern European countries. They point out that among other European states, Romania and Bulgaria have benefited from the smallest degree of attention.

Several studies analyse the two economies as part of a larger group (IMF, 2000; Afonso and Furceri, 2007; Korhonen, 2001). Ciurila and Murarasu (2007) study the trend of the real exchange rates in six Central and Eastern European countries including Romania and Bulgaria. They find that significant factors for the real appreciation are foreign direct investment inflow, current account balance and productivity differential.

Stylised Economic Facts

It is generally agreed upon the fact that Bulgaria and Romania have a lot to catch up in order to become fully integrated in the EU. We will not go into the economic details that could explain why these two countries are the laggard of the EU. Yet, it is worth mentioning that both countries experienced difficult episodes equivalent to crisis during the transition period. In the case of Romania, the first ten years after the revolution marked an environment of uncertainty, both for home and foreign investors. The prolonged communist period of constraints triggered increasing imports that were not sustained by external competitiveness. The constant problems regarding the balance of payments have reached a maximum in 1999 when the default risk seemed imminent. External financing needs outran by far the sources available or possible to resort. The crisis was avoided through a dramatic depreciation of the national currency along with restrictive fiscal and income policies. Bulgaria, on the other hand, encountered a major financial crisis in 1996 – 1997, which led to political and parliamentary instability. Public debt, budget deficit and inflation reached unsustainable levels. The measures taken by the government was based on the agreement with the International Monetary Fund and implied ambitious fiscal and structural reforms. Moreover, a currency board was implemented and the Bulgarian lev was pegged to the German mark.

The upward path of the two economies began in 1998 for Bulgaria and in 2000 for Romania. The recent period can be described by improving performance in terms of economic expansion, strengthening disinflation, reduction in budget deficit and unemployment. The expansion of the world economy triggered a boost in foreign trade of Central and Eastern European economies including Bulgaria and Romania. The region also benefited from a high attractiveness for foreign investors. It can be stated that Bulgaria and Romania are increasingly integrating into world markets and, more precisely, into European structures. But the question arises to what extent these commercial and financial linkages lead to an increased similarity between these countries and the euro area – a similarity that would eventually pave the way for monetary integration.

Among the economic indicators that can be regarded as relevant for entering a common currency area, we will constrain our attention to three of them: (i) bilateral trade intensity; (ii) foreign direct investment (FDI) intensity, and (iii) similarity in production structures.

Bilateral Trade Intensity

One would expect that the higher the bilateral trade within a group of countries the lower the cost of entering to a monetary union. Frankel and Rose (1998) present empirical evidence that supports this idea. Yet, increased trade is seen by others as a factor that leads to sectoral specialization. On one hand, trade may trigger higher economic similarity by favouring the transmission of shocks that affect all industries. On the other hand, in the hypothesis that trade leads to specialization, the primary shocks that affect an economy can become sector-specific, and this decreases the shock similarity within a group of countries.

The indicator selected for trade integration (12.1) corrects for the differences in the size of the economy. It is defined in the following formula

$$TR_{i,EA} = \frac{EX_{i,EA} + IM_{i,EA}}{GDP_i \times GDP_{EA}} \tag{12.1}$$

where $TR_{i,EA}$ reveals the degree of bilateral trade intensity between country i and the euro area, $EX_{i,EA}$ represents the exports of country i to the euro area, $IM_{i,EA}$ are the imports of country i from the euro area, GDP_i is the gross domestic product of country i and GDP_{EA} stands for the gross domestic product of the euro area.

Figure 12-1 illustrates the degree of bilateral trade intensity between the euro area on one hand and Romania and Bulgaria on the other. For comparison, we also computed the average value of the indicator for the countries that joined the EU in 2004.

Figure 12-1 Bilateral trade intensity with the euro area (1998 – 2006)

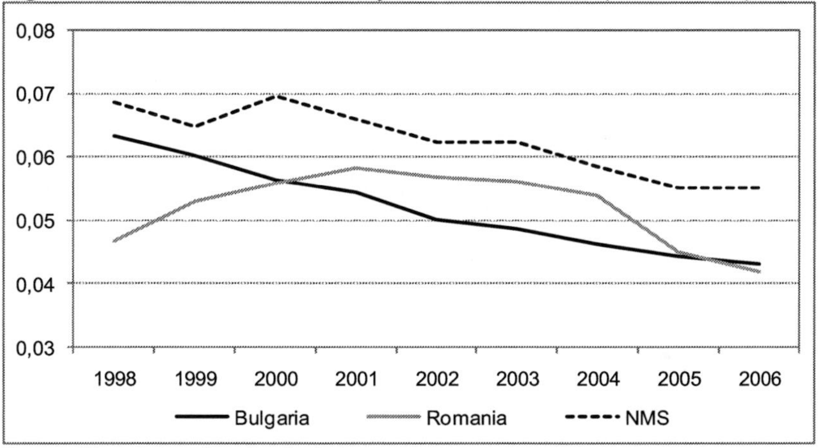

Source: Eurostat, authors' calculations

Figure 12-1 reveals the fact that Romania exhibits a higher degree of trade integration with the euro area than Bulgaria, but only during the interval 2000 – 2005. Yet, for both states the level of the chosen trade intensity indicator is lower than the average among NMS.

Foreign Direct Investment Intensity

FDI is an important factor that creates linkages and interdependencies between economies. FDI is a channel through which external shocks are propagated but can also lead to a catch up process and increased similarity in the nature of shocks that affect a group of countries. The measure chosen for FDI intensity between the country and the euro area (12.2) is similar to the trade intensity indicator in the sense that it accounts for the difference in the size of economies that are compared.

$$FDI_{i,EA} = \frac{FDI^{out}{}_{i,EA} + FDI^{in}{}_{i,EA}}{GDP_i \times GDP_{EA}} \qquad (12.2)$$

where $FDI^{out}{}_{i,EA}$ stands for the foreign direct investment made by country *i* in the euro area and $FDI^{in}{}_{i,EA}$ is the foreign direct investment that enter country *i* from the euro area.

Figure 12-2 Foreign direct investment intensity with the euro area (1998 – 2004)

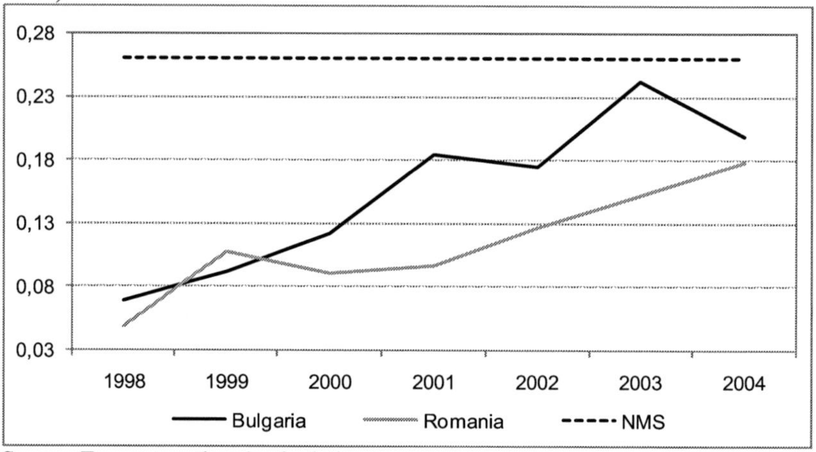

Source: Eurostat, authors' calculations

Due to data availability, the average for NMS is by the indicator computed in Eickmeier and Breitung (2006) for the year 2003. We present it as a constant just to have a grasp of where Bulgaria and Romania find themselves as compared to the other NMS. It is obvious from Figure 12-2 that Bulgaria is more financially integrated with the euro area although the trend for Romania is promisingly upward.

Similarity in Production Structures

The criteria surrounding the entry into a monetary union focus on the probability that candidate countries face similar shocks that will enable a common monetary policy to adjust successfully after these disturbances. According to economic theory, the synchronicity of economic shocks is determined also by similar structural characteristics. Figure 12-3 depicts a measure of structural similarity (12.3) initially proposed by Krugman (1991) and computed using the following formula:

$$S_{i,EA} = \sum_{k=1}^{K} | s_{k,i} - s_{k,EA} | \qquad (12.3)$$

where $S_{i,EA}$ measures the degree of similarity in production structures between country i and the euro area, K is the number of economic sectors considered, $s_{k,i}$ represents the weight of the gross value added by the sector k in total value added for country i and $s_{k,EA}$ has the same interpretation for the euro area. Six economic sectors have been considered: (i) agriculture and forestry, (ii) industry and construction, (iii) trade, hotels and restaurants, (iv) transportation and communication, (v) financial intermediation and real estate, (vi) public sector. The construction of the indicator points to the fact that the closer $S_{i,EA}$ is to zero the more similar are the economic characteristics between country i and the euro area.

Figure 12-3 Similarity of production structure with the euro area (1998 – 2006)

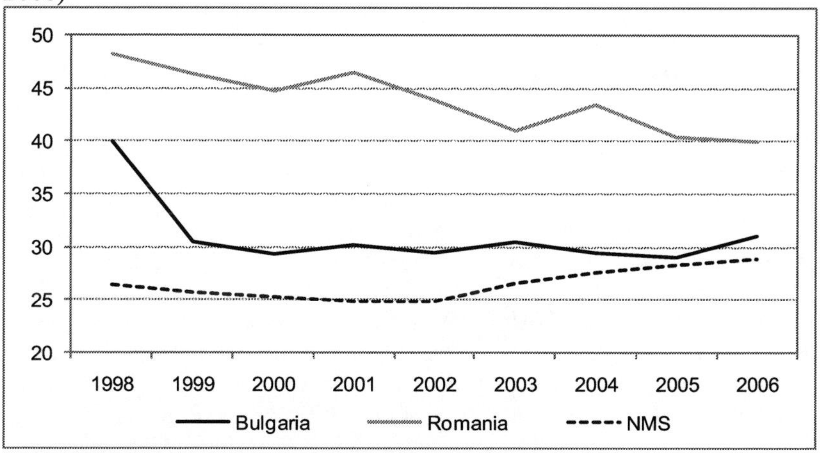

Source: Eurostat, authors' calculations

As revealed by Figure 12-3, Bulgaria appears to be significantly more similar in economic structure than Romania but less similar than the NMS average. Investigating for the causes of Romania's dissimilarity, the greatest discrepancies are explained by the agricultural sector (with an average mean 2.33 percent for the euro area and 13.41 percent in Romania), by the financial intermediation sector (26.68 percent in the euro area and 13.95 percent in Romania) and by the public sector (22.58 percent in the euro area and 13.18 percent in Romania).

Data and Empirical Methodology

Our data span covers the period from the first quarter of 1999:Q1 to the first quarter of 2007. The sample period is not very generous, comprising only 33 observations, but it eliminates serious problems inherent to the transition period (adoption of the currency board in Bulgaria in 1997, last important stage of price liberalisation in the second half of 1997 in Romania, and revision of the methodology of measuring the aggregate activity in Romania in 1998). Moreover, we do not have to deal with possible structural breaks due to the formation of the euro area in 1999. The data are obtained from Eurostat and partially from the Bulgarian and Romanian national banks.

The empirical investigation regarding shock synchronicity between Bulgaria and Romania and the euro area employs the popular technique of the Vector Autoregressive models (VAR), extensively used in macroeconomic analysis. The most important criticism to the VAR approach is its lack of economic information and the impossibility to interpret its main results, the impulse-response functions and the variance decomposition. The main three methods to identify the pure innovations are the recursive approach (triangular Cholesky decomposition), the structural approach and the long-term restriction approach (Blanchard and Quah decomposition). We chose to employ long run restrictions in sense of Blanchard and Quah (1989) as used in the seminal paper of Bayoumi and Eichengreen (1993). As opposed to them, our study takes into consideration three kinds of macroeconomic shocks: demand, supply and monetary shocks.

Accordingly, the VARs estimated for each economy (Bulgaria, Romania and the euro area) comprise three quarterly variables: (i) inflation rate calculated using the log deviation of the CPI from the previous quarter; (ii) nominal 3-month interest rate; (iii) real GDP growth rate (dy). The series are seasonally adjusted using TRAMO/SEATS (Demetra) except for the interest rate that does not exhibit seasonal behaviour.

Checking for shock symmetry is a two-way procedure. First, individual VARs are estimated for each considered economy and, afterwards, the identified shocks are isolated and analysed within a unifying framework.

The relevance of the results depends crucially on the statistical tests employed before the models are estimated. In order to specify the model, we performed unit root tests to check for the stationarity of the series. Table 12-1 illustrates the results of the Augmented Dickey Fuller (ADF) test for all nine variables. Philips Peron (PP) test yields similar results.

Table 12-1 Unit root tests

	Bulgaria	Romania	Euro area
Real economic growth	-5.82*	-3.62**	-5.00*
Inflation rate	-5.36*	-0.42	-5.07*
Interest rate	-2.73***	-3.44**	-1.97

Source: Author's calculation
Note: * I(0) at 1% confidence level; ** I(0) at 5% confidence level; ***I(0) at 10% confidence level.

According to Table 12-1, it is reasonable to consider all the variables included in the investigation as being stationary except for the inflation rate in Romania and the interest rate in the euro area. As far as the inflation rate in Romania is concerned, its lack of stationarity is due to the continuing process of disinflation that started in 2000 and is still in progress. Indeed, a closer look at the data reveals that the series exhibits a deterministic time trend. Accordingly, an exogenous time trend variable was included in the VAR model for Romania. The case of the interest rate in the euro area is not so straightforward. Although the tests do not reject the presence of a stochastic trend, we chose to include it in the model in levels and not in the first differences in order to maintain the comparability of the three models. Moreover, the results indicated by the unit root tests for short periods are very often affected by a small number of observations in the series and should be interpreted cautiously.

All models are stable (unit roots lie inside the unit circle) and according to the informational criteria (also considering the degrees of freedom constraints) the VAR models were estimated using one lag for all three economies.

The identification scheme follows the idea of Bayoumi and Eichengreen (1993) that the supply shocks have long-run effects on the economic activity whereas demand shocks do not. As supported by the data, additional restrictions have been added. For example, for Romania and the euro area no significant long-run impact of the interest rate on prices was found. The identification matrix embraced the following form.

Table 12-2 Identification scheme for Romania and euro area VARs

	dy	inflation	interest rate
dy	NA	0	0
Inflation	NA	NA	0
Interest rate	NA	NA	NA

Note: The restriction $c_{i,j} = 0$ means that the (accumulated) response of the i-th variable to the j-th structural shock is zero in the long-run.

Two other restrictions were required by the Bulgarian data: the long-run impact of the real economic growth on inflation is null as well as the impact of the inflation rate on interest rates. The over-identifying restrictions were validated by a likelihood ratio test with the null hypothesis that the restrictions are supported by the data (with a p-value of 0.93).

Results

The estimated VAR models provided the basis for the analysis of shock synchronicity between Bulgaria and Romania and the euro area. Although it does not concern our investigation explicitly, it is interesting to look at the responses of the interest rate in the euro area at the identified disturbance in the real economic growth and inflation. This could provide an informal control key that the interest rate does not affect the stability of the VAR model.

As depicted in Figure 12-4, the interest rate responds positively to an innovation in the real economic growth. The response to an innovation in the inflation rate is also positive but slightly less powerful. The visual representation of the impulse-response functions supports the idea that the monetary policy is guided by Taylor rule with the interest smoothing term.

The identified supply, demand and monetary shocks are isolated as being the residuals in the real GDP growth, inflation and interest rate equations. Table 12-3 presents the simple static correlation coefficients between these shocks in Bulgaria and Romania on one side and the euro area on the other side.

Figure 12-4 Interest rate responses to identified shock

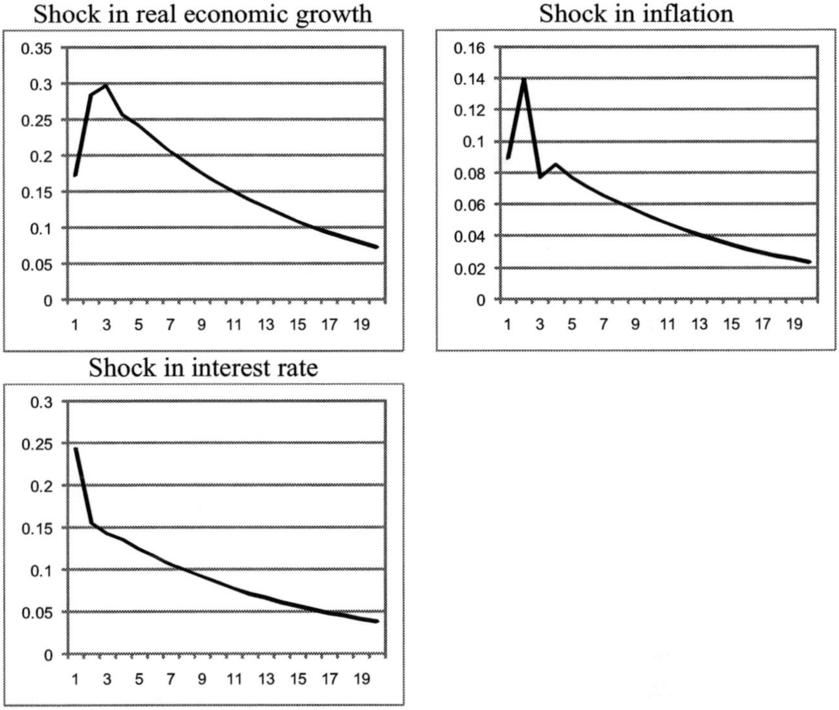

Source: Authors' estimation

Table 12-3 Correlation coefficients between shocks

	Supply shocks	Demand shocks	Monetary shocks
Bulgaria	0.2955	0.4507	0.1050
Romania	0.3446	0.1177	-0.1780

Source: Authors' calculations

Several conclusions can be drawn from the results in Table 12-2: (i) supply shocks seem to be correlated between Bulgaria and Romania and the euro zone with no significant difference between Bulgaria and Romania; (ii) much stronger correlation is identified in demand shocks between Bulgaria and the euro zone whereas the correlation for Romania is weak, and (iii) Bulgarian monetary shocks are positively correlated with those in the euro zone, Romania has experienced asymmetric monetary shocks negatively correlated with the euro area.

In order to grasp better the phenomenon of macroeconomic shock synchronization we also employed a dynamic correlation measure $\rho_{y,z}(\omega)$ as proposed by Croux et al. (2001):

$$\rho_{y,z}(\omega) = \frac{C_{y,z}(\omega)}{\sqrt{S_y(\omega) \cdot S_z(\omega)}} \tag{12.4}$$

where $\rho_{y,z}(\omega)$ is the dynamic correlation coefficient between series y and z at frequency ω, $C_{y,z}(\omega)$ is the co-spectrum, and $S_y(\omega)$ and $S_z(\omega)$ are the spectral density functions of the two series.

Figure 12-5 Dynamic correlation coefficients (1999 – 2007)

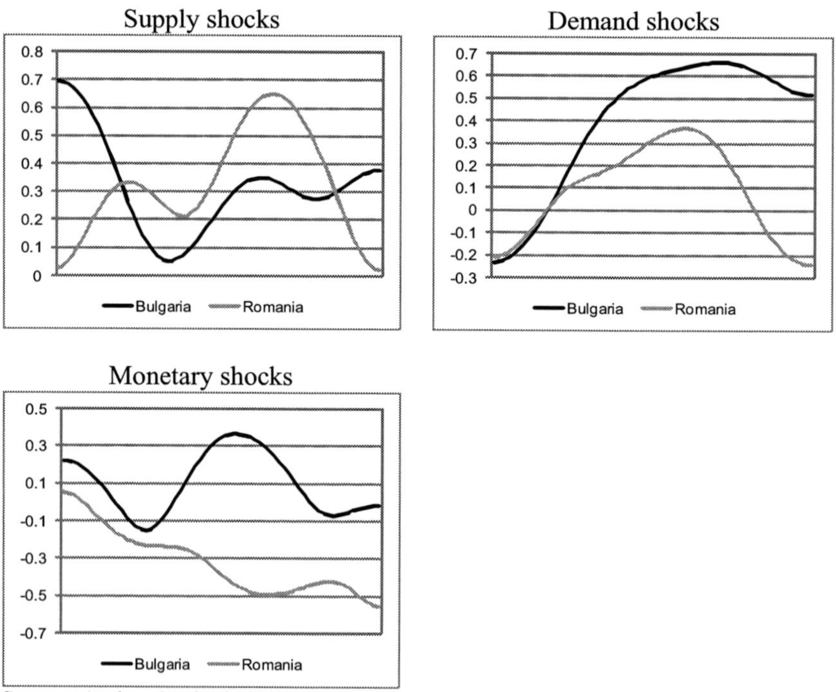

Source: Authors' calculations

Figure 12-5 depicts the dynamic correlation coefficients between the shocks in the EU newcomers and the euro area, computed frequency by frequency on 65 equally spaced points in the interval $[0, \pi]$. The dynamic correlation measure provides us with important information that is not available in the static analysis. As it is apparent from Figure 12-5, the Bulgarian supply shocks tend to be more correlated with those in the euro area as compared to the Romanian shocks in the long-run. As far as demand and monetary shocks are concerned, they are more correlated in Bulgaria than in Romania at all horizons. The results support the idea that Bulgaria is ahead of Romania on the road to monetary integration.

Conclusion

This chapter investigates the degree of shock synchronicity between Bulgaria and Romania and the euro area as this is a prerequisite for entry into a monetary union with minimum costs. The analysis suggests that although there are several features common to the two countries such as being the laggard of the EU, there should be no tendency in treating them as a homogenous group. Bulgaria seems to be more correlated with the euro area than Romania leading the way to monetary integration. The major reason that explains these results is the difference in the monetary policies promoted in the two economies. Bulgaria has a currency board which favoured an economic closeness with the euro area while Romania has an independent monetary policy and a dirty float exchange rate regime. It is beyond the scope of this study to establish whether joining the euro area would be a costly decision for the countries analysed. Considering the fact that there is strong evidence that supports the endogeneity of the OCA criteria, the empirical investigations based on ex-post data fail to predict the behaviour of the macroeconomic variables after the entry into the monetary union.

References

Babetskii, I., L. Boone and M. Maurel. 2002. *Exchange rate regimes and supply shocks asymmetry: The case of the accession countries.* CEPR Discussion Paper No. 3408. Centre for Economic Policy Research, London.

Bayoumi, T. and B. Eichengreen. 1993. Shocking aspects of European monetary unification. In *Adjustment and Growth in the European*

Monetary Union, ed. F. Torres and F. Giavazzi, 193-229. Cambridge: Cambridge University Press.

Blanchard, O.J. and D. Quah. 1989. The dynamic effects of aggregate demand and supply disturbances. *American Economic Review* 79(4): 655-73.

Ciurila, N. and B. Murarasu. 2007. An Assessment of the Equilibrium Exchange Rate in Eastern European Countries. In *Proceedings of the Third International Conference on Business, Management and Economics*. Izmir: Yasar University.

Croux, C., M. Forni and L. Reichlin. 2001. A measure for comovement for economic variables: theory and empirics. *The Review of Economics and Statistics* 83(2): 231-41.

Eickmeier, S. and J. Breitung. 2006. How synchronized are new EU member states with the euro area? Evidence from a structural factor model. *Journal of Comparative Economics* 34(3): 538-63.

Fidrmuc, J. 2001. *The endogeneity of the optimum currency area criteria, intraindustry trade, and EMU enlargement*. BOFIT Discussion Paper 8/2001. Bank of Finland, Helsinki.

Fidrmuc, J. and I. Korhonen. 2006. *Meta-Analysis of the Business Cycle Correlation between the Euro Area and the CEECs. CESifo* Working Paper no. 1693. CESifo, Munich.

Frankel, J. and A.K. Rose. 1998. The endogeneity of the optimum currency area criteria. *The Economic Journal*. 108(449): 1009-25.

Frenkel, M., C. Nickel and G. Schmidt. 1999. *Some shocking aspect of EMU Enlargement.* Deutsche Bank Research Note 99-4. Deutsche Bank, Frankfurt am Main.

Frenkel, M. and C. Nickel. 2002. *How symmetric are the shocks and the shock adjustment dynamics between the euro area and Central and Eastern European countries?* IMF Working Paper No. 02/222. International Monetary Fund, Washington DC.

IMF. 2000. Chapter IV: Accession of transition economies to the European Union: Prospects and pressures. In *World Economic Outlook – Prospects and Policy Issues*, 138-74. Washington, DC: International Monetary Fund.

McKinnon, R. 1963. Optimum currency areas. *The American Economic Review* 53(4): 717-25.

Kenen, P.B. 1969. The optimum currency area: an eclectic view. In *Monetary problems of the international economy*, ed. R.A. Mundell and A.K. Swoboda, 41-60. Chicago, IL: University of Chicago Press.

Krugman, P. 1991. *Geography and trade*. Cambridge, MA.: MIT Press.

Mongelli, F.P. 2002. *New views on the optimum currency area theory: What is EMU telling us?* ECB Working Paper 138. European Central Bank, Frankfurt am Main.

Mundell, R.A. 1961. A theory of optimum currency areas. *The American Economic Review* 51(4): 509-17.

CONTRIBUTORS

Gabriel Bobeica is a researcher of the Doctoral School of Finance and Banking – European Centre for Excellence. He is a Ph.D. student in Monetary Economics at the Bucharest University of Economics. He has received a M.Sc. in Financial Markets from the Doctoral School of Finance and Banking at the Bucharest University of Economics and a B.Sc. in Mathematics from the University of Bucharest, Faculty of Mathematics and Computer Science. He has teaching experience in the field of monetary economics, quantitative methods and financial mathematics. He participates in programs providing consulting services for the Romanian Ministry of Economy and Finance. His research concentrates on the role of expectations in policy design, policy coordination and shocks identification and synchronization. He is a member of the International Trade and Finance Association.

Elena Bojesteanu is a researcher of the Doctoral School of Finance and Banking and a Ph.D. student in Monetary Economics at the Bucharest University of Economics. She participated in numerous research projects financed by the Romanian Ministry of Education and Research, the World Bank and the European Commission as a researcher and as coordinator. Her contributions consisted in optimum currency area studies, business cycle estimation and VAR analysis using alternative identification methodologies. She is also a Teaching Assistant in international finance. She is a member of the International Trade and Finance Association, USA.

Marie Brière is Head of Fixed Income, Forex and Volatility Strategy at Crédit Agricole Asset Management, Associate Researcher with the Centre Emile Bernheim at Université Libre de Bruxelles and Affiliate Professor at CERAM Business School. She holds a Ph.D. in Economics and she is graduated of the ENSAE School of economics, statistics and finance. She also teaches empirical finance at Université de Paris IX Dauphine and Paris II Assas. She is the author of a book on the anomalies in the formation of interest rates as well as various scientific articles published in books, academic and practitioners' journals.

Nicoleta Ciurila is Assistant Professor at the Academy of Economic Studies in Bucharest, Romania. She has teaching experience in the area of money and banking and macroeconomic analysis. She holds a M.Sc. in Finance and she is also a Ph.D. student in International Finance at the Academy of Economic Studies in Bucharest. She also works as a researcher at the National Bank of Romania.

Ionela Costica is a researcher of the Doctoral School of Finance and Banking – European Centre of Excellence (since 1994), Faculty of Finance, Insurance, Banking and Stock Exchange, Bucharest University of Economics, Romania. She has received a Ph.D. from the Bucharest University of Economics, Romania in 2002. She has teaching experience in the field of international financial management and money and banking. The most important research is concentrated on monetary policy and strategies, banking sector development in Eastern European countries versus the euro area.

Gerhard Fink is Jean Monnet Professor for applied micro economics in European integration and Director of the doctoral programs at the Vienna University of Economics and Business Administration. He was director of the Research Institute for European Affairs (Jean Monnet Centre of Excellence) during 1997 – 2003. He can refer to about 200 publications in learned journals and authored or (co-) edited about 15 books. In 2005 he was guest editor of the Academy of Management Executive, one of the leading management journals in the USA. Since 2007 he is associate editor of the European Journal of International Management. His major research interests are in international business, intercultural management, business strategies in the European market(s).

Lisandra Flach is a Ph.D. student and research assistant at the Chair of International Economics, University of Tubingen, Germany. Her major interests are international trade and microeconometrics.

Dimitris Georgoutsos is Professor of the Athens University of Economics and Business, Department of Accounting and Finance. He holds a Ph.D. from the University of Essex while he is a graduate of the London School of Economics. His teaching experience involves courses of international finance, money and capital markets and risk management. He has published extensively in journals such as Journal of International Financial Markets, Institutions and Money, Journal of International Money and

Finance or Journal of Forecasting. He has also served as a referee to several international academic journals.

Peter R. Haiss is Lecturer at the EuropaInstitut and Department of Process-oriented Economics at Vienna University of Economics and Business Administration, Austria. He also works at the Institute of European Studies and is with Bank Austria, Member of Unicredit Group. He has teaching experience in strategic management, international business/foreign direct investment, international finance, European integration, and EU enlargement. His research concentrates on the finance-growth-nexus, European integration and corporate strategy with a specific focus on transition and emerging economies.

Felix Hammermann studied economics at the University of Bonn, Germany and the University of York, United Kingdom. He participated in the Advanced Studies Program of the Kiel Institute for the World Economy, Germany. In 2002 he joined the institute's research department "Development Economics and Global Integration". He was visiting student at the Universitat Pompeu Fabra in Barcelona from October 2004 to October 2005. Since his return he is in the Project Area "Beyond Europe - External Dimensions of Integration".

Florian Ielpo is a fixed income quantitative strategist at Dexia SA. He holds a Ph.D. in Financial Econometrics from the Sorbonne University. He graduated from the Ecole Normale Supérieure de Cachan and from the ENSAE School of economics statistics and finance. His research is focused on empirical finance and econometrics, with various applications including stocks, fixed income securities and the recent carbon market. He teaches empirical finance at the ENSTA school of engineer, the ESILV school of engineer and both at the Dauphine and Sorbonne universities. He published articles in various academic journals.

Elif Katircioglu is a master student in Banking and Finance at Eastern Mediterranean University, Northern Cyprus. She has received a B.S. in Economics from 9 Eylul University, Turkey. She has professional job experience in the field of accounting and marketing as well as financial consultancy. Her research concentrates on quantitative financial services marketing. She is the Managing Editor of International Journal of Economic Perspectives and Co-Chair of International Economic Society.

Salih Turan Katircioglu is Associate Professor of Economics and Vice Chair of the Department of Banking and Finance at Eastern Mediterranean University, Northern Cyprus. He has received a Ph.D. from Uludag University, Turkey. He has teaching experience in economics, international finance and econometrics. He worked as a visiting Assistant Professor of Economics at Cag University, Turkey, in 2001 – 2002. His research concentrates on time series econometrics, economic growth models, international trade and tourism models, and financial development issues. He is the Editor of International Journal of Economic Perspectives and member of editorial board of various international journals.

Lumír Kulhánek is Professor of Economics and Head of the Department of Economics and European Integration at the College of Social and Administration Affairs in Havířov, Czech Republic. He has wide teaching experience in economic and finance courses in the Czech Republic, Slovak Republic and Poland. He has published articles in respected Czech and foreign economic journals as well as in proceedings from international conferences. His research activities focus on stock markets development in developed and transition countries, inflation and monetary policy.

Petros M. Migiakis is an economist working with Bank of Greece, at the Capital Markets Section. He holds a Ph.D. in Finance from the Athens University of Economics and Business, while he holds two Master degrees in Economics and Mathematical Modelling. His working experience involves risk management and financial markets analysis in the banking sector, while his previous teaching experience involves courses of fixed income analysis, portfolio management and international finance. His research focuses on issues of financial integration, bond markets, monetary policy and the term structure of interest rates.

Bogdan Murarașu is Assistant Professor at the Academy of Economic Studies Bucharest, Romania. He has teaching experience in the field of capital markets and money and banking. He is also a researcher at the National Bank of Romania. His research is focused on macroeconomic modelling and inflation forecasting. He holds a M.Sc. in Finance and he is also a Ph.D. student at the Academy of Economic Studies Bucharest in the field of monetary policy.

Magdalena Oeberseder is a research associate at the Vienna University of Economics and Business Administration, Austria. Her research interests are both monetary integration and marketing ethics. In her Ph.D. thesis she focuses on ethics in corporate positioning. She has teaching experience in CEMS courses like the International Business Project.

Stanislav Polouček is Professor of Finance and rector at the College of Social and Administration Affairs in Havířov, Czech Republic. He received a Ph.D. from the Charles University, Faculty of Philosophy, Prague and University of Economics, Faculty of National Economy, Prague. He has wide teaching experience of economic, finance and banking courses in the Czech Republic, Poland and Slovakia and in lectureships in other foreign universities. He is the chairman of the International Program Committee of a biennial finance and banking conference. His research concentrates on financial and banking sector development in developed as well as transition countries, and monetary theory and policy.

Wolfgang Rainer is a graduate student at the Research Institute for European Affairs at the Vienna University of Economics and Business Administration. Additionally he is studying towards his CEMS Master's in International Management degree. He also studied one semester at the Norwegian School of Economics and Business Administration in Bergen. His research interests concentrate on Central and Eastern Europe, country risk studies, lending dynamics in emerging market economies and the finance-growth-nexus.

Tatiana Santos is a researcher and teaching assistant at the Department of Economics of the Federal University of Santa Catarina, Brazil. Her major research interests are international capital movements and spatial econometrics.

Fernando Seabra is Professor at the Department of Economics of the Federal University of Santa Catarina, Brazil. He holds a Ph.D. from the University of Essex and was as visiting scholar at McGill University, Canada. His main field of interest and publications is in international finance.

Ralph Setzer is an economist at the Deutsche Bundesbank. He has received a Ph.D. from the University of Hohenheim, Germany. He has teaching experience in the fields of open macroeconomics and monetary policy. His research concentrates on the political economy of exchange rates, the analysis of money demand and the global linkages between money and asset prices. He is a member of the German Economic Association

Daniel Stavárek is Associate Professor of International Finance and Head of Department of Finance at Silesian University, School of Business Administration in Karviná, Czech Republic. He received a Ph.D. from the Technical University of Ostrava, Czech Republic. He has extensive teaching experience in lectureships at foreign universities. He has published in refereed journals such as Applied Economics Letters, Eastern European Economics or Czech Journal of Economics and Finance. His research primarily focuses on exchange rates, foreign exchange markets and European monetary integration. He is a member of the Czech Economic Society and International Economic Society.

Tomáš Tichý is Assistant Professor of Finance with emphasis on financial modelling at the Department of Finance of the Faculty of Economics, Technical University of Ostrava, Czech Republic. He received his Ph.D. in Finance at Technical University of Ostrava. His research focuses on financial modelling and decision-making under risk, especially in fields related to stochastic processes, Monte Carlo simulation and option pricing.

Index